Mum, Please Help Me Die

When Cancer Meets Love

Thy Cameron

O&U
Onwards & Upwards

Onwards and Upwards Publishers

3 Radfords Turf, Cranbrook, Exeter,
EX5 7DX, United Kingdom.
www.onwardsandupwards.org

First edition. Published in the United Kingdom by Onwards and Upwards Publishers Ltd. (2019).

ISBN: 978-1-78815-729-2
Typeface: Sabon LT
Editor: Rhonda Crouse
Photography: Thy Cameron and others
Graphic design: LM Graphic Design

Printed in the United Kingdom.

Endorsements

Thy skilfully tells a gripping story that is far more, because the story is an intensely personal, vulnerable reality with a powerful, moving and multi-faceted message. Nothing can prepare the reader for the impact of the profound loss, yet remarkable victories that unfold. I could not put the book down until I'd read the last page.

A thousand emotions and tears of sadness and joy later, I finished reading this most unusually tender book... What an amazing tribute to a beautiful, most courageous girl and a faithful pursuing saviour. Thank you, Thy, for sharing this with the world.

Dr. Karen Cerff
COO: Transformational Leadership Institute

...This book gives a searingly honest account of Shirley's less-than-perfect life and, in particular, her struggle with suffering. She prayed for healing, but God had a deeper healing in mind than physical recovery from cancer.

I count it a privilege to have known Shirley and to have seen a transformation that can only come from the same power that raised Christ from the dead. It is wonderful that even after her death this story can be told by her grieving mother in such a compelling manner.

Rev. Dan Hayward
Rector, St Andrew's Church, Oxford

This exquisitely written narrative reaches the depths of both the tragedy of a life cut short and the bottomless love of the saviour. Reader, be ready to experience for yourself a wide range of ultimately beautiful emotions on the pathway to eternal ecstasy with the Lord.

Prof. William F. Cox, Jr.
Christian Education Programs, School of Education,
Regent University, Virginia Beach, USA

This poignant and moving story will take you on an emotional roller-coaster that will leave you breathless, and tearful, but also full of hope. It is the account of a young woman's struggle to trust God and how faith returns when all the odds are stacked against it.

While it is the account of a parent's worst nightmare, that of losing their only child to cancer at the age of thirty-nine, it is a bigger story than that. It must have cost Thy a great deal to tell it. How grateful we are to her for an excellent book.

Thy has a rare gift in writing. She uses words in such a way that the reader is dragged into each moment and feels every pang of hurt or movement of hope. The story ends on a magnificent note of hope. This hope would have been impossible if Christ, his cross and resurrection were not real. Thy captures the struggles of believing this great truth and places us firmly in the presence of Jesus and at the foot of the cross.

Rt. Rev. Frank Retief
Retired Presiding Bishop of CESA, now operating as REACH SA

Thy's beautifully written and searingly honest book struck a chord with me on many levels. As a mother, daughter, Christian, and as someone who has struggled with a serious disease, I found that Shirley's journey from emotional torment to deep spiritual peace made me want to find that peace for myself, for now and for always.

But it is in Thy's depiction of Shirley's growing understanding that God loves her that my heart soared. Shirley changes from someone who feels she can't please God and needs to perform in order for him to love her, to someone who has experienced, tangibly, God's presence, and knows that she doesn't need to do anything for him to love her; that his love is unconditional. That knowledge, and the trust it engenders, is utterly beautiful. In Shirley's case, as Thy writes, God has been knocking on her heart for a lifetime, but "cancer turns the key". I put the book down wanting to keep my heart open every day, and to remember always that God loves me – as his daughter, unconditionally.

Katie Cartwright
Wife, mother, consultant researcher,
with MAs from Oxford and Cape Town Universities
and a diploma in freelance and feature writing

Because I have a daughter too and have witnessed some of Thy's immense suffering, I found it really hard to get down to reading this book. While it addresses so many issues very relevant to modern life, in me it stirred deep emotion. Times without number – when I could at last speak to God again – I whispered, "Why so much? Why like this? Why allow hope when you knew you would take it away?" At times I wondered if I would ever again believe he heals.

What was I left with, that last late night when I had finished reading? Strangely, one thing only: that his name is "I will be what I will be". My mind floundered, but my very bones knew he is the Eternal, he is my Father, I want no other.

I cannot find words to speak of what I experienced. This book is so relevant, so powerful...

Marzanne Leroux-van Der Boon
Experienced popular writer of Christian historical fiction set
in modern-day Israel

Acknowledgements

Soon after Shirley died, I saw a picture of her in a relay race, running towards the baton-exchange. I was there, and I know there was one other whom I can't identify. Shirley passed the baton on, and I came to understand it was to me. She wanted her story told to honour God, and it seemed she was passing that task on to me.

In the confusion and distress of grief, I couldn't concentrate and found it very difficult to write. I had never written a book before, and no part of me was functioning fully. I believe my editor, Rhonda Crouse, was the right person to steer me. I thank her for her patience, wisdom and expertise. Her insight and direction have enhanced the end product, for which I am very grateful.

I had many resources. These included a great deal of material from Shirley's interactions with her very special group of friends, who did so much for her; her diary, journal and texts; our emails and, in particular, her testimony[1], recorded at great cost to her one week before she died. I also recorded in my diary and journal testimony from those who knew her. Being with her for eight of the eleven months she suffered etched a great deal into my memory.

The care, practical and prayer support of Shirley's Secret Helpers, Greyfriars Church in Reading and others was remarkable – a living example of Christian community. Her best friend, Nick Crowder, went far beyond any call of duty and out of deep love gave all he had to her. He also blessed Brian and me, especially at the time of her passing and in the months that followed. How can I ever communicate how grateful I am to you all?

While I was away, my husband Brian, supported by many meals and much kindness and prayer, bravely held the fort. Brian, I don't know how to thank you enough for all your support, your daily texts and Skypes, and your wonderful welcomes every time I came back home for a while. Thank you, above all, for sharing grief – our grief – over and over again. And for being prepared to help the writing process along in any way you could. I know every time you've read through the manuscript again, it has brought fresh pain.

---

[1] See *www.onwardsandupwards.org/mum-please-help-me-die* for excerpts from the video testimony and details about the DVD.

I also want to thank those to whom I could email a round robin and know you would pray with us. Thank you for financial assistance from so many of you. Thank you too to those who sent me texts, emailed or phoned to encourage me while I was with Shirley in the UK. You were my lifelines.

Thank you to those who kindly allowed the use of their names in this book. Pseudonyms have only been used where necessary.

Thank you, too, to each of you who has been prepared to give your time to read the manuscript and has sent me a review.

That this book exists is, therefore, only partly my doing. Time and again, when I had nothing in me to continue, God gently lifted me up, encouraged me and gave a strength not my own. He also helped me to know what to say.

In the four years since Shirley's passing, I have learnt a great deal. And I owe God a great deal.

Thank you, Shirley, for longing to tell your story, and for passing on the baton. I ask God to use it so that what you longed for happens, and he is glorified.

Contents

Preface by Dr. Derek Morphew

As a partner in a small publishing company I have read many manuscripts from many authors over the years. None have brought tears to my eyes. This one did.

This is not a story for the faint-hearted, or for Christians who want convenient answers to difficult questions. It will force the reader to face agonizing theological questions about the origin of evil and suffering. It will also equip others who may face the same overwhelming challenges. How does one cope with dying of cancer or caring for a close family member who is? Can one find God – yes, really find God – in such circumstances? This story gives the answer: yes, you can!

The narrative is intensely personal. There is Shirley (who eventually succumbs to cancer) and her relationship with God. There is Thy's relationship with Shirley. There is the relationship of caring Christian friends to Shirley, part of the wider Christian community. Through them the reader is invited into inner struggles, agonizing questions, fears and hopes, faith and unbelief, and eventually the loss and triumph.

There are salutary lessons to be learned as well. Has the church equipped its members for suffering? When faced with a similar crisis, will others have to go through all the same agonizing questions? Or can we do better? This book will be one of those resources that will assist us to do better.

Shirley is not the average Christian facing the prospect of suffering and death. From childhood, and into adulthood, through many on-and-off romantic relationships, marriage and divorce, and life crises, Shirley is a deeply troubled soul. She is deeply insecure, craves love and acceptance, suffers from clinical depression, and at one point attempts suicide. All before the dreaded discovery of cancer. The question then arises, how will this Shirley cope with dying of cancer? The triumph of her story is that from struggling with her relationship with God through her whole life, she actually finds God, profoundly, through this agony and eventual loss of life. From being a deeply unhappy person, she becomes deeply happy, at peace with God. She determines that she will die well, and she does!

Her discovery of God is ground out, day by day, through hope and disappointment, fear and faith. It is made more profound by the fact that Shirley is a 'clergy-kid'. Her father is a Church of England clergyman and her mother a member of the Vineyard movement. Thy has an Ed.D from an

American Christian university. Everything is cast in the context of people who know the Bible.

When cancer hits, Shirley's questions about God's love for her only deepen. How can God love me if he allows me to die of cancer? At one point, she visits Holy Trinity Brompton, where she meets a radiant young woman who has been healed of a terminal lung disease. And she lives in an environment of various churches known for their healing ministry. How does she deal with the mystery of why some are healed but others are not? One of her milestones is the moment when she decides to turn away from her previous emotional issues. Her priorities and hopes for life, if she is given a second chance, change. The questions arise and are faced one by one. Does God send sickness? If not, can I love him if I am not healed? The centrality of the cross begins to make its way into her dialogue with God. Because of Jesus, Shirley knows God is love. She enters into a fellowship with him in her sufferings. She comes to know and believe that God is good and God loves her. She has increasing moments of his presence. Some of them overwhelm her. Her God is bigger than all circumstances. As her physical pain increases and her body slowly succumbs, she finds increasing joy and peace in him.

Thy's story has milestones too. How should a mother love and care for a deeply troubled daughter? Can one care too much, cross personal boundaries and be 'enmeshed'? How does one handle the anxiety of knowing that your daughter is perhaps drifting away from God? How do you deal with a prophetic word from a close Christian friend that proves to be accurate in the long run but not easy to hear when it comes? Most painful of all, how do you watch your daughter slowly waste away? But all this becomes so much more possible to bear as Thy is privy to the way Shirley finds God in Jesus.

How should loyal and close Christian friends relate to someone going through such a struggle? Should we support the faith and expectation that God and/or medicine can heal? Is it responsible and loving to participate in a naive kind of faith that is unable to face suffering? How do we support faith in miracles whilst also encouraging the requirement to face the hard reality that healing may never come? This group of friends does not falter. They provide heaps of practical love and support, and an abundance of prayer. They face the hard questions with Shirley. They also participate in the fellowship of suffering.

As a theologian, I am challenged by this story in a particular way. Have we taught subjects like the sovereignty and love of God with clarity and balance? Granted, topics like the origin of evil and the goodness of God in the face of evil have challenged the church for centuries. On reflection, my conclusion is that we can do a better job on teaching about the genuine availability of miraculous healing while at the same time equipping our people with a robust ability to endure suffering and sickness without doubting the love of God. Put differently, any theology of healing and sickness must pass the test of being able to dialogue with stories like this. It is not the only story Thy has faced. She has journeyed with me through the death of our wonderful young pastor, also from cancer. What makes Thy, the author, more remarkable is that she endured both stories, the one following soon after the other, and never wavered in her walk with God. This book witnesses to a very solid and mature Christian faith. Those who read it will find it will edify and strengthen. Those who face a similar crisis will find it profoundly helpful.

Dr. Derek Morphew
Academic Dean, International Vineyard Institute

Foreword by Prof. James Swezey

In this compelling book, Thy Cameron takes the reader on a heart-warming and gut-wrenching journey. There is no way to fully understand the depth of grief a parent experiences at the death of a child, but Thy gives us unsparing insights into that pain. This is not just Shirley's story; it is also the story of those who loved her.

Thy often draws upon Shirley's own words. She paints a beautiful portrait of Shirley's full and rich life, both as it appeared on the surface, and also the profound struggles that lay beneath. God's grace was ever-present – even once cancer struck. During one time of searching, Shirley wrote, "While on a lonely, windswept beach, I felt moved to pray for a long time. Nothing dramatic happened, but I thought that maybe God was glad to hear from me." And so Shirley began "factoring God back into the equation of her life". And therein lies the heart of this tale.

More than anything else, this is a love story – the shared love between a mother and daughter and the God who loves them both. I encourage anyone who is sincerely seeking God's presence or desires to experience his great love to read it. It will provide much-needed light and sustenance for our dark days. Thy and Shirley remind us that we never need face those days alone.

Prof. James Swezey
School of Education, Liberty University, Lynchburg, USA

Foreword by Rev. Costa Mitchell

You, dear reader, are holding a beautiful thing in your hand. You are holding the redeemed, restored soul of a young woman. As you read this story, you will learn that soul, and you will discover an answer to the question, "Why suffering?"

In this gripping rollercoaster ride, we discover that God is less concerned with changing our circumstances than with changing our lives. Written with harrowing honesty and beautiful poignancy by a mother who thus bares her own soul as she describes her daughter's journey, this book filled me with awe as I was granted the privilege of watching God transform Shirley Cameron's soul.

Shirley was raised in true faith, but her soul was broken by a deep sense of not being worthy of love. Beautiful, highly intelligent and adventurous, she tried every remedy until, facing her growing awareness of brokenness, she encountered the love of God.

We read how cancer ravages Shirley's body and challenges her faith. We hold our breath as her renewed commitment to Jesus is tested, and we gasp in wonder as we see her rising to the test and coming through it refined. As physical healing eludes her, she writes, "If God loves me, I have no need to fear. His love is huge – therefore, I'm not afraid because God loves me!"

I know that this unputdownable, heartbreakingly beautiful and inspirational book will make you weep. But its message is simple and strong. If you discover the same love of the same God, you will echo Shirley's gladness and perfect triumph.

Rev. Costa Mitchell
Retired National Director of the Association of Vineyard Churches, South Africa

Mum, Please Help Me Die

CHAPTER ONE

Just a Bump

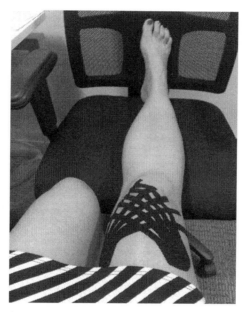

"Mum, they are pretty sure it's a tumour in the bone."

"I HAVE JUST BUMPED MY LEG ON MY DESK AT THE OFFICE, Mum," Shirley says over the phone, "and it's really sore."

It's a week or two since she flew back to her home in the UK after a lightning weekend visit to her father and me in Cape Town. Since Shirley left South Africa in 2000, her visits here have meant a great deal to us. And this short stay – in March 2013 – has really delighted us.

When she arrived at the airport late that Friday night, she looked stunning. She'd just come from doing presentations in Johannesburg for her IT firm in Bracknell. Still dressed for the presentations in very high heels and a filmy, autumn-coloured dress, she was breathtaking. Gentle waves of long, flowing, now golden hair rounded it all off.

She lives in the leafy green village of Wokingham. It's a winsome mix of farmlands – horses sometimes clip-clop down Sandy Lane – and housing developments. Now back home, she curls up on her old leather couch, phone held firmly between shoulder and ear.

"Mu-um," she says, I've been gym-ing a lot. At first, I thought the leg thing was just that. In the end, I went to a physio because it didn't go away. Sue felt that something was not quite right. She sent me for X-rays."

Doctors' appointments, scans, tests and biopsies fill the next few weeks. Shirley passes a lot of time sitting in waiting rooms with somewhat dishevelled magazines.

"What was the worst," she tells me, "was when they took tissue from the lump in my leg."

Her thoughts are anxious and somewhat dishevelled too.

Still the swelling increases; it stretches the skin of her right thigh more and more. Her leg begins to shine and glow deep pink. It's now quite clear that this is very serious. For our small family – Brian, Shirley and me – the days become anxious and stressed.

"Oh, Mum, the pain just gets worse and worse," Shirley confides. "And they can't give me anything for it until they know what's going on. The only way I can get upstairs now is to sit on my bum and drag myself up backwards."

Every time she does this, macho boy-cat Wilf comes alongside. In his beautifully groomed, thick, white coat, he struts his stuff as she slides from step to step. After all, he has made the mink-coloured carpeted stairs truly his. And he loves to welcome company.

There's a day when Cullum from next door calls to his mum. "Shirley's sitting in her car crying."

Amanda goes to have a look.

"It's the pain," Shirley tells her. "It's just got too much for me."

Shirley can't sleep. This is not new, thanks to bouts of depression and stress. Now it gets worse. She comes to hate tossing and turning in her upstairs bedroom. Her three cats don't like it either – she disturbs them as they stretch out on the bed beside her. So she often stays downstairs in front of the TV, hoping to get sleepy. Many times, this doesn't happen until the early hours of the morning.

She watches current movies and lots of repeats. *The Matrix* is a favourite. Amazingly, *Indiana Jones* is drawn into the loop. She loves to escape into sci-fi, and finds as much of it as she can. Even *Buffy the Vampire Slayer* serves as some sort of distraction.

Resourceful as ever, Shirley tries to ease the pain by strapping the leg. She creates an attractive crisscross pattern with black tape. It matches the black and white stripes of one of her dresses. She comforts her aching limb with a hot-water bottle. She also heats a happy hugger filled with beans in the microwave. When none of this works too well, she applies a cold compress.

"Ha, ha," she writes on Facebook, "I drove to Leeds with a bag of frozen peas on my leg."

Still the leg swells and the pain increases. She finds some attractive baggy pants online. And orders three pairs. The skin over the sore area stretches yet more. It continues to redden and feels shiny-tight.

She really can't sleep, and she dreads the struggle up the stairs. Often, she sips the dry red wine she loves until late in the night.

Every day now, Shirley calls from the UK. She details her growing alarm. "Next thing, I get this scary phone call. 'Please come down to the hospital to discuss your results,' they tell me. What do you think it means, Mum?"

Shirley googles. She scans through a lot of possibilities, some of them pretty serious.

"At least it's not the big C," she quips on Facebook.

Then, one day, Shirley phones.

"Mum, they are pretty sure it's a tumour in the bone," she wretchedly tells me, her voice distressed and teary. "It is cancer, but they think it is only stage 1, or at the worst, stage 2."

Stage 2 would mean the tissue around her femur has also been impregnated with the murderous, malignant cells. Stages 3 and 4 would mean advanced cancer.

Time passes, and Shirley regains some control. She tries to make light of the situation for everyone's sake – if you *can* make light of something as serious as this. She's doing this because, typically, she can't bear to cause anyone pain.

All this is such a shock. Shirley's always been so amazingly fit and well. So many of her favourite things depend on excellent health, physical strength and full-out action. Of late, to help with excessive restlessness and stress, she's been spending time at the gym and swimming more than usual.

She discovered the benefits of a little exercise as a nine-year-old, when her very wise teacher sent her to run around the sports field. As usual, she had finished the classwork first. Rather than have her get in everyone's hair, Miss Kok would send her off for a jog.

Not during her university days of snoozing and partying – but from the time she was married, she got into exercise in a big way. Orienteering, mountain climbing, hiking, sky-diving, skiing and a little bit of rock climbing were all thrown into the mix.

She even tackled DIY, but found out that it's not as easy as it looks. So she got the curtain rails up in her three-bedroomed house with one or two endearingly skew.

Once we've recovered from the news to some small degree, Brian and I and many friends and family have to ask, "How can you – of all people – have cancer?"

Yet she has.

CHAPTER TWO

Early Years

"...to be a mother is the most wonderful thing in the world."

BRIAN IS ORDAINED AS A CURATE IN 1970. AS A PASTOR'S WIFE, I have a heart for the work too. I want to support my husband in every way I can. And I have a strong desire to serve God with all I've got. I run the women's work with its Bible studies and jumble sales. I take on Kids' Church. I counsel, visit and do admin. I even write the monthly newsletter. I am expected to become fully involved – and, as usual, I go over the top.

In 2000, I enrol first for a Master's degree in education at a Christian university in America, and then enter their doctoral programme. I love all this, as well as doing some lecturing online for the university.

From 2002, I create and present all sorts of programmes for a national Christian radio station. I interview for my magazine programmes. I work on relevant themes for my music programmes. I write women's and children's talks for my other programmes. In 2004, I resign, overcome by a mild form of Chronic Fatigue Syndrome or ME.

It's obvious that I love to keep many balls – too many? – in the air. But perhaps there's more to it than that. It's so easy to pass it off with, "Oh, I'm just a workaholic." But what does that really mean? It means I need the comfort of work as some need drugs – or adrenaline rushes, or TV. In fact, Brian and I are in the same boat. We don't play much, and we don't play often.

In 1970, Brian and I decide we want to start a family. We want and want and want a baby. But we can't fall pregnant. The disappointments are too many to count. I find myself thinking God is engaging me deeply in a painful refining process. It really hurts to have your hopes go up and down, up and down like a yo-yo – month by month.

We put our names down for adoption. Two more years of heart-anguish go by. At one point, knowing how the adoption society works, we have a pretty strong suspicion that they have a baby for us. We begin to get a little excited. It won't be long now. Then an amazed gynaecologist has to admit we might be pregnant.

"I can't believe it, I just can't believe this!" he says, wiping his bald head, perhaps more thoroughly than necessary. "Go away," he says gently, taking in the surprise on our faces, "and come back in two months and then we'll know."

So after a very long two months, we come back. And, shaking and wiping his head all over again, he has to admit, "You really are pregnant, four whole months pregnant."

I find it all such a joy. I decorate. Using pictures from colouring books, I paint a frieze of bunnies, kittens and puppies in soft, pastel colours to run right around the baby's room. I design – and Brian builds – a cupboard for the baby's clothes. The banging as we put it together makes the baby kick hard in the womb – a precious moment.

Shirley is born in 1975. I am sure no baby could be more loved or welcome. I think many times that to be a mother is the most wonderful thing in the world.

A pastor friend says, "You haven't lived until you've had a child."

I say many fervent amens to that.

For me there's another side to Shirley's arrival. Here's my chance to love unconditionally. I feel it's safe to love a baby like that. I know this precious baby will wallow in all I have in my heart for her. So I set about providing her with a background in which she can flourish. (In fact, Brian tells me later he was jealous at times – because I gave her so much love.)

At first, we spend our time together doing very simple things. It includes tickles and cuddles. I think I can still hear her baby-chuckle. I love to watch her sleep. I don't like the idea of putting her down with a bottle. So I make sure I always hold her for every feed.

As a little child, Shirley is a delight. She loves to chatter, learns very quickly and likes to do things for herself. She loves cheesy bread, but vehemently rejects banana custard and pawpaw.

She never runs short of ideas, to the point of sucking three dummies at once, always with a mischievous twinkle in her large green-brown eyes. When she is out of line – like taking a liking to dog biscuits – a stern voice is all that is necessary.

One special day, on the way to nursery school, I spot a single little yellow daisy on the pavement. I stop the car and show it to her. I want her to learn to delight over such a marvellous thing. I want her to learn to appreciate what is special in this world.

Once Shirley begins to talk in earnest – she is soon very articulate – we talk non-stop. I work at this because I know it's very important at this stage of her development.

At bedtime I read *Winnie the Pooh* and other stories before tucking her in. I start to make up stories for her. Every night she now begs me for one of mine too.

"Ple-e-ease, Mum?"

There's a favourite about cupcakes "with icing on the top and a cherry in the middle".

During Shirley's teen years, I run a youth group in our home on Friday nights and Teen Church on Sunday mornings. We produce a musical together. We sell Boerewors[2] rolls every Saturday until we have enough

---

[2] a South African sausage

money for the group to fly from Pretoria to Cape Town for four days' holiday with no sleep.

I do it for my teens. But I do it all for another reason too. I do it for Shirley. I see it as creating lots of space for her; and compensating, in some way, for the siblings she doesn't have.

Shirley is born with only two – not three – blood vessels in her umbilical cord. This suggests to our paediatrician there could be trouble ahead – problems at some later stage in her life.

I dismiss any suggestion of possible trouble as absurd. Foolishly, I assume that since we've waited so long for Shirley, there can't be anything wrong with her.

At no point does God say he is giving us a perfect baby, but I assume it. I also think that after all we have been through in the struggle to have a child, we deserve a totally normal, healthy one. So I never follow up the two-blood-vessel story and its possible implications.

In time a shadow of concern does creep ever so slowly into my heart. I don't want to face it, but I can't deny it anymore. Maybe the missing blood vessel is significant after all? Maybe, while there's nothing physically wrong, it symbolises the absence of something else? Something psychological? Or maybe something ominous lies ahead?

School days bring the catty interchanges of little girls. This is distressing for most of them, but Shirley goes to pieces. I am always comforting, holding her on my lap and gently drying the very many tears.

She always seems to be crying. At first, I accept it all as normal. But I come to see that her troubles are way beyond that. In fact, they're extreme and intense. Eventually I do have to admit that Shirley really struggles. I can't put my finger on it, but it's not how it should be. I become incredibly distressed for her.

One day I take her to the beach on holiday at Scottburgh. Nine-year-old Shirley takes off her thick glasses. She doesn't want to lose them in the sea. There is a moment when I look up to see her coming up from the water, totally lost. I see my child as bitterly isolated and alone. She just can't see where we are. I run to fetch her, aching for her and how she must feel.

In a strange way, pictures of Shirley utterly alone always stir up the ache in me. Her lostness is what I see – a figure on the beach on the Isle of Harris in the Hebrides; her lone, retreating figure hiking on top of Table Mountain; her lime-green-jacketed figure way down a ski slope with masses of empty white snow all around. Perhaps – even now – I begin to see that to struggle with life as she does leads to intense isolation and loneliness.

Growing up brings Shirley a series of challenges – deep insecurity, a poor self-image, a battle to find satisfying friendships. All these things whisper the trouble she's in and that trouble lies ahead for her. Tears drench each new challenge. Unconsciously, I work harder and harder to help her.

The hints of trouble ahead are, as yet, only the faintest suggestions. But they are there. And I know something is amiss, although I can't put my finger on it.

At this point – in the midst of growing distress – my pain for her begins – pain that will last for a very long time.

CHAPTER THREE

Shirley's Last Visit

*"Having Shirley with us makes everything we do
that weekend just that much more wonderful."*

SHIRLEY'S HAD HER FAIR SHARE OF ACCIDENTS. ONCE WHEN
out jogging, she fell so badly that she couldn't put her skinned hands into
water for more than a week. So when she bumps her leg on her desk, I'm
not too worried at first.

The level of anxiety in her voice as she tells me about being sent for X-
rays raises my concern considerably. The agony of the leg biopsy leaves me
hurting for her. She doesn't complain easily, so I know it's been terrible.

She talks more and more of increasing pain. When she asks the question,
"Mum, what can all this possibly mean?" her angst is deep and dire.

Her question undoes me. I don't know what to say.

I think back to her last visit, in March – before all this began…

———————

For Brian and me, waiting at the airport on a Friday night, the anticipation mounts. The doors swing open. It's late and Shirley's tired. But she still manages to take our breath away. She's still dressed for work. And – once again – her great dress sense hasn't failed her. No wonder her friends have changed her surname from Cameron to Glameron. We're glad she hasn't had time to change. It's lovely for us to see her like this.

And her smile's the winning smile we all celebrate.

Shirley's deeply tired. She sleeps a lot. She munches her beloved cheese-flavoured Niknaks on an ageing, weathered sunbed in the backyard.

We are thrilled to have her with us. It's been a very long time. We savour the Brass Bell at Kalk Bay. Waves crash against our window as we talk. Having her with us makes everything we do that weekend just that much more wonderful.

We also eat out at sunset at Maestro's, where we watch the sun gently dressing Table Mountain in golden nightclothes.

Between courses, Shirley scrolls through the pictures on her iPhone for us. She's obviously glad to be here. That makes her unusually chatty and expansive.

She still has photos of her skydiving days near Citrusdal, close to Cape Town. She's done eighty-eight jumps. She describes the first one:

"I managed to land in a prickly orange tree. The only nice thing about it was the wonderful scent – it was in full bloom."

More pictures follow. One is of her landing in a beautiful field of white daisies. Next we see a picture of her – in her sky-blue and cerise-pink jumpsuit – in a formation jump with two others.

As we wait for our meal to arrive, she scrolls down until she finds the pictures of her full marathon runs. One comes up of her obviously in pain during the London Marathon. I remember a phone call about that, when she said, "Mum, you should've seen the blisters on my feet." *Hmm – I can just imagine.* Now, she says, "I look a real mess, don't I?"

Neither of us thinks so.

Shirley's deft with her thumbs. When she finds her New York Marathon pictures, she grimaces.

"I was so stiff and sore, but I did have a day to spare in the Big Apple. So I walked – and limped – for miles through art galleries. You don't want to know about my feet."

We peer at two pink, puffy feet.

Dinner is served. We fall silent, busy now with the business of eating. When coffee arrives, Brian asks for more pictures. She hesitates. But she scrolls down and finds a picture of herself... spread-eagled in the snow.

"Oh, look at this." Shirley titters at the sight of herself, skis wide apart, in a heap in the snow. "I've improved, you know. I actually avoid trees now – I used to give every tree I hugged a guy's name. Now, if I have to, I can find a pile of soft snow in which to land."

She loves to get the adrenaline pumping as she clocks 70mph down the slopes. At last – to everyone's great relief – she buys a helmet. Very anxious for her safety, her ex-boyfriend Stuart has bullied her into that.

She scrolls down a bit more.

"Oh, now just look at this," she says again. And sniggers.

It's a short video from Nick of 'Glam Bum', as her friends on the slopes call her. She and Nick met on the ski slopes in Austria after Christmas 2011, and they have been close ever since. Nick's managed to photograph that part of her anatomy many times – or so their friends tease – as she whoops away at speed. For a moment or two she's quiet, remembering that day in the sunshine on the Austrian Alps.

The next picture is of her getting into a Lamborghini.

"Our IT team was completing team training. The prize was to drive this wonderful machine round the race track – and I won!"

(On the phone to me previously, Shirley sounded smug – seeing that all the others competing were men.)

"They all drove too fast," she explains, "but I drove really carefully."

She does quite a bit more scrolling while we wait. Then she finds some pictures of her kitted out for scuba-diving. There's a murky picture of her having a tête-à-tête with a whitetip shark. She's named him Bob.

I remember that on her first dive in the Red Sea, she came face to face with a deadly poisonous stone fish. Her diving-instructor friend 'freaked' and whisked her away.

A few more pictures follow, this time of the ski slopes near Salt Lake City, home of the Winter Olympics of 2002. She's just been there with her workmates in January this year.

Her panoramic photos of the Wasatch Range impress us deeply. She becomes wistful. Her voice grows soft. It's obvious she absolutely loves outdoor action. And such unusually downy, powdery snow.

We are really very sad when Shirley's lightning visit comes to an end. Her presentations to four different banks have gone well, and she's clearly been very happy to be back in South Africa, so she's been far more spontaneous than usual – and we've loved it. She's genuinely sorry it's been so short. She tells us enthusiastically that she plans to come more often – and that she's coming back soon.

That was March. I don't know why, but now I jerk back to reality. *What can April bring us,* I wonder. Shirley's already had so many struggles to 'do life'. How do I react to the bump on her leg, the worried physio, the X-rays, tests and biopsies? Dread squeezes my very soul. As her angst – and pain – increases, so does mine.

Chapter Four

Denial

"Mum, what can all this possibly mean?"

NEXT TIME THE PHONE RINGS, I GLARE AT THE INSTRUMENT for several moments. I don't want to pick it up, but I *do* want to – and always do. Time after time – and this time too – I feel the distance between us. Shirley's in Wokingham near Reading and we are six thousand miles away in Cape Town.

The talk of a tumour in the bone deepens my dismay. How can I even contemplate the possibility that it is cancer?

"Mum," she says mournfully, "they think it is only stage 1 or 2."

"Oh, God," I say under my breath.

I haven't even been able to say the word, let alone consider the possibility of the prince of dread diseases, so great is my struggle with denial.

I certainly can't even think about stages 3 and 4 – anything more is off the charts for now. Helplessly, I reason, *okay – if it's only stage 1 or 2, there's hope, isn't there? Maybe they've found it early enough. And – maybe? – they can just remove it all, in one fell swoop, and we can move on with our lives.*

I recall the massacre in 1993 during the evening service at St James' Church, Kenilworth, Cape Town. The day after the shooting, I had a strong desire to clean up the damage in the auditorium. I suppressed my feelings. I had just been shot at – with the AK47s that killed eleven people in the church around me and wounded fifty-eight others.

What I wanted was to 'fix it', so that everything could be back to the way it was before. We'd just wipe it all away, as if it never happened.

Once the police had given us permission, a team of us went in to clean up. We wiped up bucket after bucket of blood. Pathetically, I straightened the books in the pews. As if that could make it right again!

Now it's the same thing again. Again, what's happened is so terrible that I can't allow it. I need to wipe it all away – to deny all of it. As if that could set things right!

I toss and turn on a restless pillow, hating the long hours of the night. Next morning, I wake up from an eventual fitful nap, surprised to find myself sobbing.

"No! No! No!" I cry, the words crescendoing from the depths of my soul.

I shriek the words. They shred the silence of the house – and Brian's heart – as he holds me close. Who could think that such a small, two-letter word could express so much shock, so much horror and agony?

And who could think – how can *I* think – of what might lie ahead?

CHAPTER FIVE

The Worst Day of My Life

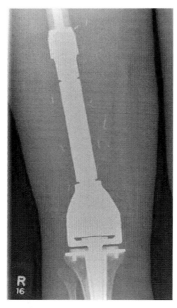

"Your new femur will be made of titanium…"

"HELLO, YOU. CAN YOU PLEASE DRIVE ME TO OXFORD ON Friday, 14 June, for the PET scan results?" Shirley asks, hoping so very much that Nick can.

Glad to help, he drives her to Churchill Hospital. Here she's to meet her oncologist at the Osteosarcoma Clinic for the first time. Nick's probably her closest friend, so it's great to have him with her.

Neither Nick nor Shirley notices much of the gloriously green country-side along the way. Irrigated fields, fallow and cultivated meadows and bottle-green trees flash by. Tranquil sheep graze in the lush pastures of Oxfordshire. An occasional fighter jet streaks across the azure sky, cutting large fluffy clouds mercilessly in half with its vapour trail. It's the turmoil in Shirley and Nick that makes it impossible for them to notice anything much.

Nick steers Shirley's silver-grey Beamer with the swift, confident manoeuvres of a racing driver. Shirley adjusts her hefty right leg – until the throbbing pain subsides and she's a little more comfortable. Her right thigh now resembles a polished watermelon in size. She pulls her flowing, full-length, dark-blue patterned skirt out from under it. A pillow supports the aching limb. Every now and then she rubs the leg affectionately.

Not surprisingly, Shirley spends much of the journey deep in thought. Nick glances at her every now and then. Wisely, he says nothing.

Old skeletons in her cupboard seize the opportunity to try to make mischief. They suggest, "You haven't been looking after yourself properly, you know."

Shirley remembers how many times she's been too tired to do anything else but pick up a takeaway and chips. She remembers boxes of creamy Belgian chocolates, polished off in one or two sittings. She remembers drinking too much wine.

More accusations filter through. For ever so long now, Shirley's felt that when God does deal with her, it's always to punish and condemn. So it's not surprising that another dark thought assails her: *Nobody – not God, not anybody – loves you, or so you believe. If you are that unlovable, why shouldn't unlovely things happen to you?*

And so the distress of the day steadily increases.

Shirley shivers.

"Hey, you," Nick says, "take my jacket if you're cold. It's on the back seat."

Shirley shakes her head. They drive on in silence. Now and then, she catches Nick smiling sympathetically at her. She manages to sort of smile back. And then she feels a little better.

Not far from Oxford, they begin to talk – about the consultation that lies ahead. Her brimming eyes cloud behind her sunglasses. She shivers even more, though she's wearing a pale-blue hoody and soft, flowered scarf. From time to time, Nick gently pats her besieged right knee. And she shifts a little. The warmth of their friendship certainly brings some relief.

The hospital has a new, modern front. It conceals a past – rickety buildings with old, black rubber doors dating back to the Second World War. Shirley hangs on to Nick. She slowly shuffles the whole length of the foyer, past rows of shops. They turn left at the lovely indoor waterfall that flows gently down, its walls and mosaic floor turquoise and aquamarine.

Halfway along the long, sterile white corridor, they turn left again. The receptionist steers them to that colour-coded circle of seats under bright skylights that is dedicated to sarcoma patients.

A digital screen repeats endlessly, "We are sorry to have to inform you that the following clinics are running late."

A list details which ones and how late.

It's all so very strange. Shirley's long, abundant, wavy golden-brown tresses caress her delicate face. But she finds little comfort in anything other than her soundless praying – and the warmth of Nick's hand.

"I'm really sorry to have to tell you," Professor Agit Kumar says, "but you have osteosarcoma."

Vicky, the Macmillan nurse, present because of her dedication to cancer patients, sits absolutely still. Her bright blue eyes moisten with compassion.

At first, Nick and Shirley do not hear a single word. Their focus is not on the consultant's words but on what they see. They find themselves staring at the display of scans and X-rays on the grey, luminous box on the wall in front of them.

The tension is tangible. It feels as if the entire world has come to a standstill. Since osteosarcoma is very uncommon in adults approaching forty – Shirley is thirty-eight – they have been clinging to a slender thread of hope that this is not her problem. Now, as they see the evidence before their eyes, their agony is intense.

"Well – okay," Shirley concedes very reluctantly under her breath, still looking at the screen. Then she mutters, "But it can't be in my lungs. Oh, God, please – it just can't."

Nick asks the professor to repeat what he's just said. Vicky leans forward, full of sympathy, her blue eyes matching her blue uniform. Kumar runs his hand through his curly brown hair.

For a moment or two, there's nothing but silence in the room. Then the professor speaks. This time, his words penetrate.

"The red areas represent the cancer," he murmurs, somewhat apologetically.

Shirley squeezes Nick's hand so hard she crushes his fingers into a distorted mass of grinding bone.

"You can see the cancer is very advanced in the right femur," Kumar continues.

The right leg certainly is a mass of red, the whole thigh area riddled with the dread disease. Nick and Shirley look at each other. The ice-cold fingers of fear grip their trembling hearts.

"We need to operate to remove almost the entire femur from hip to knee."

Nick and Shirley struggle to take any of it in.

"Your new femur will be made of titanium," the professor continues. "We'll have you walking by Christmas."

Considering the seriousness of the situation, these last words seem somewhat out of place.

(Later Shirley explains to her friends, "It's a big op. They have to replace a large part of my leg with exciting metal bits. They also have to replace my knee and all sorts.")

Now Nick and Shirley shift their focus from the leg. They frantically scan the image of her lungs. Rather like ripe apples hanging from a laden tree, a number of small groupings of dots glow red – not just from one, but from both lungs.

As Kumar looks at these too, he murmurs under his breath, "There are so many."

Alarmed, Nick takes Shirley's hand in both his. This time they feel the fear gnawing deep.

"The secondary tumours in your lungs are going to be a lot harder to get rid of," the professor explains, even more apologetically. "We've got to tackle those as soon as we can."

Nick looks at Shirley. Life has just thrown her a major curveball.

("I was expecting a flood of tears," Nick later tells Jo, a close friend to both of them. "But what do I see instead? The most remarkable composure." He shakes his head in disbelief. "I was totally amazed. Either this was shock or it was something else – perhaps an inner strength? The reserve the struggles of her life have taught her?" Whatever it was, he found what he understood to be her mysterious strength quite beautiful.)

Shirley's soft, melodic voice breaks the stony silence. She asks the hardest question. "What are my chances of surviving this, Professor?"

For a long, hard moment, Agit Kumar looks at her. "Because it is in your lungs, the chances of survival drop from sixty or seventy per cent to just ten per cent," he says gravely. "If we can remove the whole tumour from the leg – and successfully treat your lungs – you could have a bit more than five years," he explains. "If we can't catch the lungs in time, you could have up to a year."

Blow after blow crashes down and lays siege to hope.

But, Shirley reminds herself, they are talking of operating on the lungs at some point, aren't they? If they can even talk like that, then they think it's possible to win – that's hopeful, isn't it? Otherwise why would they even try?

Yet – unbelievably – her prognosis, as it stands, allows only a year if the lungs can't be cleared.

All of this is utterly overwhelming. Shirley and Nick are absolutely numb from the shock. This whole experience is something else. It really hits home as Nick drives them back. Tears and words erupt in a mingled flood.

"I cannot do this," Shirley keeps repeating. "No way – I just cannot do this!"

"Dear, dear girl," Nick replies, "I don't think God is asking you to do this. All he's asking you to do – for now – is to get back on your feet."

She becomes quiet and thoughtful. *Okay – hmm – maybe I can get back on my feet... Maybe I can do that much...*

Nick weaves the Beamer through the heavy Friday afternoon traffic. Shirley hardly notices. Her focus on the pressing catastrophe is so intense, she's oblivious – even of the swollen, aching mass that is her right leg. Occasionally, her flowing skirt billows in the wind. And occasionally, soft hair wraps her damp face. *I know this huge thing is about to happen to me, but what it's going to be like, what it's going to feel like – any of that stuff? I just have no idea. What also freaks me out big time is the rush to get me on chemo. Only two days and the chemo starts? It's just a complete whirlwind. Go figure – how terrifying is that?*

Nick's lost in thought too. His thoughts go back to when he first met Shirley on the skiing trip in 2010...

To Nick, Shirley's a most intriguing and captivating thirty-four-year-old woman. He gives her the once over. *Oh, my life, you're pretty.*

Next thing, he checks to see if any other guys are interested. Then he sets up a dinner with her and a few others in town. The others actually all bail out, as they're too tired and want an early night. So – really happy now – he tells her, "It's just us, if you like."

For him, the butterflies move up a gear as they walk out into the freezing night. Snowflakes flutter past their eyes. He discovers that she has a sense of humour "that could deck you with belly cramps from laughing, and a smile and laugh that are contagious".

She's got a brain sharper that a samurai sword, he says to himself, *and an ear that listens so acutely and hears what you are saying (or not!) All with a beautiful, soft feminine voice – like incense washing over you. And a most wonderful and beautiful creation to look at too!*

The evening is bliss – the chemistry, the spring in his step despite very weary ski legs – as they walk back to the hotel.

Now, as Nick drives, he glances at Shirley, so pale and withdrawn. He remembers they dated for some months. Then he saddens as he remembers her insecurities coming to the surface. So did her struggles with deep depression. They intensified as the weeks went by. They also put the relationship on hold.

He frowns. Quite some time ago, he invited her to work with him on a Tech charity project he'd launched. Working together became the opportunity to cool things off a bit. This was bitterly hard for him, but he couldn't see what else to do. But they forged a great friendship and spent a lot of time together. Amazingly – although they stopped dating – their friendship deepened.

Since then, they've continued to share – trials and tribulations, and the highs and lows of each dating others. He chuckles as he remembers going to the same pub, one of them with a date, the other to sit in a corner checking the date out, in order to report back later.

This time, as he looks over at Shirley, his glance is tender and his heart is full. *Hardly a day passes when we don't make some sort of contact with each other. We both know we're walking a parallel path that can, should the circumstances be right, come back together. You just know when there's that silent – yet tangible – dynamic with someone. There's peacefulness, an ease, the ability to have a whole conversation – in just a glance. Then life throws you a curveball. At first you think it's manageable – just a little blip – then a piece of news comes that truly takes your breath away. You think things can't get worse, can't hurt any more – until they do.*

On this Friday afternoon trip home after Kumar's news, Nick and Shirley are each so busy with their own thoughts that they hardly talk at all.

In her testimony, filmed ten months later, Shirley recalls:

The doctors decided to rush me straight into chemo ... so literally within three days, I was on chemo. Go figure. I didn't have time to think – it was just a complete whirlwind.

The other thing I can remember about the day of the news – by far the worst day of my whole life – is a sort of shock, initially. I felt completely numb. Perhaps it was denial? Then there were tears, even bravado. I guess it was bravado in front of the prof that made me seem very calm and composed. Dear Nick helped a world.

I remember towards the end of the day, just – virtually everything inside of myself falling on my knees – saying, "I can't do this, I cannot do this. No way!...

Shirley hesitates.

"...Nothing in me has got what it takes to do this!"

I looked at Nick. He seemed to be praying or something. Not me! I'm in a place of pure disbelief. Um, no... disbelief isn't the right word. I did believe what was happening to me. But I think I had no concept of what that was actually going to mean. So, it was kind of like... I know this huge thing is about to happen to me, but what it's going to be like, what it's going to feel like... any of that stuff, I... I just have no idea...

I just made this determined decision...

Shirley flicks the hair out of her eyes.

...that, you know... I can give up completely right now. Or I can take on what lies ahead; I can fight for my life with everything I've got. There's a lot to come. This is just the beginning. For me, it's a no-brainer: of course I'm going to fight.

CHAPTER SIX

Shock

*"...the dusty, grey colossus of a rhino ambles
purposefully across the road..."*

"THERE'S SOMETHING BIG UP AHEAD!" BRIAN'S VOICE RISES
with excitement. "Just look at all those cars!"

The short, golden veld of the Kruger National Park shimmers in the
midday heat. Right in front of us, the dusty, grey colossus of a rhino ambles
purposefully across the road, ponderous head swaying from side to side.
Cars struggle to manoeuvre, some to see better, some to reverse out of
danger's way. We thrill to see a second beast beginning to cross the tarmac,
head heavy with horn.

Today's game drive has failed to get us interested in the way it would have done in the past. It's taken these two animals in the open grassland in front of us to get our attention at all.

Brian and I booked this trip a long time ago, so – in spite of Shirley's horrendous news – we decided to do it anyway. But we're not really enjoying this. Our thoughts are with Shirley and her cancer consultation in Oxford. We are waiting for news from her later today. We don't have any idea what this will mean. We do know we can pack up immediately if we have to.

Now and then, we chat a bit. Then we pull up in the dust outside our hut in Satara. We know there's mobile phone reception only in the rest camp. We wait out the afternoon. We need to make absolutely sure we are there for Shirley's text – when it comes.

Back in our hut, we find the hours becoming steadily longer and emptier. They drag their feet like really old men. We can almost not believe it when, at last, an incoming message agitates the all-too-quiet phone.

Shirley writes:

> *I am so sorry to have to tell you this in a text. But there's really no other way to get hold of you. The scan shows that it is cancer; the cancer in my leg is advanced to stages 3 and 4. They say they can operate for the leg. The problem is that it's also in my chest. The prof says this will be harder to deal with. They want to do chemo a.s.a.p., via a 50-hour drip, starting Monday. This means being admitted for a few days every second week for six months. Please pray for me. Much love, Shirls.*

Time stops. We stare at the phone forever. A cold, clammy fear wrings our hearts, encircling them like wet fog. Leaden, they sink down, down, down to the bottom of our shattered souls. Pain shreds every inch of our beings. We feel hysteria rising in our throats. We want to scream and scream.

Instead, we are so sickeningly silent – absolutely paralysed. We can't react, not for at least an hour. Denial pins us down. Colossal disbelief packs its punch. Again, we force down another unbearable wave of hysteria. Then we become aware of a great feebleness, turning heart and limb to jelly. When, at last, something does stir within us again, it's a pain-drenched cry to God.

At long last, we respond – just a little – to the news. Our first attempts to process it are very, very feeble. We text Shirley. We scrabble together all the most comforting things we can think of to say. Pain oozes through the cracks, and we struggle to put stray, frightened thoughts into words.

"Let's go home," one of us rasps. It's a no-brainer.

Hysteria rises again and again – and we battle to keep it down. We hold each other. We sort of pray. Shakily, we make some plans. We are so very grateful now that just before we came away on holiday, God prompted us to book me a flight to Shirley in the UK at the beginning of July.

Brian brings forward our flights from Johannesburg to Cape Town to the next night. He cancels the last few days' holiday in Mpumalanga. Now we just need to get back to O.R. Tambo International Airport tomorrow, in time for the flight home.

Hand in hand, we go to see the Camp Manager.

"Please sir," we ask, "can we leave camp before the usual 6 o'clock opening of the gates in the morning? We have a very long way to drive. When we came up, there were detours along the road that delayed us big time. Now we have to get to Jo'burg in time to catch a plane home to Cape Town tomorrow night."

The large, tubby black man shakes his head reluctantly. We tell him of Shirley's plight. He's full of sympathy. However, he pushes his glasses up his nose and shakes his head again, even more emphatically.

"I can't do it," he says. "It's just not safe." Then he asks her name. "I'll pray for her," he promises.

As we set out at six in the morning, Brian and I are very quiet. There's quite some distance to be covered. We feel the pressure to get there on time. Stress levels begin to rise.

Brian concentrates on his driving and I concentrate on it too. I can't make a difference, but I so badly want to help. So I watch the road with him – the road signs. I will us safely past the potholes and slowly trundling trucks.

Every now and then, I put my hand on his knee to encourage him. I feed him peppermints and water. In fact, I drive every inch of the way too. Many times, I brake for us, often when Brian doesn't even think of braking.

At times, words bubble out. They go nowhere – except round in circles. We express our bewilderment, denial, confusion, sheer panic and intense longing to be with Shirley. Emotions are at high tide. In desperation, we look for the footprints of God in all this. We know instinctively that his presence will bring comfort.

When we finally get home to Cape Town, Honey, our Labrador, wags a delighted welcome. We switch on lights and begin unpacking. Just then the phone rings. It's Shirley.

She tells us she's been overwhelmed by the support, love and encouragement she's received. And she's very brave, open and honest. Her honesty makes it possible for us all to be real with each other. It becomes easier to talk about chemo and her chances of survival – now only ten to twenty-five per cent. Then she tells us she's factoring God back into the equation of her life. It's the right news at the right time.

For us, past experience with lung cancer in others overshadows any hope we might have. I'm so confused, so unable to believe any of this is real. Yet I have to hope.

The doctors talk of perhaps operating to remove the lung tumours. *Surely that will deal with the problem?* I refuse even to think that the lungs have beaten us. I refuse to think she might die soon. Shirley has a normal life-span ahead – of that I'm totally convinced. Eventually, I do very reluctantly consider the possibility of just five years. I get pushed that far – but I can't and won't consider less. I just can't. I'm weakened to the point where I'm not doing reality right now or anything remotely like it.

All weekend long, the phone calls between Shirley and me crisscross the ocean. It's such a comfort to talk – to hear her melodic voice – even when we don't know what to say. It's a very long weekend.

A glass of wine or two with her housemate, Johno, brings Shirley brief comfort. They hardly talk. Shock thwacks her ability to feel and numbs her pain just a little. There are so many aspects to her suffering.

Although Shirley says later, "I didn't have time to think," she finds out that she does – and plenty of it – before her treatment in Oxford on Monday. Her thoughts weave their way through a bewildering tangle in her mind. Ours follow a similar course.

All weekend long, the leg aches. Shirley and Nick tell friends – and ask them to pray. Brian and I also tell all those close to us. Group after group encircles Shirley with their love and compassion. She's being swaddled in sympathy and concern – and we are too.

Her friends come and go. They text, email and phone.

"Mum, they're so shocked," Shirley shares, "and some of them are teary. What I find really hard is that they actually don't know what to say."

Awkward silences from caring people are our difficult experience too.

"Mum," Shirley says, "John took me to Oxford for my consultation. Mum, he cried."

John's nearly eighty, a big, gentle man and a pillar in the church; so shocked and saddened by the news, he can't find the right words – any words – to say to Shirley.

"Sheena also cried," Shirley says.

She's a close friend, about Shirley's age.

It's hard to handle the feelings of others as well as her own turmoil.

While she waits, Shirley relives what – until now – have been some of the worst days of her life. *And now this?* Shirley catches herself shaking her head. The disbelief's ponderously slow to leave her. This tops them all.

She moves a heavy, completely black cat off her swollen leg. Chloe resembles the peanut-butter cat on supermarket bottles. Shirley stretches out in her tracksuit pants on the worn, grey leather couch. It's a tight fit, as the purring feline – now next to her – clearly has middle-age spread.

She mulls over the situation again and again. *They're telling me I have cancer… I'm most probably going to die? Perhaps I have only a year to live? A ten per cent chance of making it through? This has just got to be the pits! Nothing has come close to being as bad as this. The news Kumar gave Nick and me yesterday makes yesterday by far the very worst day of my life.*

Brian and I share the denial. The passing of time doesn't seem to make the news real. Disbelief hovers about us too, not showing any sign of leaving.

Interrupting her own reverie to stroke the slight body of another cat – the small, delicate Shelley-cat – Shirley fondly murmurs, "What a little kitty brain you have."

The brain in that ball of beautifully mottled fluff knows only one thing right now. Both her stomach and the cat feeder down the passage are alarmingly empty. Shirley gets the message and obliges. Soon all three felines have taken a turn at satisfying the inner cat. Shirley realises she's hungry too and fetches a slice of bread and Marmite.

In Cape Town, we put out Honey's dog-biscuit dinner and open Savannas from the fridge. Cape Town is one hour ahead of the UK. We suppose Shirley's having a drink too. And we are right.

"Fill my glass please," she asks Johno, who just stands there, a bottle of wine in his hand. A little bit of *The Big Bang Theory* on TV – she really can't concentrate on anything much – some chatter about Johno's job hunting, and roasted chicken from Sainsbury's follow one another. All of this does help – a little – to pass the time.

Reactions come and go and whip up a storm. Every now and then Shirley tears up, moaning, "I… can't… do… this."

Brian and I cling to each other, sad that we are not with Shirley. Her friends hover protectively.

Shirley becomes more and more tense, quiet and withdrawn. Even her beloved cats know to tread lightly. A restless frown keeps creasing her high forehead. She can't believe time can pass quite so slowly.

The phone calls between us become increasingly more difficult. Shirley becomes tight-lipped and silent. Quietly, we all wait for Monday, 17 June, for the chemo to begin.

We dread the great unknown. But no one dreads it more than Shirley.

CHAPTER SEVEN

Loss and Despair

*"In her Art class, Shirley paints a huge sad face –
her face."*

MILE AFTER MILE SLIPS BY. IT'S THE BEGINNING OF 1991 – NEW
Year's Day, in fact. Shirley is now seventeen. I drive the little pale-blue Ford
Escort, its hatchback down to make a bed for Tigger, Abby-cat and Sugar.
Next to me, Shirley stares out through the window. Brian follows – with the
canary – in the metallic-brown Sapphire. Our little family is moving from
Pretoria to Cape Town.

The little white Toy Pom is fine, but it's a different story with the two
cats. The tabby and ginger tom are doped, but every two-and-a-half hours,
they begin to fuss. We pull up. Brian, in the Sapphire behind us, pulls up

45

too. He takes out the canary in its cage and puts it on top of the car. All around us farmlands shimmer in the hot sun. This promises to be a very long journey. We have over a thousand miles to cover.

Shirley is absolutely silent. She has said hardly a word all day. Her thoughts are her own. I hate this. I hate what they're doing to my cats. They keep forcing more dope down their throats. And why does Dad have to put the canary where everyone can see it? What a weird present anyway, from a very weird old lady in his congregation. Why would anyone give you a silent canary – this bird never sings – as a parting gift? This is all so embarrassing – and now even the goats are coming across the field to stare at us.

The job done, we drive on. Soon the drugs take effect and the cats stretch out to snooze once again. Abby-cat snores ever so gently. It's hot and we don't have air-con. A landscape of grey-brown Karoo bushes stretches out on either side of the N1. The scrubland only just holds its own. The fields of blackened rocks are shiny hot from the relentless sun. Now and then a dusty sheep crops at meagre offerings on the slopes of the koppies[3].

Soon Shirley is miles away in thought again. No matter where she turns, she sees nothing but loss. She was probably going to get provincial colours for netball; to be part of the school's debating team; to sit on the junior city council of Pretoria; to get distinctions for all her subjects in matric. She was almost certainly going to be a prefect, or more. Loss is just everywhere. *I'm totally 'freaked out', shattered, heartbroken. In one vicious thwack, I've lost everything: all my friends; Deon next-door, who was my "brother"; my youth group – they were my brothers and sisters. I've lost Tracey – we became friends in nursery school; and I've lost Brendan, my brand-new first boyfriend.* She can see his blond hair and handsome face. She wonders for a moment what happened to the little fluffy pink bunny – with one ear up and one down – he gave her when they said their sad, tender and very costly goodbye. The pain of this parting is, for her, such a big thing.

Shirley is also losing her extended Johannesburg family, her netball team friends, her church community, her school friends and the friendly lady at the tuck shop. She's such a people person that nothing can bring her more joy than being with her 'peeps'. She needs people – and her connections to them – even more than most. When she was two or three years old, she latched on to Tommy who was six weeks older, the son of a friend of ours. In her mind, she needed him to belong to her alone. If he toddled off to play with someone else, she cried as if her heart would break. Later, she felt the

---

[3] gentle hills

same about her nursery school friend, Anne. On another occasion, she'd come back from a birthday party hungry because she hadn't bothered to eat – she'd been so busy enjoying her little friends. And she cried bitterly when any visitors left us to go home.

Now she's devastated to lose nearly all those she knows and loves, in one mighty blow.

More than that, Shirley's really very sensitive. She has such a gentle heart. It's a beautiful thing to have, but in her case, it also means she's fragile. In particular, she has a brittle sense of self. To feel good, she needs her connection to the people in her life. This kind of need is a family thing. Others in our family have, or have had, it too – it's a dependency or co-dependency of one sort or another.

Shirly has much time to think and does plenty of it. *After we arrived in Cape Town, we were upstairs in this huge old house. I just felt so miserable. I caught Mum's eye and I knew she knew how desperate I was. I saw the panic in her.*

Some weeks later, she finds herself in the playground of Westerford High in Newlands. It's a beautiful setting because of the Cape Mountains, lawns and ancient chestnut trees. But she continues to yearn for the people 'back home' who energised her and brought her to life. *This is the absolute pits – a whole two-hour recess when we're supposed to go to our clubs. Every single day. And I've nobody to talk to. Nobody cares a hoot. The school psychologist says I'm mourning, as if my brothers and sisters have all died on me. He's only seen me once, but he's so dead right. Brendan, Tracey and Deon promised to write – but they don't – not even one single email. I pick up chestnuts under the huge old trees. I can't think of anything else to do.*

Once more it's loss, the loss of being left out. Her classmates have been together since nursery school. Her teachers are investing in learners they've watched grow for years. School families from her class – the backbone of the school – have met socially, also for years. Her new youth group – as they have done for so long now – tease and laugh with each other, not with a sad-looking stranger.

In her Art class, Shirley paints a huge sad face – her face. She makes the eyes green so they swim in pain. She paints huge cracks in the face, illustrating her whole world falling apart. And she fills the cracks with a chaotic jangle of music notes to document her anguish.

What's to be done? Moves – especially such a big move – are hard for everyone in a family. And we are all trying to find our feet. We're trying to adjust to a new city, a new church and a new home.

I'm very sad to see Shirley so extremely unhappy. But I'm not surprised. In fact, I've dreaded this. I've always known that she would find the move the hardest of all of us. Even before we left Pretoria, I was worried sick about how she would manage; how I dreaded having to break the news.

I am alarmed by the true extent of Shirley's loss. I can see so many of the things she's losing. And some of them on their own are huge for such a very insecure teenager, let alone all of them together. So far, life for her has been basically uphill. This I know only too well. And now this?

Almost every week, I end up holding her close as she lies sobbing in my arms.

For the first year, I refuse to get involved in anything beyond housework. The church work must wait. What I know of Shirley convinces me this is necessary. I must always be there for her, no matter what, for as long as it takes. While I ache for her, I tell myself that she will recover, but it's going to take a very long time – and huge 'TLC'.

I know the situation is very serious. But no one connects the dots and sees that she needs professional counselling. And I don't either. I do what mothers do – pour out love and care unreservedly. But she needs a professional counsellor. Tragically, not one of us realises that.

I want to do more. What I come up with is a very little thing, but still I feel it's worth a try. I set out to buy her a cuddly puppy to hug. Perhaps burying her nose in soft, golden fur, getting enthusiastic licks across her face, and smelling the special smell that is pure puppy, will do something? I don't for a moment think this is the answer, but it is something, isn't it? I certainly cannot – *cannot* – do nothing.

Shirley badly needs to feel loved right now – with no strings attached. She needs someone with whom she has no history. Puppies give their love so unconditionally. Having a little monster that is totally hers and that loves her, when no one else seems to, might – just might – be a bit of magic...

Juno arrives, flown from Warrenton, doped and in a little cage. The Labrador puppy chews up Shirley's contact lenses, a knob off her chest of drawers and Brian's new shoes.

I have only a poor understanding of the depth of Shirley's depression. No one else seems to have even that. Her heart is awash with pain. And her thoughts are very dark. *I can't do this. I can't see a single thing to live for. All I do is flounder in pain.*

Often, she sits on her bed, knees up against her chest. Arms hugging them, she rocks slowly – monotonously. She rocks and rocks and rocks. *Every two weeks I seem to have this complete meltdown. I lie in Mum's arms and just sob. Often, it's past midnight before I can let her go. One time* – Shirley giggles just a little, her wonderful sense of humour has not let her down yet – *I suddenly realise that it's very late. "Mum," I whisper, "I don't want to spoil your birthday." Looking at the time – half an hour past midnight – Mum chuckles very gently. "Sweetheart, you already have," she says. So – together – we chuckle just a little bit more.*

CHAPTER EIGHT

Love with Strings Attached

"Mum, you will fix my cat?"
(Photograph of the cat that the vet operated on.)

BRIAN CHERISHES A PRECIOUS MEMORY OF FOUR-YEAR-OLD
Shirley who is supposed to be following us to the car. She stops halfway
down the path. We are going out and are already late. But she just stands
there. Quite exasperated, he calls her to hurry. She looks at him, taken
aback.

"I am looking at the rainbow," she explains. "Isn't God beautiful?"

Brian also remembers her coming into his study holding a fragile, broken
plastic toy.

"Fix it, Daddy," she pleads.

He knows there's no way he can – it's just too smashed up. His heart aches. The last thing he wants is to let her down. He grieves his utter helplessness. He hopes she understands.

Shirley's about twelve when her cat crawls into the lounge very badly hurt.

"Mum, you will fix my cat?" she asks, green-brown eyes – now swimming – round and pleading.

Abby-cat lies under a lounge chair, obviously in very big trouble. I scoop the tabby up, ever so gently, on to a soft cushion. She whimpers in pain. Her back seems to be broken.

"She must've been hit by a car," Brian surmises.

I marvel that she's been able to drag herself this far.

The vet confirms that both hips are broken. He suggests an operation to put screws in. We know it's going to cost. The look in those large, green-brown eyes makes any hesitation on our part impossible though. We've just had a nice fat tax rebate for 1987.

When we see the vet's bill, we joke, "The tax man giveth, but the vet taketh away."

Sadly, as the Babygros become T-shirts, and the T-shirts change sizes, a devastating misunderstanding grows between Shirley and her dad. She never receives the message that he loves her. She sees him as someone she just can't please. Sometimes her head droops. She shakes her blonde pigtails as crippling beliefs take root in her. She always falls short of his expectations. And she's just not good enough to deserve his love. She cries silently within.

These most damaging beliefs play out as pain throughout the years to come. Shirley comes to see God too as someone she just can't please. He always requires her to perform – and she always comes up short. She doesn't meet God's conditions and therefore she can't believe he loves her. And so, while from time to time she believes God's there, much of the time she's not too keen on him either.

This is the perspective from which Shirley does life – for her, love is always conditional. No wonder her concept of love makes life so difficult. Year after year, she becomes more disillusioned. From there, it's a logical, sadly inevitable step to conclude, "I'm just not lovable."

Later, Shirley brings this need to please and meet others' expectations into her relationships with men. She works on being what she thinks she must be so that they will love her. Years later, Loren, her 'bestie' at university, says, "Those days at uni... Except for Mark, she had such strange taste in men."

Very, very sadly, Shirley actually briefly considers that the cancer, when it comes years later, is a punishment from God – because she hasn't performed well enough.

In 2010, Shirley writes:

> *Mum, you know that I'm currently working through some of my issues with Dad in counselling, but I must do it in my own time.*

Phyllis, her counsellor, is leading her through a discussion of nature (her own) versus nurture (by her parents).

At one stage her dad writes:

> *I know things haven't been right between us. My heart is very sore about it. I have always loved you. There are times when I feel your being so far away from us almost with physical pain.*

Shirley understands this to be love with strings attached. It's always asking something from her. Such love can't satisfy. It certainly fails to satisfy the longing in her heart. She finds it a poor, strangled experience – a mere shadow of the real thing.

I've experienced it too, so I understand. I know the emptiness.

So does Brian. And to make matters worse for him, he was only two when he lost his dad.

CHAPTER NINE

Missing the Boat

"...all Shirley longs for are the old friends she's lost."
(I flew the youth group she loved from Pretoria to
Cape Town. Shirley is in front, third from the left.)

MANY TIMES, I MISS THE BOAT WITH SHIRLEY.

When Shirley is about twelve, a friend moves away. For her, this is the pits. I explain to her that people are like ships passing in the night. They bless us for a while and often move on; we must be thankful for what they've given us, but not count on them staying; the only one we can count on staying is God.

Shirley gets very angry with me for saying this. For her, the suggestion that friends – anyone dear to her – might go away and leave her is absolutely unthinkable.

I don't get it. I don't see the unusual emotional angst. I don't see what pain a separation – even the suggestion of a separation – stirs up for her. I don't understand her fear – no, pure panic – at the possibility of abandonment. This is unusual behaviour but I fail to realise that something extremely serious is at play.

Even the most compassionate and loving support is not enough. With her difficulties, Shirley needs more than that. This is the bitter bite and the depth of her mental and psychological incapacity.

Later, in 2012, at her counsellor's suggestion, Shirley lists in her diary some of the things that made her angry. I find out that she was angry with me thirty years previously for being in bed so often when she was little.

"Why're you always sick, Mummy?" she asked, when she was four or five. "Are you going to die?"

I could see the very serious look on her little face as she stood in the doorway to our bedroom. We didn't want her to be an only child and were trying for another baby. This meant I often stayed in bed, hoping not to miscarry.

What she saw was being abandoned if Mummy should die. Worse than that – because of her difficulties, she believed that such a thing would destroy her.

"I'm really much, much better already, you know," I told her. "We are sometimes sick, but then we get better."

I wanted her to come to me. I was surprised when she walked off. My heart ached. I had no idea what was going through her head – what she was feeling. And I didn't know how to explain. How do you explain a possible miscarriage to a five-year-old?

So I did the best I could, on the spur of the moment. But I knew I hadn't said the right thing – just knew it. And I groaned because I knew I'd failed her miserably. I managed to miss the boat so badly that the terror of that moment stayed with her for more than thirty years.

Shirley was also angry with me for walking out on her and her dad. Brian and I used to argue quite a bit. I don't think it was abnormal, but it was real and intense. One of us would storm off somewhere to fume and calm down.

One time, on my way out, I was very concerned that I couldn't get to Shirley to take her with me. But I comforted myself that surely she was alright because she was with her dad. As usual, Brian and I kissed and made up and all was well – or so I thought.

But now, thirty years later, Shirley writes in her diary that Mum "walked out on me and Dad". Again, she was being abandoned – and was going to be destroyed by it.

It was always unthinkable to me that I might hurt her. How painful it is to realise that I did.

Now in Cape Town, I am convinced we are heading for a difficult time. I can feel it in the pit of my stomach. The best I can do is to give Shirley my full attention. I do it very willingly, wanting nothing more than for her to be happy again.

I ponder Shirley's silence as we drove to Cape Town. I remember thinking that there were better ways to spend New Year's Day.

Shirley's deep withdrawal concerns me. We used to talk so much when she was little. But recently, long, uncomfortable silences have become part of our lives. Now she talks to no one except her friends.

I see this in most of the teens I work with. They talk passionately to each other but talking to their parents is the pits. Parents are regarded as unsafe. Perhaps my track record of misunderstanding has made Shirley angrier and angrier with me. Perhaps her unwillingness to confront – a tall ask for most people in such circumstances – and say what is bothering her has added fuel to the fire.

It's complicated. Silence comes when pain curls you up into yourself. Is this another side to what is happening? Shirley has such brittle self-confidence. Does she pull up the drawbridge to secure herself? When her pain is deep, does it scrunch her up – out of our reach? Whatever the reason, there are many silences between us.

I really don't understand why the move is this bad for her. I try to encourage her with the prospect of new friends, a wonderful youth group in one of the biggest and best churches in the denomination, and on and on. This is what those at the new church are saying, and I have bought it wholesale.

But all Shirley longs for are the old friends she's lost. How far I am drawn off target by the advice of others! (Later, I live with a regret that tightens its nasty grip on my heart from time to time.)

It all gets worse. I resist for a long time, but eventually I listen to the advice of our new pastor. After all, he is well known and very popular; many turn to him for advice. He believes Shirley is misbehaving because she is spoilt. I know in my gut that he is wrong; this is something very different to that. But under all the pressure, I tell Shirley to pull herself together and to stop misbehaving.

(For years after, I find myself so sorry that I did that; sorrier than I've been over most other things. This is the last thing you do to fragile bone china. How could I allow myself to be pushed? I instinctively knew she was in real trouble. I can't even imagine how deeply I failed – betrayed – her. And this time, more so because a pastor was involved, it impacted her trust in God. I think missing the boat this time was one of the worst errors of judgement I ever made. It makes me wonder how much else I got wrong that's been no good for Shirley. It is true that sometimes the areas in which we are deficient and broken are the very areas where our children – and others in their brokenness – need us the most! But getting it wrong is never what we intend.)

I certainly don't miss the boat in my belief that Shirley needs all the encouragement she can get. Especially as she keeps asking herself, "What's the matter with me? All of this can only mean I'm the problem."

In 2001, I read a book about individual differences between children. I find a description that fits Shirley to a T. To me, the child they describe in these pages is especially lovely.

That's it! I say to myself. *She's a grown-up compassion child, as fragile as bone china, but just as exquisite.*

I sit down to write to her. I want to help her to understand and appreciate herself better. I want to uplift, affirm and encourage her. Throughout her life, I've had glimpses of the unique quality of her true nature. These are some of the treasures I hoard.

> *Sweetheart, my book describes you as the most lovable, the gentlest compassion child. You are the most creative of people. You dream noble dreams – and go off into your own wonderland of fantasy.*

I thrill that she's like this, because I especially like these kinds of people.

> *You truly, truly love people, detect their emotional needs and can't bear anyone to be hurting. You're an excellent listener with a depth*

of empathy. You're also hell-bent on rescuing and relieving others of pain. You need us to love you as deeply as you love.

I think this will truly encourage her – I'd love people to say these things about me.

You can be so full of fun with a sense of humour to die for. I'm writing this letter to tell you I celebrate and salute you and thank God for the privilege of knowing you.

But I also need her to understand:

You're also the most vulnerable to hurt. The rough world we live in makes you insecure and fearful.

"Thanks, Mum," she responds.

God knows, I too really need encouragement. Am I doing the right thing by her? I am trying so hard.

(Later encouragement comes through a powerful message I receive in 2005. I am training teachers in Johannesburg. I share with my hostess, Paula, my ongoing, deep concern for Shirley. I am surprised when, some months later, Paula phones. "I think I have a message for you. God seems to be saying, 'I know the deep anguish of your heart over Shirley. *Hush,* be still – I have her gently in the palm of my hand.'" *Oh, wow.*)

Chapter Ten

Flexing Her Muscles

"Shirley and Loren become like sisters."
(Shirley is bridesmaid at Loren's wedding.)

UNIVERSITY LIFE BEGINS FOR SHIRLEY IN FEBRUARY 1993 IN beautiful Stellenbosch. She's eighteen and life looks promising.

The historic town nestles against mauve-grey peaks like Simonsberg and Stellenbosch Mountain. Red and white roses fringe the vineyards. Oak trees shade the stately Cape Dutch homesteads.

Shirley moves into a residence called Irene. In her second year, she moves into a flat, and then shares a flat with Loren. The two become like sisters. Often, weeks go by when I don't hear from Shirley.

Years later, when Loren and I 'do coffee', I ask lots of questions about Shirley's time in 'Stellies'.

"Oh, Thy," Loren says, "we laughed such a lot. What an amazing sense of humour! And we went to all the student events advertised in the Neelsie. We got jobs waitressing to earn some money but soon gave up – too much hard work and too much sore feet. The other thing we did was sleep – or at least Shirley did. I had to work my butt off. But she would hardly open a book and still cream her subjects, especially English and Psychology. *Cum laude,* no less – I found it so frustrating to watch."

I watch a frown flit across Loren's face.

"One thing Shirley really hated was to take Prozac."

"That was for two whole years," I say.

Because of her struggles to settle in after our move – and later – our GP prescribed Prozac at the end of her matric year. He thought it would help her get through – and it did. But this left Shirley shocked: *she needed to be on anti-depressants?* That was bad enough. But what was worse was that the doctor also sent her for a short spell of counselling.

Apart from one visit to the school psychologist, this was her first experience of therapy. She found these new experiences strange and alarming. They stirred up and added to buried fears. It was not long before she was thinking, *there you are – I always knew it – there's something very wrong with me.*

One of the guys Shirley goes out with at the time introduces her to skydiving. Soon she's diving herself. To make money, she packs parachutes for the club. Multitasking is one of her strengths – she loves keeping a whole lot of balls in the air at once.

Of those years, Shirley later writes:

> *Somehow I managed to miss discovering how very much God loves me. I was sure that he loves everyone in a general sort of way because, after all, he's good. However, I was convinced that I didn't deserve any special attention. I kept interrogating myself – I wanted to know what I really thought. My childhood years had tattooed me with Christianity. It seemed that instead of setting me free, my faith was causing me feelings of failure, guilt and unworthiness. For a long time, I struggled to keep these inside. Surely then, the logical thing to do was to leave the church and religion behind?*

Shirley enjoys her new-found independence hugely. So do I. It encourages me that phone calls home become pretty rare. This feels normal – as I think normal should be. I dream of seeing Shirley standing firmly on her own two feet, happy and fulfilled in her relationships, normal and flourishing, healed. I pray and pray for healing – rather than cry incessantly.

When she does come to Cape Town for weekends – not too often – she borrows my car. She's flexing her muscles and I am glad; some of these are hopeful developments, or so I think.

She drives the little grey Fox off into the night. It's definitely best not to ask where she's going. Those are the nights when Brian doesn't sleep at all. I fall asleep until midnight. Then together we lie in bed restlessly listening for every car. Eventually – at three or four in the morning – she turns in at the gate.

CHAPTER ELEVEN

Shirley's Wedding

"It's a lovely wedding under twisting, fresh green vines
on a wine farm outside Stellenbosch."
(Left-to-right: Brian, me, Shirley.)

"I MET MARK FALLING THROUGH THE AIR."

A beautiful Shirley impresses her guests with her confidence, poise and charm. She's speaking at her wedding on 16 December 1998. As always, people bring out the sparkle in her.

She said, "I don't want a dress that makes you look like a balloon." So she wears a slim, flattering white gown, really great for dancing.

The skydiving in Stellenbosch becomes skydiving near Citrusdal, west of Cape Town. Shirley and Brent prefer conditions there – everything is bigger and better. For a start, there is a bigger plane and a nicer crowd.

It isn't long before Brent becomes history. And Shirley meets a number of guys. Blond, greyish-blue-eyed Mark is one of them.

Soon falling through the air together leads to much more. They find a flat and move in together. Every week they bring their washing. I am grateful – otherwise we would probably not see much of them.

On those evenings when the Cape is spectacularly beautiful, they fetch us to meander up Chapman's Peak Drive. We share sundowners and 'nibblies' and watch the sun set. Another favourite spot is Signal Hill. The blue sea all around us turns to gold; the day ends in splendour. It all feels good.

Then Mark proposes – outside Pirates Steakhouse – and they set the date.

I feel really hopeful. For me, marriage is the answer for Shirley – it just has to be. This is the light at the end of the tunnel – the first real light, that will make her life normal and fill her chronic sense of need.

I want to do something really special to encourage her. I inherited my mum's half-carat white diamond. I want Shirley to know that, no matter what, I will always love her. Somehow, I know I must communicate that. Granted, now Mark loves her, it seems. But I still want to do something too, to reassure her. Her constant pain always stirs pain in me. So I make the sacrifice – a cherished reminder of my mum – and give her the diamond. I feel it's okay to do this because she and Mark don't have money. But I don't discuss this with Mark. Not wise. So I trespass.

During the build-up to the wedding, Shirley is particularly unsettled – rattled and uncertain. She is more fragile than usual. What doesn't help is her scramble to finish her dissertation for her Master's before December.

Then, about two weeks before the big day, Mark tells Shirls he's not sure he wants to marry her. She's devastated. I try to console her. Surely the only thing it can be is a fleeting attack of nerves? But it leaves me concerned.

Shirley becomes very high maintenance – which means I work very hard. I don't like the role I feel forced to play at all. My plan is to remove myself to an appropriate distance from Shirls and Mark as soon as possible.

Time is slipping by with much to be done. I don't mind walking my feet off to find serviettes the right shade of dark-green.

Shirley asks my florist friend and me to do all the flowers. We drown in the sweet scent of the St Joseph's lilies we drape around large white candles.

Shirls and I fill little dark-green boxes with chocolates for her guests to take home. While we're doing this one Saturday afternoon, just before the wedding, Shirley has a terribly frightening meltdown. Her mood blackens to the point where she feels as if she is sinking into a dark, sooty-black pit. I try and try – but I can't reach her. This is the worst despair I have ever seen. Fear threatens to panic my soul. Helplessly, I stroke her back – very tentatively – as I sit beside her. I do not know what else to do.

I don't quite know when I made the decision but for a very long time now I've propped Shirley up. After this new trauma, I try even harder. I think of it as something like a tennis match: the game flows if both players keep their end up. Each one must make sure that they receive the ball and send it back. But what if one of them can't? Because it's Shirley who can't, I'm willing to do her bit as well, trying to hold the fort for her until she can. So I hit the ball. Then I run to her side to help her hit it back to me – always a holding operation at best, never a permanent solution.

At this point, I don't realise how very long I'll have to do this. Nor do I realise that passive aggression will build up in me – and have very destructive consequences in my relationships, especially with Shirley. Foolishly, I think I can hide it completely.

I know it's essentially her problem and her call. But I won't let her down until she takes control of her life.

I would find such an invasion of the boundaries of another person unthinkable under normal circumstances. In fact, this is something I'm strongly against. But I see my child being pulverised. This is a major crisis – so what do I do?

I'm convinced that at this point, to help her 'do life' is the lesser of two evils. I believe that not to help will result in something much worse. I wouldn't do this willingly for anyone else. But this is my child. I can't just watch her perish. I love her too much.

I certainly spend no time considering whether I'm making things worse. A rescuer who is by nature gentle and compassionate will hopefully do the least damage. So the question becomes, not should I rescue at all, but what kind of a rescuer am I? I know how gentle Mrs Fix-it is trying to be, but does she pull it off?

Twice I've done the Boundaries course.[4] I know the authors see what I'm doing as a flagrant trespassing on someone else's space. But I do remember a very significant conversation with a friend. She said, "I can't put in place for my husband the boundaries the book suggests. I can't stop compensating

---

[4] Based on the book by Cloud and Townsend; *Boundaries;* Zondervan (1992).

for him. That would be far too unkind." I come to see that she makes a very important point. Where is kindness, given the serious weakness in Shirley's make-up?

The wedding day – 16 December – starts out cloudy.

Shirley wails, "How can I be radiant on a day like this?"

But the day improves. At sunset we sit outside drinking in the beauty of a golden sky. It's a lovely wedding under twisting, fresh green vines on a wine farm outside Stellenbosch. Sun dapples the green leaves as the ceremony progresses.

"I promise to love you always."

Shirley continues with her speech, her voice soft but clear. She faces Mark, her eyes fixed lovingly on his face. She and Mark are so sincere in their promises to each other that tears secretly slip from a number of emotional eyes. The low sun filters red through the wine in our glasses as we all wish them the very best.

Before we drive home from Stellenbosch, I sneak up to their cottage for the night. I leave chocolates, candles and matches in the middle of their bed. I remember how much Shirley loves candlelight.

I'm very hesitant. I really wonder if I'm doing the right thing. Eventually, I decide to do it anyway. I'm not thinking of their feelings but am consumed with mine. I want to underline my absolute support for them. But I never feel completely comfortable about my intrusion.

Very soon after the wedding, Shirley and Mark move to Johannesburg. I say to myself, "This is really good." I think the distance between us is a very good thing.

Two relatively happy years follow. But then, in 2000, Mark is transferred to London...

CHAPTER TWELVE

Heartbreak

"Mark and Shirls drive us from London to Wastwater."

"I CAN'T BELIEVE THIS IS ALL WE CAN FIND, MUM," SHIRLEY wails over the phone. "And it costs so much."

In London they live in a stuffy, one-bedroomed flat in St Margaret's. Rather like beads on a necklace, its musty rooms string out in a row along a narrow passage. There's a bit of grass out back, and that's it.

For Shirley, everything about coming to the UK has been a large mountain to climb, rather like our move to Cape Town in 1991. She finds it so strange and alarming. And she still hates change.

But there's more. About a week after they get there, Mark's IT firm sends him to work in Ireland for a month. Her self-confidence is a brittle thing at the best of times. To face the challenges alone now is something else: this is abandonment again.

For Shirley, the wheels come off big time. She becomes the frightened little girl alone in the playground all over again – this time with a mountain of boxes to unpack. And the pressing need to find a job.

So she keeps my phone extra-busy. And I keep trying – extra-hard – to comfort and encourage her. Some days she doesn't hear from Mark. That spells nothing but total disaster for her. Her pain is intense. No one understands quite how terrible this is for her, or why.

Mark doesn't get it. All he knows is that this is a great opportunity. He can't get a grip on what it all means for Shirley.

The months slip by, full of ups and downs. At the end of their year in London, Brian and I visit them for Christmas. The dark skies make the fairy lights on the little Christmas trees in the windows a delight. Fresh green holly garlands on the doors give the faintest aroma to the chill night air. And the cold makes our cheeks glow pink.

Two days before Christmas, Shirley presents me with a chocolate birthday cake for breakfast. We grin to see the cat's face decorating it. Later, she takes her time to cook us an appetising Thai dinner. That evening, we all catch the train to see – you guessed it – *Cats*.

When Shirls and Mark come home from work, they pour a glass of wine. Then they cook together – they love their wok – and chat away about this and that. As time goes by, I find myself looking continuously for reassurance that the marriage is working. And to see this reassures me.

"Mark's my soul mate, Mum," Shirley tells me. "I've found my soul mate."

I do a watercolour for them of two half-empty wine glasses standing on the ironing board – they glint red beside the iron. At the foot of the board is their large black London cat – I couldn't leave Chloe-cat out – and pink scented lilies from Sainsbury's on the dining room table. This is what their lives in London are like. Using some licence, I paint the open doors of a church beckoning through their window. Not very subtle, I'm afraid.

Two years later, when we visit again, things are very different. One Friday night in July 2002, Mark and Shirls drive us from London to Wastwater in the barren western Lake District.

Just before we set out, Shirley tells me, "I have to do things like this for the sake of our marriage." She means the outdoor things Mark likes. This is news to me. It leaves me fearing the marriage is under strain. "I have to work to make this marriage work," she adds.

Mark takes in his stride the highways, then the narrow country roads and finally the overgrown, barely visible tracks. We have no idea where we are. We hope he knows. We arrive at midnight. Our 'cottage' is attached to the farmhouse. We know we are in the right place because we can smell the lambs – penned almost at our front door.

In the morning, we begin the walk towards Scafell Pike. "The wrinklies" – as Mark calls us – soon peter out; we sit down on the grass with such purpose it seems we don't plan ever to get up again. Mark and Shirls do a whole lot better with the walk.

The times when Shirley is clearly being very high maintenance deepen my concern. How well I know what that's like. And I see it happening quite often.

Now, in 2003, after five years of married life, three of which have been spent in London, there are big problems. Mark wants to spend money on DIY equipment. He's set his heart on fixing up the ground-floor apartment they've bought in Teddington after leaving St Margaret's. Shirley wants the money for a fantastic holiday – going halfway round the world and ending in New Zealand.

The arguments are many and bitter. Their struggles over all sorts of things – like her desire for a successful career rather than a family – intensify.

The cut and thrust of their recent quarrels occupy Shirley's thoughts.

Mark feels I bullied him into skiing. How was I supposed to know he had such a fear of falling on ice?

We're so different. Mark feels inferior because of my abilities – he resents me. This is one of the major things that makes our marriage so unhappy. He says I want to wear the trousers all the time. We don't meet each other's needs. So we feel lukewarm towards each other. In fact, we have never been particularly close.

When I asked him, "Have you been happy in our marriage?" he said, "Actually, I have been most unhappy." That leaves me wondering whether there's any future for us. There've been so many misunderstandings – so many. And now Mark says he's not willing to go for counselling anymore. So now what?

Mark stands in front of Shirley, greyish-blue eyes swimming with pain. His fair complexion reddens as he stresses out. Startled, she looks up at him.

"Shirls, I've been thinking," he murmurs.

She looks away. Her heart plummets like lead. Alarm rises throughout her being. There's a particularly uncomfortable silence. Then Mark struggles on.

"Don't get me wrong, you're great." He pauses and hunches his broad shoulders. "I just can't make the changes in me that you want. I can't deliver on that score. There's something you want that I can't give you. So I'm not going to try."

Dread knots Shirley's stomach. She goes ice cold.

"I don't know how to say this," Mark murmurs. "I'm sorry. So I just have to tell you that I'm leaving you. It's taken a long time to decide. But I can't go on any longer, I just… can't."

His voice breaks. He stumbles away to their bedroom. Silence – a long, heavy silence. Much later, he comes back to sit on the couch. More silence. Shirley's forgotten to move.

Then he says, "Um, I'll be down at the pub for a while."

Shirley hears him close the door very firmly behind him.

The minutes tick by. These minutes are different. They drag by, heavy, slow and pregnant with meaning. Like a waxwork at Madame Tussauds, Shirley continues to sit dead still through each one of them, one by one.

Then she packs a bag, feeds Chloe-cat and walks to Phil's. He's her boss and they're working on an IT project together.

"Mum, I have some really sad news," the email reads that I receive on 24 February 2004.

I haven't been able to face telling you before now, as I know how upset you will be. Even now I can't face phoning you, as I know I will break down completely. The thing is that Mark broke up with me on Thursday night. He says that in his heart he doesn't believe he can love me the way he should and that we're not right for each other.

I have cried a great deal, but I think I'm still in shock at the moment. Mark's gone to Ireland for work and will be there for three months. It feels as if he's just away on work.

Later that same day she writes:

Listen, I know you are going to be dreadfully worried about me, but I'm okay. I'm very, very sad and no doubt going to get sadder. I suspect I may be suffering from a bit of depression. These last months have been so hellish, it's not really surprising.

How disappointed Brian and I are. Her email saddens but doesn't surprise us. Shirley says she's in shock – so are we.

The emails that follow use phrases like "hellish", "at a loss" and "really scared". As I read them, I can't react. That's actually what I need to do – give vent to what I'm feeling. But I can't let anything unhinge me. I can't let myself feel all I want to feel right now.

Right now – *especially* – I have to be able to help her. So, for now, I stem the rising tide of distress inside me.

"I knew we had issues, Mum," Shirley shares, "but I've been horrified to find out the extent of them. The thing that hurts the most is Mark's conviction that he doesn't love me anymore."

Many times, when life has delivered her another curveball, it's been about being lovable. Each time she's concluded, "I'm just not lovable – not even by God."

These words from Mark are one of the worst possible things for her to hear. There is a blade that's already plunged into her heart. Now Mark gives it a twist.

I know the pain this causes me. I can only imagine what it does to her.

Shirley's thoughts run on.

After Mark leaves me, I don't want Mum to come. I've been sharing much of Mark and my troubles with Phil. He's a real comfort to me. He listens to my complaints about Mark and gently sympathises. I know he has the hots for me. We never become an item. But I know he'd like to. I know Mum desperately wants to comfort me. I don't want her to see Phil and me together. And – actually – where is she going to stay?

Mum accepts my decision without saying anything. This is a big thing for her, as I know she is longing to come. She reminds me – gently and sympathetically, "You have to make your own way through all of this." I know she really believes no one else could or should make any of my choices for me. So, hard as it is, she stays away. But in utter desperation to do something – (Shirley smiles – Mum must have been desperate to do something quite like this) – she sends me a little soft, white teddy bear from South Africa. It is good to stuff him under my pillow. And pull him out any time I need to. I know she doesn't want to make any comment. So to her, this is a way not to do that, but still to send the message that she so badly wants to comfort me. I do tell her, he is certainly very good at hugging.

Mark's rejection puts pressure on the cracks in Shirley's self-image. Her thoughts become increasingly negative.

When we split up, I thought my life was over. I felt crushed by an overwhelming sense of loss. Now I can't believe that life will ever be good or that I will ever be happy again. In fact, I have a tremendous feeling of failure. Surely, I did something dreadful to cause my husband to leave me after more than five years? I am really scared. I am afraid of being lonely. I'm not well, feeling real angst, at a loss as to what to do. I'm not sure I can cope with the consequences of more mistakes. It feels as if all the things I've really cared about in my life have come to absolutely nothing. It is just one disappointment after the next. One minute I feel nostalgic, the next regretful. So often I am just so sad.

The pressure on her flimsy self-confidence mounts. And deep despair threatens to overwhelm her.

I cry a lot, and drink a lot, and cry some more. I just don't believe I can survive. I know God keeps our tears in a bottle – the bottle he has for me right now must be the size of a wine vat. I know this sounds melodramatic, but things keep happening to remind me just how fragile I am. And how thin I'm stretched emotionally.

A dozen things crowd in upon her all at once. She's thoroughly tempest-tossed by her own brokenness. Her emotions contradict – jostle for attention. This is deep emotional suffering.

A month after Mark left me, I am utterly alone on my birthday with not even one phone call from a friend. Or from a brother or sister – seeing I never had any. Certainly no family in England. I've had so many unhappy birthdays, and now here is another one. I've decided never to do birthdays ever again. I feel like nothing but c**p through and through. What am I to do? Where am I to go? I am dawdling around all alone in the playground all over again.

To help with this birthday, I pathetically suggest Shirley goes to the pub because at least there are people there. I long to help, but – as many times in the past – cannot really do a single thing. My helplessness is complete.

What a horrible, aching, sad time 2004 is for her. And for Brian and me.

Phil says Shirley can have the couch in the office. My heart aches that for a whole year she doesn't have a home of her own; or any of her things, which are all packed in boxes. Nor does she have a landline, so we can only email each other.

For that whole year, Shirley wrestles through round after round of torment. We talk about it all – especially her perspective on life. It's skewed by a huge sense of rejection; her steady belief over the years that she's a loser kicks in.

I can see that right now her self-confidence is at an all-time low. I try to help her make sense of it all, to help her make choices. I believe if she does, she'll feel a little bit better about herself – more empowered. Patiently, I stay with her as her pain unfolds. All the nattering between us is very real and honest – that makes it sweet and precious. Many, many emails connect us. She shares – much as she used to a very long time ago – and is open, honest and loving. How precious – how thankful I am. We connect with an intimacy of a special kind. I rediscover her inner beauty, integrity and loveliness.

I make my messages as warm and loving as I can. I know that her fragile sense of worth has taken a huge knock. It's always hard work to encourage her, but right now it's harder than most times.

"Oh, Mum," she groans, "will I ever find someone to sweep me off my feet? Will I ever marry again?"

I believe she will – at her best, she's so attractive and so fun, such good company and, above all, such a treasure. So I tell her so. Behind all this is the nagging fear that she could easily crack up completely.

She confides to her trusted diary:

> Been wrestling with questions around worth. What is it that gives a person worth?
>
> Question: if one is not loved and accepted by others, does one still have worth?
>
> Question: even if one is loved and accepted by others – but doesn't experience that – how does one feel worthy?
>
> Why do I not have the love and acceptance of others I long for?
>
> Easy answer – I'm not worthy.

The divorce is horrid – absolutely impersonal and online, no less! To do it in England means waiting out a year of separation before it can even begin to happen. So Shirley and Mark decide to do it in South Africa. They're talking to each other and making practical decisions in an almost friendly fashion.

Accordingly, she comes out to South Africa in January 2005. We go to a lawyer's office in Wynberg. She signs some documents. And it's done. I can't believe it. Six years of marriage and – *poof!* – it's all over. As we drive up to Rhodes Memorial for a Thai chicken salad lunch, I feel sick. I'm aghast that it's all so heartless – almost inhuman.

Shirley says nothing. I don't have anything to say either. I feel that I mustn't intrude but give her as much space to work through this as she needs. To be very still is the gentle and kind thing to do. So I sit quietly by her, hoping she can feel my empathy.

In two days' time, she's on a plane back to the UK. She's still too wounded to indulge in words. I do understand. But I'm so sad that she retreats into herself and can't share what she's going through.

Actually, I can't share either. She's on her own in her pain – and I'm on my own in mine.

CHAPTER THIRTEEN

Picking Up the Pieces

"I thought maybe God was glad to hear from me."

HALFWAY THROUGH 2005, SHIRLEY SEEMS IN A BETTER PLACE. She's definitely – very tentatively – picking up the pieces of her life.

> *Part of what I plan to do to recover is a dream holiday in New Zealand. There'll most likely never again be such a good time for me to do it as now. Very few my age can take time off their grown-up lives and jobs and mortgages.*

> *This is so important to me that I feel it's worth doing even on my own, and I will have lots of fun. I plan to do various walks and*

activity tours... I don't have any financial commitments at all right now, not even rent to pay. And my job is willing to give me time off.

This sounds reasonable – but perhaps she's blanking out the emotions that are too painful to face? She leaves me wondering if she's not trying to have the holiday she wanted in spite of Mark. Giving up on this dream was one of the things that made her so mad with him. Whatever else this might be, it's stubbornness for sure.

She hopes to find someone to share her adventure. In the end, there's nobody. In October 2005, she goes anyway, isolated – again – and alone.

———————————

Shirley packs leather boots, a goose-down jacket, a small red tent, her music on her iPod, her iPhone in her pocket and a few other essentials. Thinking, nibbling, sleeping and reading get her through the long flights. Soon she's in a little grey hired sedan, map in hand and GPS at the ready.

Stopping, relaxing, nibbling and exploring, she covers South Island. She camps in national parks. She delights in squirrels and birds. She does the excursions that appeal. One of those is a helicopter flight to a very white glacier. Another is a boat trip uncovering the beauty of fjords, waterfalls and snow-capped peaks.

She turns her music up loud as she drives. Some of the time she sings her heart out. But some of the time she cries and cries. She stops to shop, collecting earrings and a few other bits and pieces. She submits to a neat, abstract tattoo at the base of her spine – which does, at first, ache quite a bit. There are moments of stress when all her socks take their time to dry in the back of the car.

In another of her coveted emails, she writes about watching South Africa play rugby against – and lose to – New Zealand, in Dunedin.

She also says:

While there, on a lonely, windswept beach, I felt moved to pray for a long time. Nothing dramatic happened, but I thought that maybe God was glad to hear from me.

———————————

Once back in England, Shirley's full of initiative. She finds a new job in 2006 – this time as a Project Manager for an IT firm in Bracknell, west of London and close to Reading. Many emails describe how hard it is for someone as unsure of herself as she is to do this.

They also reveal how daunting it is for her to look for a house on her own. She badly wants a picturesque – possibly Victorian – cottage in a nearby village. Such houses are just way too expensive. So, later in 2006, she buys in Wokingham.

Her home is a semidetached double storey set alongside other homes fronting a small green. In all her heart-searching, she's discovered, to her surprise, that what she really wants is a husband and family of her own. The three bedrooms upstairs, a back garden and large kitchen are a step in the right direction.

At the end of her first week in the new house, she writes:

I've had a scary/fun/good week. I'm thrilled to have moved out of London. There's a gym down the road. And a squash club – whoo hoo!

I'm doing a singing course again – in Richmond. So I'm thinking of buying a keyboard.

My eyes are lighting up at all the possibilities of nice long runs. I'm surrounded by farmland and green fields. Sometimes I hear horses canter by. I'm really doing okay. If nothing else, I love the change.

Mum, it's happening again, things are working out for me! Please pray that I will make lots of new friends and be at peace with being single for a good long time.

Shirley's certainly very different. She's moved on; and is active again and full of initiative. She's able to function and is in control of her life. It sounds so normal. Her courage and resolve impress. I'm relieved – and, at this point, really hopeful.

Shirley brings Chloe-cat home, the cat that belonged to her and Mark. A neighbour to their Teddington house has kindly taken her in all this time. No longer orphaned, the tubby black cat soon leaves her usual paw-prints in the bath. And once again it's necessary to keep the toilet lid closed.

In fact, Chloe leaves paw-prints everywhere – in all the dust Shirls is stirring up everywhere. To make the house really her own, she scrapes, strips, paints and varnishes. This is courageous DIY, amateurish and enthusiastic, but with a vengeance. While Chloe revels in dust, Shirls seriously speckles her hair and face with white spray from her roller – and takes a selfie to prove it.

Some months later, the furniture arrives from South Africa. Mark and Shirley have agreed that what they had left in storage is to become Shirley's. She's delighted. And so is Chloe-cat. She takes to a back cushion of Shirley's white two-seater couch in front of the TV. From there she can do her best purring.

Shirley writes:

> *I need to tell you how wonderful it is to have my furniture and things. My house feels completely different – it feels comfortable and homey. At last I have a nest, a haven that's all mine. I feel blessed. God is so good.*

CHAPTER FOURTEEN

Grey Days

"If you would ask her, at this stage, 'What colour is life?'
her reply would be, 'Very grey.'"

SHIRLEY HAS HER NOSE IN A BOOK. LARRY CRABB WRITES:

> *I need a break. Mindless entertainment helps. I turn on the TV. I*
> *understand our addiction epidemic: But we're foolish. When we tire*
> *of effort we live for relief.[5]*

"That's exactly it!" she says. Larry Crabb obviously understands. She
jots down a great deal from the book in her diary.

---

[5] *The Pressure's Off;* Colorado Springs, WaterBrook Press (2012).

She sits on the couch, TV tuned in to *Master Chef, NCIS* and *Friends,* even *Who Wants to Be a Millionaire?* – or whatever. Often, her fingers aimlessly work the keyboard of her laptop. They search for something – anything. Absent-mindedly, Shirley strokes whichever cat is within reach – apart from Chloe-cat. She's got her ex-boyfriend Stuart's two cats too; he couldn't resist when she pleaded to keep them.

Sometimes the candles Shirley loves light the room with a warm glow. And she inhales the sweetness of incense burning. At times, she cradles a glass of red wine, watching the red liquid reflect the soft light. In her university days in the wine capital of South Africa, she learnt to love it – white or red.

Shirley's discovered the comfort wine can bring. Once a month, a large box arrives from the wine club. And she savours many a sip. A favourite wine – sometimes a little whisky – soothes her for the moment. She admits drinking doesn't fill the vacuum for long – but it's better than nothing. So every time circumstances rough her up, she turns to this old friend.

"Chris," she courageously confides one day, "I'm drinking too much."

Her special confidant aches for her, and then gives good advice. So does her counsellor, Phyllis. And her pastor. When she tells me, I ache too.

Nick, now a very particular friend, remembers her sleeping over at his cottage when she'd had too much to drive home. That's when she wrote in her diary with typical honesty:

> *I come off the back of a bad week, having had issues at work, drank too much.*

Shirley also shops to feel better. Often, she comes home with a bulging shopping bag hanging from each hand. She plonks them on her bed. Then she eyes her bedroom cupboards.

"It's going to take a miracle to get all this in there," she tells Katy. Her close friend has found the time for a very welcome visit.

"Oh, Katy," she says, eyes sparkling, "look what I've found. Nick's taking me to the Royal Albert to see *Madame Butterfly* and now I've got just the thing. Isn't it to die for?"

Shirley pulls a charcoal-coloured, off-the-shoulder long dress from its packet and holds it against her. The lighter grey trim to the unwinding layers – as they flare out – makes magic.

"Wow, Shirls," Katy gasps, "that takes one's breath away! I kid you not; you're going to knock 'em sideways in that."

Miss Glameron lays the dress gently on the bed. Giggling and chatting, they go downstairs for a girlie chat and catch-up over coffee.

Much later, Shirley climbs the stairs again. She looks at her bed. The new things she's bought soothe her soul. Then she looks at the pile of clothes on the basket-weave trunk just inside the door. These poor garments have been whining for quite some time to be put away. Now they're no longer whining; they're rioting.

"There's nothing for it," she sighs. "Time to do a throw-out and repack my cupboards."

Dresses, jeans, tracksuit tops, T-shirts, shorts and jerseys fly into a heap on the floor.

"Oxfam, here we come," she mutters, and then pulls an empty box down from the attic. She packs it full. Now it's the box that bulges – and the bulging cupboards that bulge far less!

When she was eight, Shirley made a beautiful pottery lady in a long dress with hat to match. She's been making beautiful ladies ever since. Selfies and other pics record the unending changes and often stunning results.

While the beautiful clothes help her turn heads, they don't solve anything for long. They do lift her spirits though – but only for a little while. Then they add to her angst.

"Oh, Mum," she wails, "now I'm really in debt."

Most of the time, Shirley's trying to feel better. Especially after another sleepless night. Often, she stands in her PJs in front of her two bookcases stuffed with fantasy and sci-fi. She skips over *Harry Potter*. And smiles at Frank Perretti. *Long time since I read him,* she thinks.

It's not too long before she finds just what she wants – a fantasy world in which to lose herself. It's soothing to forget – for a while, at least – the overwhelming reality that threatens to drown her. And if the bookcases fail, there are always e-books galore.

Or she opens a full box of Belgian chocolates. Sometime soon she'll feel guilty and go for a run to tackle the extra kilograms. But not right now. Now it's okay to have a binge. In any case, it's just a little one. And all the exercise to follow will help in another way too. It will help to reduce her stress.

During this time, she writes:

> *Didn't feel peaceful yesterday eve – quite distressed, didn't feel session with Phyllis went well... painful, painful road. I'm experiencing a lot of emotions as a result of the lid coming off.*

Over the years, being in counselling has consoled Shirley many times. It brings intense pain, but the new insights she gains are worth it. Phyllis has listened so patiently, gently and wisely, without a shadow of censure. Shirley couldn't have done without her. What a comfort that someone's listening to her so attentively, at least once a week.

In her efforts to feel better, Shirley takes herself off for a weekend in the Lake District. She pitches her little red tent in a field near Rydal Lake and goes for long walks.

She feels free and safe – and tells no one in particular. She's reminded of her New Zealand holiday in 2006. Back then, as she drove around the South Island, she did a lot of talking to no one in particular too.

This time there are sheep on offer.

I've talked to my cats for ever so long, she thinks to herself, *so why not sheep?*

Curious, a nearly full-grown lamb comes over to check her out. He sniffs at the sandwich in her outstretched hand, decides it's not really his thing and moves off, pulling at tufts of grass.

Prompted by the beauty of the place – the Lake District's always been a true haven to her – Shirley enjoys the light-hearted moment, and feels close to God.

She later explains in her videoed testimony:

> *Holidays became my life. They meant everything to me. So I spent an awful amount of time planning them. They were really all about either scuba diving or skiing, whatever. It was all about kind of being on the go and being out there.*

No sooner is one holiday over than she's planning the next. She believes if she does not do this, she'll sink.

Her diary's always been a truly safe – no, probably her *very safest* – place.

"Oh, I cried so much," she often tells the much loved and dog-eared book when her skies morph from grey to near black. It's a real haven. No one's ever been able to set foot in there, so she can truly be herself. It's in there she describes her deepest anguish:

Feeling/believing that I don't have worth. Intense fear about giving up self-sufficiency (who will take care of things if I don't).

The big picture really doesn't look good. The cavern of her empty heart still echoes. Her soul still pulsates with pain. And it all keeps getting worse. So she becomes more and more frantic.

If you would ask her, at this stage, "What colour is life?" her reply would be, "Very grey."

Chapter Fifteen

Searching for Love

"Scott's told me I'm very special to him."
(A Valentine's dinner prepared by Scott.)

IN AUGUST 2005, SHIRLEY GOES TO A PARTY IN LONDON. HER royal-blue dress offsets the blonde streaks in her long brown hair. As usual, she begins to sparkle when she's with people and has a great time. Next day she phones.

"I met an attractive guy. I haven't been able to think of dating – until now. I haven't wanted to risk rejection again, I guess. But Dale's persuaded me it's time – and with him!"

Dale's an ex-teacher turned 'bobby'. After their first date, old uncertainties fragment her composure. So many times, she's worried about the same thing: *Will there be a second date? Will he ask me out again?*

This unravels her as in the past. She flips from fear to hope and a multitude of other feelings, rather like turning the pages of a book.

"I'm both surprised and actually pleased to find out that Dale's a Christian," she says. "Actually, since Dunedin beach, I've given God and religion a second chance."

But Dale's involved in a serious car accident. He's quite badly beaten up. It's some time before they meet again. This time Dale tells her she's perfect for him in every way, but there's a check in his spirit that this is not the right time for him; can they just be friends?

"I was seriously shocked when Dale dumped me," Shirley tells me. "Can you imagine – rejection all over again – and so soon?"

I hear a lot in the silence that follows.

Then she says, "In an instant, I realised how desperate and broken and afraid I still am. I've tried to heal myself, but I haven't managed it. I thought of God. And cried out to him. I told him I'd tried everything I could think of."

Early in October on a Saturday morning, Shirley phones and asks if I am sitting down. I feel for my three-legged stool.

"Mum," she says, "God answered me. I have a new birthday somewhere in the wee hours of 1 October. God has made it quite clear to me that I long for two things. I want the love of a man – and I want God's love. God wants me to make him my priority – I must come back to him first. He doesn't want me to focus on getting a guy. That, I've discovered, doesn't work. I need to seek God as my biggest, most important quest. Once that's in place, God himself will sort out the rest."

This lifts my heart. I know how many times I too have taken a big step forward in my faith, only to slip back again. It's like the capture of a position by advancing armed forces. We manage to hold the new position only briefly before we retreat. Because of my own repeated failures, I wonder a little, will she also slip back again? *Oh, Thy! You pessimist!* I think. Maybe not.

"You know how good I am at crying?" she goes on. "Well, I've cried and cried. But it's been different, because I am crying with relief. And joy – joy in God. I'm so changed! I actually went to apologise to Mark. He didn't know what hit him, poor man." She giggles just a very little.

Shirley accepted Jesus for the first time when she was four in a caravan park at Blyde River Canyon. When she was twelve, on a Veld School camp, she gave herself to him again. In her final year at Westerford High, she dedicated the study schedule she drew up to him: "So whether you eat or drink, whatever you do, do all to the glory of God."[6]

Clearly, over the years, her faith has blown hot and cold. Not so with God. He has always been there for her. Her coming back to him at times like this is always a response to his constant pursuit of her. Now, at this point, she's seeing God as the supreme goal of her life.

To believe God doesn't love her is a flashback from the past. And for her now to feel that God does is huge. Perhaps she won't be able to hold on to this realisation – but the fact that she's got there is amazing.

"Mum, it feels as if God has let me take a very long bungee jump. And instead of letting me fall any further, he's reeling me in. Why do I feel that God just crooked his little finger at me?"

Not long after her move to Wokingham in 2006, Greyfriars Church warmly welcomes Shirley. So does the tall, dark, rather handsome Scott. It takes a while for her to settle in. Scott certainly helps. Soon they're going out together.

It doesn't take long before Shirley's emails are full of him.

> Scott's told me I'm very special to him. Do you think that equates to 'I love you' in boy language?

Experiences from the past caution her:

> I'm trying not to put any pressure on him, but it is sometimes difficult to be cool when I've fallen so in love! Luckily, I think he's in the same boat. Okay, you – enough love-sick babble.

And she signs off.

Very soon she writes:

> I think God wants me in this relationship. I know he loves me and is working things out for my own good. I think Scott cares about me a great deal (he still hasn't told me how he feels about me, though). I also know he's afraid of losing his independence. I need courage, Mum. Half the time, I just want to run.

All too soon, old tapes play in her head.

> I'm not a terribly happy bunny, I'm afraid. I'm having a rough week... I've been a bit anxious about Scott. He's been rather quiet. I

---

[6] 1 Corinthians 10:31

*want to give him space as he hasn't had a girlfriend for seven years.
As a result, I find myself wondering whether to email him/call him,
etc. I don't want to crowd him.*

*I told Scott I'd been anxious. He was very gentle with me and gave
me a huge hug and a very nice whisky.*

She's so keen on this relationship that she acknowledges, "I'm a little too
much in 'eager-to-please' mode, if you know what I mean."

She and I both know what she means. And I sympathise – we've shared
about this before. Something else she does is to create attractive masks to
wear. She has a whole cupboardful. She wears her best ones non-stop for
Scott. It's all about being accepted and loved. She's convinced it's her bouts
of depression that frighten guys away, so she must hide any sign of that. But,
sadly, masks have a sell-by date. After that, they come off.

———————

Four years of ups and downs follow. Scott helps a bit with some of the
DIY on her house. She has marriage and a future family in mind now. Sadly,
Scott tells her clearly that he doesn't like the house and he doesn't want to
live there.

Shirley's housemate, Carolyn, comes home night after night to find her
depressed and withdrawn. Stepping in through the front door means
stepping in to gloom.

"You're so miserable, Shirls," Carolyn says. "Every time I look at your
face, I see nothing but despair."

Shirley admits she's struggling. "Scott and I are going through a difficult
patch and I feel overwhelmed. I guess I'm at a place where I'm questioning
everything. Surely it shouldn't be this difficult? Right now, it seems a lot
easier to walk away from it all."

The flood of emails increases.

*I'm feeling really hurt and angry right now – why can't he make up
his mind about me? I feel quite inclined to throw my toys and say
that's it.*

*Mum, please could you pray for a few things? Should I end things?
I'm trying to seek God on this – and keep my heart open to hearing
from him. Thus far God continues to shower love and assurance on
me.*

With her typical sweetness, she dreads hurting Scott. The uncertainty
causes her anxiety to spike.

I feel peaceful, but my body is telling me otherwise – I'm having trouble sleeping, and I'm having a bad time with spastic colon and headaches. Why, Mum, why? Why can't he say he loves me?

Just like all those times before, this time too she concludes:

I'm just not lovable – not even by God.

When Mark left her, it was because he could not love her as he should. So, unknowingly, he pressed the blade, already in her heart since childhood days, deeper. Now Scott's silence, even after four-and-a-half years, increases the pain in the old, familiar wound because he too – also unknowingly – gives the blade another twist.

Watching Shirley with Scott tests my long-suffering to the limit. Again her strategies haven't produced the results she yearns for. I so long for her to have what she wants, but I know her strategies don't work. She needs to discover for herself the futility of sowing fig leaves to hide behind. That exercise leaves her deeply exhausted.

I groan as I watch. Of course she can't keep it up. Sooner or later, she ends up unmasked and tired out. Often, I'm tired out too. Our hearts pulse with pain. It's a relief when she ends it.

Sadly, Shirley's relationships with men frequently break down. Since her divorce seven years ago – and apart from the four plus years with Scott – she's ploughed such a lone furrow.

In September 2011 she writes to me:

I feel God is teaching me lessons about trusting him and leaving everything in my Father's hands, which is hard for a control freak like me. In the end, this Scott-thing had been weighing me down big time.

You know what? Now that it's gone, I'm starting to feel more and more like me. I've weathered the storm, if you like. I'm even starting to feel cheeky again.

I miss Scott's friendship, but I don't miss the pain and struggles. The events of the past few weeks have confirmed to me that I'm attractive with a lot to offer. So I'm sure I will find someone at some point. My Scottish friend in Denmark certainly seems to have the hots for me! I also know that I'll be okay on my own. I really believe God will provide what I need. (He's already provided a great group of friends!)

But any change – like Dale or Stuart or someone else not being particularly nice over the phone – throws her completely. She scribbles in her diary:

I get into manipulation mode, trying to ensure I don't get hurt – regardless of whether I like the bloke... if he's right for me... giving away my power... I guess, ultimately, I'm afraid of being hurt and disappointed again. It's all self-protection, not love.

Her next email asks again for help.

Hey you, if you have a moment today, please could you pray for me? Tom's invitation to rugby in Dublin freaked me out a bit, painful head, couldn't sleep – too much coffee and Nurofen?

But Stuart comes to believe the distance between Leeds and Reading makes their relationship unworkable.

Quite some time later, Shirley writes:

Feeling very stressed! Trying to unpick why – work, counselling, Greg. Third one is a new revelation! I've realised that, after the initial stages of a relationship, I get very stressed and fearful. I feel like I'm losing myself, because I'm being governed by fear. To some extent this is natural – given the past – but I don't want to be governed by it. Perfect love drives out fear.

The relationship with Greg is very brief. It ends when Greg says he needs to focus on bringing up his two young children.

Many months later – in late 2012 – the telephone rings. I know it's Shirley. And my heart sinks.

"Hi, Mum," she says. Her voice is flat. Those two words in that tone of voice always trigger alarm. They have done for years now. Partly because it's more of the same old, same old.

"Oh, Mum," she tells me, "Dylan's decided to take a job in Australia."

The ruggedly handsome, blond Dylan is an online date she found on a Christian website in early 2012. He did say, "Of course, I'd never go out with a girl on anti-depressants." That was a blow to the gut. So Shirley masked her brokenness from him too – as she had done with the others – but with even more effort. She tried doubly hard to come across as effervescent and fun all the time. She made sure she always looked beautiful.

And, at great cost to herself, she suppressed everything about herself that she thought he wouldn't like.

Hot tears begin to fall slowly, and then become a gushing riot. So often she does nothing to wipe them away. Now, too, the streaks dampen her face, left to evaporate in their own good time from hands and tousled hair. I'm not there to see it happen – but I know it is. And I ache.

"He hasn't phoned or replied to my text," Shirley agonises, like so many times before. "What should I do? Perhaps I should move to Wimbledon, Mum," she suggests. "Then I can pop in and see him as often as I like – without invading his space, of course."

Predictably, she asks, "Should I call him?"

She invariably does contact the guys again – and again, and again. She needs to talk every day and to see the guy every second day. It's what Phyllis calls her "peekaboo problem" – she has to see the guy physically, or she panics and doesn't believe he's there. And the guys don't come, and they don't call.

Shirley's really very gentle – so much so that she has to make friends again after a break-up. And so, true to form, she sends Dylan a carefully worded email. "What went wrong?" she asks.

"Work's a demanding mistress," he replies, "and you've been so miserable seeing me for quite a while – I can't remember the last time you were happy with me." And she thought she'd played her cards right this time! Not deceived by her efforts for a moment, Dylan explains, "When I was with you, all I could see was your unhappiness, sad face and disappointment. You were very, very miserable. I just wanted you to move on in your career and excel."

Shirley goes to see her pastor about the large number of single women in the church. He's not impressed with the single church guys either. He agrees that "a number of them are wusses".

"Oh, Mum," Shirley wails, "please, Mum, I can't have a wuss."

I hear her.

"I'm so scared, Mum, that I'll never find the right man."

There's that tell-tale sniff again. I feel it.

"Because I'm gentle and kind, I tend to attract needy, sensitive, nice-guy types. Kind of like a mother hen. Apparently, Bruce is coming to London for a few days. When I heard, the first thing I thought was, *here comes another one of my chickens!* Unfortunately, although I like this kind of man very much, they don't excite me! There's no spark. And yet the ones that do excite me aren't as nice. Go figure."

Over many years, Shirley and I repeatedly talk about her passionate search – and the old chestnut of the merits of pursuing God so that he can direct her search for a man. She seemed to get it right when Dale dumped her. And now? My sadness is deep, because she seems to be right back where she started – thinking finding the right man is the answer.

With each failed relationship, she takes strain. She doesn't factor in the dysfunction of some of the broken people with whom she goes out. So every break-up is her fault. But she does also – with characteristic astuteness – factor in an important truth: "When you get into your late thirties, everyone available is in the same boat. All 'recycled' – divorced or whatever – and carrying baggage that now inevitably gets in the way."

Towards the end of 2012, a small, sleek, powerful pleasure boat rocks gently on the Red Sea. The spectacular sunset turns the gentle ripples along the sides of the boat golden. Tired divers relax, drinks in hand. Tomorrow they look forward to tumbling over the side again, entombed in their sleek diving suits, looking for adventure. Now they lazily swop stories.

Shirley's turquoise bikini shows off her perfect tan. She seeks out the comfort of the luxurious cushions at the front of the boat. Steve comes over to join her, beer in hand. The gym instructor's suntanned body reddens in the twilight.

Meeting him seems to be the most wonderful, plump, glistening cherry on the top. But he doesn't want a relationship. This time her disappointment is the worst it's been.

On 19 November 2012, she writes in her diary:

> *After a fab time in Egypt, hit rock bottom coming back to... what? A dysfunctional life! Have decided to chuck in the towel with this version of life and follow my dreams!*

At this point, something snaps. I know it does. And Shirley gives up.

Now she talks frequently about selling her house to finance her new dreams of comfort and satisfaction through the pursuit of pleasure. She takes a huge step – this is a major decision – and casts all caution to the winds. She puts her house on the market.

CHAPTER SIXTEEN

Mum's Dearest Wish

"Her lostness is what I see – a figure on the beach."
(Camps Bay, South Africa)

WHILE BRIAN WAS AWAY FOR A WEEK IN SEPTEMBER 1997, GOD blessed me in a special way. Every night, I encountered the Holy Spirit. As he fell upon me, I found myself lying on the carpet. Gently, he poured himself into me, so that by the end of the week, I was blessed beyond measure.

Ever since then I have, on occasion, discovered the exquisite wonder of living face to face with Christ. For many years, I've known about him through my study of the Bible, but face to face is different. This completely changes life. Knowing God – rather than knowing *about* him – has become the most precious relationship I've ever experienced. How much do I long to know him? With everything I've got! Not surprisingly, I want Shirley to share this – to know him intimately, as the best thing of all.

I want this so much for her that I pray "whatever it takes". Actually, I pray "whatever it takes" more than just once.

"If you have a belly button, you have baggage," a wise friend said recently.

My own baggage skews my understanding of reality – and of Shirley. At times, I'm overanxious and push too hard. That's when Mrs Fix-it does the most damage. God only knows what other unhelpful baggage I bring in to clutter our relationship. As we do life, I find out not only how broken Shirley is but also how broken I am.

It seems she suffers from an anxiety disorder – and dependency – and probably clinical depression as well. I don't know what it is. Apart from the GP prescription of Prozac, it's never been diagnosed. No parent wants to believe something as horrible as this.

I refuse to see Shirley's mental and psychological challenges as permanent, or beyond fixing. But she's so fractured, there's no easy fix – everything can't just 'come right' as I expect it to, given time. She's mentally ill and that won't change. We need a miracle.

I don't realise how much a mental disorder skews our perspective. It makes it so much harder for Shirley to see, and understand, and progress in knowing God. I don't realise that my fix-it behaviour is also the result of blindness. But the astounding thing is that God can use the flaws in one of us in a positive way to compensate for what is lacking in another. So perhaps this is one of the times when he's doing that? Oh, how I hope so.

I remember paging through a glossy magazine and being stopped in my tracks. A picture filled the page of a bronzed, most athletic figure, muscles bulging. What hit me between the eyes though were the thick metal chains twisted round his body – hardly a good place from which to do anything much.

It reminds me now of what 2 Corinthians 10 says about strongholds that imprison us. One thing's certain – this is a spiritual battle for Shirley's soul.

Often, before we talk, I pray, "Come and fill me with your Holy Spirit. Show me how to help Shirls, dear God."

I don't know how – and I don't want to blow it, if I can help it.

Many of the beliefs God has instilled in me are not Shirley's. But, because of my dearest wish for her, I push – feel it necessary, because of her disability, to even *bully* – her into accepting them too. That's not what she needs. She needs to have the space and time to respond as God – who alone can open every sort of closedness – works in her life.

Shirley's silences flummox me. Because she does not answer, I have no idea how my efforts towards her knowing Jesus are going. That leaves me with only gut-feeling to go by. It's like speaking into a vacuum that merely echoes. The less she responds, the more I try to help. I suspect – actually, I know – I'm going too far. She no longer feels safe with me. But my faith is weak and I believe I've got to get her into God's Kingdom somehow.

Every time Shirley is caught up in struggles – old or new – I remember that struggling figure. The odds against her are powerful and intense too – like the chains. Sometimes I see the chains break – some of mine too. Sometimes I see them multiply. Only very occasionally do I see any vanish.

And so I sit with her in her shadows – pretty myopic myself – longing for things to change.

I try to apologise to Shirley – quite sure I have wronged her. I really want her to tell me. Then I can do something about it. Then I can do more – mend my ways, if necessary. She never responds, which leaves me sad. Sad and powerless. I'm way out of my league. And that leaves me feeling very unsure – I know what I want for her is the right thing – but am I doing it right? In my journey, I have not yet learnt how to wait on Another. I need to 'let go and let God' – trite but true. After all, he prizes intimacy with Shirley far more than I can ever understand.

Respecting Shirley's boundaries crops up again and again. Mrs Fix-it doesn't do well on this one. Confronting her over something like her drinking brings me face to face with the possibility of trespassing once more.

The drinking does disturb me deeply. Clearly, it disturbs her too – which leaves me even more disturbed. What makes it worse is that I really don't know how bad it is. I wish I could see for myself but in some ways I don't want to know.

I visit – only extremely fleetingly – the idea that I can tell her she must stop. But that would be a parent-to-child response, not the adult-to-adult relationship I'm trying so hard to cultivate.

I'm so concerned about this kind of thing that I write:

> *Are you going to be mad at me for writing what I really believe? I hope this doesn't sound too 'mummyish' but just 'mummyish' enough to bless you today.*

Very early on, I abandoned my previous assumption that because we had to wait so long, God must have given us a perfect child. I realise my love for Shirley has nothing to do with whether she's perfect or not. So I write:

> *You amaze me with the courage you've had and the road you're travelling. You also enchant me with your integrity – I see it as pure gold.*

My efforts to encourage her never stop.

> *For some time now, I've been aware that you're blossoming and catching the sun. You're exposing to us some of the loveliness God had in mind when he created you. I say some of the loveliness – there's a lot more to be revealed over the years ahead!*

Year by year, our hearts ride many ups and downs together. When Shirley sounds in a good place, I'm relieved. It's hard to put into words how wonderful those rare moments are – when I hear a positive, happy note in her voice.

I don't want her to stop confiding in me. She's so fragile. I believe she's too brittle for me to ever vent my feelings. Much of the time, I can't be myself. I feel I always have to be there for her and be safe for her.

I can't afford to let my patience run out – ever. At times I feel resentful – and hurt – but I can't ever say so. There are times when I struggle with sheer exasperation – followed by despair. It's such a long journey and so little – actually it seems like nothing – ever changes or improves.

That I suppress what I really feel impedes the quality of our relating. But to me the prize is that if I'm gentle enough and not too confrontational, she'll continue to confide in me. I don't want to lose anything more in terms of real communication. And I don't want to lose the opportunity to influence her in the right direction.

I agonise. Can I make her strong without wounding her? I see our relationship as some sort of anchor for her. She must have someone. I can't bear the thought that she might have no one at all. This is about keeping both ends up, otherwise she'll implode.

"Hey, you," Shirley says one day, "I'm sorry I'm always dumping on you."

"Well, actually," I reply, "I would like to enjoy your other side too, you know."

"Sorry, Mum, I know it's not fair on you," she sighs.

We share the regret.

I have also come to learn – through the study of character formation that is part of my journey – that making your own choices empowers. Shirley's self-confidence dips seriously low much of the time. So I must encourage her to make her own choices – particularly the best one of all. I make this my focus as I interact with her.

If I can help her think straight, she'll be in control and cope better with all the rest, I argue. After all, we connect well on a cerebral level. It's when I go too far in that direction that I eclipse the warmth I always intend.

What rattles me are the decisions that I think are less than wise – like selling her house to finance holidays.

And then, I find myself thinking, what happens when the money's all gone?

I've pleaded with her not to sell the goose that lays the golden egg. When she sells anyway, I say nothing and walk away. But I'm really not happy.

On our separate – though sometimes parallel – journeys, there are such ups and downs. And different things challenge. But the way forward is always choice by choice. At times I mess up with those and at times Shirley does. More often than not, on an emotional level, we live right past each other. Or we both queer the pitch.

While I've set my heart on Shirley knowing God in a profound relationship, I know – but often forget – that in the end it is God alone who can bring that about. All along the line, he has her – us – safely in his hands and on his heart. If I only look out for them, I will detect the very many gentle interventions from him along the way. The redeeming factor is that as we do life, neither of us is in ultimate control.

CHAPTER SEVENTEEN

Deep in Thought

"Shirley's black-and-white kitten was all soft fur,
bright avocado-green eyes, sharp claws and fun."

ON A BAD HAIR DAY, IN MORE WAYS THAN ONE, SHIRLEY
phones the salon for an appointment. Perhaps a new look will help. In spite
of the hum of the hairdryer, she's thinking deeply. *Must I move to London?*
Is that a good – or a bad – idea? What about success? And happiness? Go
figure: I wanted a great career, which was something Mark and I couldn't
agree on. Now I'm sold on having great holidays – and a beautiful body –
and a husband and children. Have I built my house on the sand – again?
What she feels again is that huge, very familiar void. *I feel I need to take*
time to sort out what I really want and need, and my relationship with God
without a man. I really need God.

Down at Ye Olde Leathern Bottel, everyone orders battered cod, chips and mushy peas. Glasses clink as Nick proposes a toast. Jo, Katy, Shirley and he are enjoying a pub supper. It's been a long time and there's a lot of catching up to do. There are lots of giggles – many of them from Shirley – and oodles of animated chatter.

Somehow the conversation turns to the question of trusting God. Jo and Katy share a little. Then Shirley puts down her glass.

"Hmm… I used to think God was basically there to make my life comfortable and to sort things out for me. He was there to make sure I got what I wanted. Oh, I did love him – and, yes, I thought that what he did at Easter was pretty cool – but it was all very, very mediocre, very lukewarm, and it wasn't meeting the desires of my heart." She shakes her head. "But, yeah, I kind of… was pretty sure that" – she laughs softly – "God's role as a sort of companion on my journey was to answer my prayers and to do the things I wanted."

"Like providing a parking place when you have to have one?" asks Katy, smiling.

"Or giving you a great date?"

Everyone laughs. Jo's just met Colin, so she has dating very much on her mind.

"All that and much more," Shirley explains. "I actually thought God was some kind of useful and supremely competent servant. He comes along for the journey – to do for me what I want."

"And when he slips up?" Nick asks.

"That's when I get mad with him. I've thrown my toys out the cot a lot when he's not delivered. And stomped off angry – again."

The arrival of the waitron balancing platters of cod, peas and chips cuts the conversation short. Not too much later, the girls head back home.

As Shirley and Nick sit on the couch at her home in Wokingham enjoying one last glass of wine, she opens her heart a little more.

"You know my dad's a vicar?" she asks.

Nick nods.

"I've known about God all my life. I think I gave my life to God when I was four." She takes a dreamy moment or two to remember. "So God has always been in my life – but it's not been an easy relationship – to say the least. Hmm… I was a Christian – going to church – but it just seemed to me that wherever I looked for love, I couldn't quite find it. I wasn't quite sure that God loved me. You know, come to think of it, my life's journey's been a search for love. I felt like I'd asked and asked and asked for things, and God hadn't really heard me. It felt like I was doing something wrong... hmm... and I think the hurt and the frustration with all of that just kind of built up and built up. So I had a big fight with God."

In the silence that follows, they take a few moments to sip their drinks.

"About – gosh, I think after the Scott-thing ended as it did in 2011 – I just said to God, 'I believe you're there. But I don't believe you care about me, 'cause how come you've just ignored me? How come you've not answered any of my prayers? Why do you let my journey be so tough and unhappy?'"

Nick looks intently into her eyes. "Do you still think that because God doesn't give you what you want, that proves he doesn't love you?"

He holds her gaze for quite a while. Then she looks away.

"Well, doesn't it? But there's more – there are other things too."

Shirley's black-and-white kitten was all soft fur, bright avocado-green eyes, sharp claws and fun. Summer would play in the shadows at the front door, tear up the staircase and flop on Shirley's snug pillow and, sometimes, her face. Now she's been run over by a car.

When Shirley's tears dry up – just a bit – she phones.

"Mum, why did such a horrid thing happen? Surely, she didn't deserve to die? Who did this?"

The issue for her becomes: *Just who's to blame? God? If he's always blameless and beyond fault, whom do we have left to blame? Satan? He's the opposite, it's true. But what about whoever was driving too fast? Then God permitted it, but can't be held responsible for it, can he?*

"You know what, Shirley," I say, "you've been praying for hours. And you've got a lot out of Phyllis's counselling of late. Then the Summer thing happens. Maybe Satan doesn't like the direction your journey's taking. Then, through what Satan intends for evil, God actually plans to offer blessing. We often don't understand how that can be – and we don't escape the pain."

As part of her journey, Shirley ponders, questions and tries to find answers. It's a journey to find truth and to shake off deception. She goes to many Christian conferences. She's really very intellectual – a bit of a brainbox.

Besides copying into her diary the gems she's found in Larry Crabb's book, *The Pressure's Off*,[7] she's underlined screeds in the book itself. Nick told her about it. He was so enthusiastic that he bought her a copy in the hope that it would help her understand God's heart for her. She's amazed to find so much of it absolutely spot on for where she's at now – in 2012, probably the darkest year of her whole journey so far. She can't wait to call in at Nick's cottage in Shiplake.

"Hey, you," she says, book in hand, "look here."

They pore over a page together.

"Crabb says striving to figure out how to make life work is slavery. The one thing above all else that we must have are actual encounters with Jesus Christ. I've had some, you know – and I know you have."

Smiling as he remembers, Nick dishes up the 'spag bol' he's made.

"True," he manages to say as they twist spaghetti and scoop up sauce. Shirley can't eat and read, so she stops.

"Crabb also says only God – in person – can satisfy the depths of our human desire. There's nothing better than this. We can count on him to do it for us – to draw us to him through circumstances. It is God who keeps the hope alive that we'll be able to taste joy, no matter what goes wrong."

Shirley twists spaghetti round her fork – and swallows, getting tomato on her chin. Nick laughs and wipes it off for her.

"So the journey we make through life is really mapped out circumstance by circumstance? And how we deal with them – choice by choice? I must say, I never saw it that way before."

Nick's still not really listening but concentrating on his next twist of spaghetti.

"Look here, Nick." Shirley turns to something else she's underlined. "Crabb also says that to reject the best of heaven – which is what God is offering – is what Satan encourages. Satan wants us to head for something else. He claims our life's futile anyway. Oh, I fall for this line – over and over again!"

Nick points at the rapidly cooling spaghetti. Shirley gets the message. Not too long, and Nick takes the dishes to the kitchen while Shirley stokes the fire. Then she turns more pages.

"Crabb points out that pain teaches us to value intimacy with God over blessing. It leaves us full, alive and happy. In fact, we learn to live – still in our pain – but with joy. Hmm… I need to think about that."

---

[7] WaterBrook Press (2012)

Nick's mobile buzzes so he remains distracted. Shirley reads on. Once he sits down again, she says, "Crabb believes the challenge is to change journeys. The Spirit advances God's route for us and we come to thirst desperately for it. He convinces us that we are fully loved – so our future's guaranteed! And we can rest in that, in his love for us. Everything – any kind of baggage from the past – can be redeemed. And we come to enjoy Jesus and to reflect him. Hence the pressure's off! How cool is that? As you know, a major part of my 'baggage' is my struggle to believe God loves me."

Nick smiles. At last, his attention is on the book – now that the spaghetti's all gone. "That's such a biggie for you, Shirls – so absolutely huge! Let's drink to our journeys with God – mine and yours – into truth, love and freedom."

They fill and clink their glasses once more.

As Shirley struggles through 2012, she often sits with her Larry Crabb book open on her lap. Sometimes she texts Nick about what she's read, but mostly she ponders – typical Shirley – in deep contemplation on her own. *There's God – that's a real biggie. Maybe he's actually hands-on in caring for me? He's certainly always around. Then maybe I actually have to factor him in – permanently?*

Her eye falls on another of the many quotes she's copied. *God, I don't know how you can produce the fruit in my heart of a consuming love for you. I seem to find so much more enjoyment in the good things of life, and sometimes in sin... I experience more pleasure in other things... It will take a miracle to change that.*

She knows she's on such a journey. On a new page, she scribbles:

Still need to move to that place where I am passionately in love with God. Currently, I feel grateful, thankful; love him, but not passionate, ready/willing to give up my all – in a heartbeat, on fire, etc. Does this grow in time?

Lord, I come to you, just as I am. One thing I ask – let me see your beauty. And – seeing your beauty – let me love like you and live like you.

Often, as she spends time thinking, a supernatural comfort settles over her like a soft, downy blanket.

Sometime in 2011, as a counsellor with Christian World Revival (CWR), Shirley has to report to mentors for guidance and advice. So she goes to see Christine. She knows Chris through their joint involvement in a prayer ministry. As a friend and counsellor, Chris listens intently. As a mother and grandmother, she's full of compassion.

Chris has thrown out a lifeline for Shirley many times before, and this time too Shirley comes away really encouraged.

She writes to me:

> I had a great time praying with Chris! We rebuked the lies about me that I've been living under for so long. I repented of accepting and believing them.
>
> The first time Chris prayed for me, she started to cry. She saw a picture of my heart with a blade in it causing a deep wound. Together we 'pulled out the blade' and prayed for healing.
>
> This time I think it really worked. I feel like the old, familiar pain is gone. I feel light and free and happy.
>
> The other thing God did for me – which moved me deeply – was that he gave Chris an overwhelming sense of his love for me, and also of his pain that I have been hurt. Chris was so overwhelmed that she cried and cried – and I ended up comforting her! We were really touched by God, Mum. It was so precious. I feel better than I have in ages.

CHAPTER EIGHTEEN

When Life Takes a Serious Dip

*"She's sitting in her Beamer
in the gathering dark outside her house."*

THIS TIME WHEN SHIRLEY PHONES, SHE'S SITTING IN HER silver-grey Beamer in the gathering dark outside her house. It must be autumn 2012, because there are piles of caramel-coloured leaves all around her.

I've no idea how long she's been there in the shadows.

"Oh, Mum," she chokes out, "I feel so, so terrible." There's such heartbreaking sadness in her voice. "I just... can't... go in."

She's sobbing now, and she really means it. This is crisis. She slumps behind the wheel, shoulders heaving and tears flowing freely.

"Oh, Mum, it's so empty. The house... so dark... There's no one there."

101

Her front windows glint alien black in the semi-darkness.

"I don't want to go in… I can't go in. How can I? I am so alone, Mum." Pushed by pain, the sobs crescendo. "I just can't do this anymore."

Sickened beyond measure, I wait. As I wait, I ache. Compassion and searing sadness struggle up inside me. I feel gutted. How hard I pray.

Later, Shirley manages to whisper, "I hate my house… I hate my horrible life… I hate everything!"

All around her, neighbours are inside, lights on, glad to be home after the day's work. They fill up with pizza, chatter and TV.

I pray – absolutely incoherently – and wait. Eventually it's a little quieter.

"My darling, I'm so sorry," I soothe. "Tell me more. Take your time. Just take your time. I'm not going anywhere."

All sorts of things spill out. She looks at her life; so many broken dreams, with so many sides to them.

"My life's dysfunctional, Mum," she cries. What's the point of going on when she feels so lousy all the time? Again, as so often of late, she asks, "Is there any hope?"

Every time, that pushes my panic button. And I fill with dread. Because it sounds truly suicidal. My desperation is complete. How can I, still in Cape Town, rescue her? *Talk, Thy, talk,* I tell myself. *You can at least do that.*

Next – because this feels right – I try gently to comfort, warm and soothe her. I see a series of steps I have to walk her through – to rescue her. I want to get her to the point where she can respond. How I wish there were somebody there nearby whom I could call. But, sickeningly, there is no one but me.

I sense that we're not there yet – Shirley's still freaked out – so I keep talking, encouraging, telling her I love her, and *we'll get through this.*

When I feel that the time is right, I talk her into taking her key and getting out of the car. Then I talk her up the path to her front door. Finally, we get the door open – it always sticks – and she's in. And the lights are on.

"Phone me again in half an hour," I say, "and let's see how you are then."

The phone call is as much for me as for her. While I wait, I try to find comfort. Rather pathetically, all I can find is the thought that at least the cats are there – fur soft and soothing under Shirley's every stroke.

When Shirley phones – an incredibly long half hour later – she sounds a lot better. I'm endlessly grateful. It's clear the immediate crisis is over. Relief is immense, but deep foreboding shadows the future.

Much of the time, the beautiful Beamer is just plain dirty. The dust coat thickens so much that someone decides to write on it: "Please wash me... soon?" He adds a sad, round face.

Nothing happens.

So the distressed artist adds a date.

When he gets to adding the third date, Shirley angrily takes the long-suffering vehicle off to the car wash.

Thankful to see the change, her next-door neighbour Mark comes across as she parks. "Wow, what a difference," he calls out. "Now what about the lawn?" he mutters.

Inside, the kitchen tells the same story. Dishes stand about. The dishwasher fills very slowly as Shirley's not really doing any cooking. Regularly, the grocery cupboard's empty. That's when toilet paper gets rationed. The post overflows the basket besides the door. Dead pot plants collapse in despair. The cause of death is always ravaging, unrelenting thirst.

Every now and then, Shirley gets into clean-up mode. "Oops, here's another dead soldier," she mutters, as she tosses out tired, half-empty jars of mouldy pastes, pesto and spreads from her fridge. They crash, one after another, into the garbage bin.

When she does do a bit of cleaning, she actually feels a little better. She does titter when she finds a dried-out mouse behind her desk. But it's not often that a clean-up spree makes it up the stairs. So the increasing mound of clothes crinkles and creases behind the bedroom door.

As 2012 progresses, Shirley's life spins out of control. The break-up with Scott the year before – her most promising relationship yet – has a lot to do with it. She plunges into deep depression.

"Thy," Nick tells me over the phone, "Shirley keeps turning up for work really late. I text and phone, but day after day, she arrives bleary-eyed and half-asleep – and very late. I take her for strong coffee and a talk. Only then can we get to work."

Shirls is very distressed too. "Mum, I'm battling to sleep. I hate that I'm going to toss and turn. So I put off going to bed. I read – mostly watch TV – sometimes until three in the morning. Trouble is, when I do fall asleep, I can't wake up. The alarm goes, but I can't get up. I'm always late for work, but I don't know what to do."

Today she's too depressed to get out of bed.

Nick tells me, "She doesn't know this, but they're talking of firing her."

I'm not surprised – I've been thinking that too, and of how that will devastate her. Fortunately, it doesn't happen. But Shirley's despair deepens.

Nick also confides, "She's such a confused little girl in a woman's body. She comes round to my place in Henley full of smiles. After ten minutes, her face crinkles up and the tears just flow. She pours out her troubles – always lots of them – and eventually comes to a stop. At this point, she's feeling much better. We drink some red wine together. And I take back my soaked hanky. Next time she visits, it's more of the same. I always feel I need to support her by building a scaffold around her, she's so brittle and fragile."

More and more, Shirley fails to keep appointments. She misses sessions with Phyllis. She falls asleep instead of meeting Jo and Katy for curry at the pub. They phone her, she apologises, says she's coming – and falls asleep again. They get so hungry – and mad – that they order and tuck in without her.

She doesn't come to band practice, although she leads a worship team on Sundays. After being extremely patient, Eileen her worship leader suggests, as kindly as she can, that she step down for a while: "I think you need to take some time out to look after yourself, so take a break for now."

Still her despair deepens.

Shirley's due to see Chris, but she cancels. She's down to take a turn on a Saturday morning as a member of a church prayer team. She just doesn't pitch. Worse, at times she's due to lead the Saturday worship – and she just doesn't turn up for that either.

"No excuse. No apology. And no Shirley – grrrr..." wails Chris. She writes:

> It seems like Shirls is in such deep despair that she's saying, "No one loves me, so I might as well ruin my life anyway." I hate to say this, but she's her own worst enemy. From the concern I am hearing from mature, grounded Christians at the church, she's not helping herself. And they're saying they can't use her in ministry – even though she has so many gifts – until she's back on even keel.

I sense growing frustration. And annoyance.

As Shirley's depression deepens, her faith fades. God vanishes and she can't find him anywhere. Actually, she's not able to look too hard. Clearly, all of life's gone steeply downhill. And it's spinning further and further out of control.

For Shirley, the depression is so deep now that she can't hide it anymore. I can imagine how acute her distress becomes because "people know". Knowing how much this must distress her brings me fresh anguish. Now she has this too, on top of the anguish she's been feeling deep within herself from knowing she's out of control. And every time she blows it, she sickens with more angst and feels more and more vulnerable and exposed, incapable of making a course correction.

On her Red Sea holiday – the best holiday ever – Shirley reverts to her old belief that finding a man is the answer. She is prepared to date anyone, no longer necessarily a Christian. So there's a brief relationship with Steve, who actually also works in Bracknell. This brings more pain and nothing else.

"I am so cross," she tells me. "My life's the pits, and what does God do about it? Nothing – absolutely nothing. I'm mega-hurt and frustrated. So now I'm having this big fight with him. Why can't I feel him here? Where is he?"

She's come back to believing God "needs to do the right thing" – or else. And, once again, God 'lets her down'. The disappointment is huge. So is her angry reaction.

She tells Katy, "God and I are not talking at the moment."

When Katy discovers Shirley will be alone on Christmas Day, she's quick to ask, "Why don't you come and join us for Christmas dinner? You know my family and it'll be fun. Amelia's so excited about the size of the heap of presents under the tree already – you try to work out what's going on in my four-year-old's little head!"

Shirley doesn't even reply to Katy. This – like much of what she has been doing – is out of character. Alone in her lounge, she watches the rain. Then she notices that Chloe-cat has left black hair and muddy paw prints all over her white couch.

"Oh, damn," she says, and a bit more.

Annoyance lingers for a moment, only to be overtaken by the ache that's always there – familiar, rather like an old friend, except this is no friend at all.

Tight-lipped, she attacks her Christmas tree. She rips the electric plug from its socket. The flashing lights die. Baubles bounce across the carpet. She bundles tinsel and trinkets into a plastic bag. She breaks the reluctant tree in half. She wrestles the pieces into a blue garbage bag. Cats cower in the corners.

Still tight-lipped, she flings open the front door. Unnoticed, Christmas lights twinkle in the warm, inviting windows of her neighbours. She marches the offending decorations through the cold. Round the corner, she tosses them into the garbage bin. Wet from the incessant rain, she hurries back. Cold drops trickle down her neck. She slams the front door.

It's Christmas 2012, and she's furious with God.

CHAPTER NINETEEN

Hitting Rock Bottom

"I have never been happy."

OVER THE YEARS, SHIRLEY TELLS ME A NUMBER OF TIMES, "I have never been happy." As 2012 drags on, she says it again.

I hear a shrug as she describes the last five years as "just five years unhappier". On miserable, grey days, rain streaks the window next to her favourite spot on the couch. She drizzles pain.

What she quotes in her diary from Larry Crabb adamantly declares that nothing can prevent God's redemption and glorious final victory. She concludes with:

God wants me to be happy!

She's not completely defeated but there is only the slightest hint of hope.

Shirley talks about "chucking" the job she's come to hate. She's moved on from working with Nick, back into the IT industry. Her present job leaves her thinking that she's too gentle to make a career of IT, where it's every man for himself and they take no prisoners. Perhaps she should also change church? Move to London?

Or stay in the IT world and move to Utah? A vacancy could be coming up in Salt Lake City – and the skiing's terrific. Perhaps a radical change is what she needs? Moving to a different culture may help?

Next moment she talks about going back to study – at London University – to qualify as a counsellor.

Then again, perhaps it's time to wipe the slate clean? Start all over? Should she pack everything up and come back to South Africa? She could stay in our little flat. And take the time she needs.

All this talk is desperate. And it's very drastic – perhaps dangerously unrealistic – for someone as insecure as Shirley. Will sweeping away nearly all the support she now has (besides mine) be a good thing? She's made so many bad choices – *her* words. Will this just be another one – a huge one?

She's very discerning and asks an insightful question: "If I do all this – and get into a job which is more suited to my gifting – will I perhaps find that actually I don't feel any better?"

"Sweetheart," I gather my courage to ask (I don't want to, but I feel I must), "what if the problem is inside you? Then you'll simply be taking it with you? And it'll continue to cause havoc – as it's always done."

On one of the visits Brian and I make to Shirls, her neighbour Amanda catches me on my own in the garden. She comments on Shirley's busy life. But I come away convinced that that's not what she wants to talk to me about. As a mum herself, I think she's saying, *Shirley's not coping, and you ought to know, Mum.* I'm comforted that there's someone actually on the spot that notices – and cares. I'm alarmed that others are concerned too. And I'm very grateful to God for the many times Amanda takes Shirley a mug of soup.

I write to Chris, whom I hardly know at this stage:

> *The last two weekends with Shirley on the phone have been harrowing – so negative – and she cries and cries and cries. Worryingly, she keeps saying she can't cope anymore. She's cling-wrapped in fear. She says she can't take much more of this.*

I panic, what if I have a call from Shirley that leaves me thinking she's at the point of suicide? What do I do then? Who can get to her really fast? I do not have a single phone number.

I email Chris and Nick. Chris organises some phone numbers for me – one of the pastors, for a start. She writes:

> *Your dear daughter needs much prayer, and I know that folk at the church have a heart for her and are praying for her.*

Many, many times Shirley does find comfort in going up for prayer after an evening service.

Nick replies:

> *Thy, I feel the thing that you most need to know is that Shirley is incredibly well supported. She's loved, prayed for, and protected by a number of wonderful people. No matter the situation, they'll be there for her... Being a father of three myself, I understand what it's like for you to love so deeply, be so far away, and so unable to 'cover' your child.*

> *Rest assured, Thy. If circumstances were to come to my attention of such a critical nature that I genuinely feared for her safety, I would, with others such as Chris, be in touch. I trust and pray that our faithful Lord, however, will never allow this to occur.*

I'm comforted by both Chris and Nick, but only to a point. I don't think I've managed to get them to realise how serious this is, or how serious I think it is.

These days, I am on the alert for anything – or anyone – that will tell me more of what's going on. I understand that Shirley's depression is very serious. That she can't sleep or get up in the mornings is some indication of how bad it is. But, unfortunately, none of us realises the full significance of such severe insomnia. And her worrying about it – and about being late for work – piles on the layers of anxiety for her.

Often the sadness in Shirley's voice makes me take down the bedroom phone and sink on to the floor. I sigh – and prepare to listen, comfort, pray under my breath and encourage. In winter, I pull the heated towels off the rail in the bedroom and wrap them around myself. Time after time, I put the phone down feeling wrung dry. Nothing keeps out this cold.

What else can I do but soothe, encourage and envelop her in love? So I empathise: "I hear you and bleed inside with you when you cry out that you have never been happy. This unhappiness thing is why you are getting increasingly tired – so terribly, unbearably tired." And I encourage: "I admire you because you're made of great stuff. And I love you, precious friend of my soul."

I suspect I know why very few come round over weekends or ask Shirley out. Depressed people withdraw into themselves. They're not good company. So often she's on her own all weekend long. Her despair wipes out her usual resourcefulness and drive, leaving her totally paralysed. For hours, she just sits.

I'm reluctant to step in – to trespass. But, in the end, I decide it is better to do so than not to do so. "At the beginning of every week, try to set up something for the next weekend," I advise. "Phone around until you find someone who's happy to meet you at the pub. Or get someone round for pizza – or go Chinese and get the crispy duckling you love – and a movie."

———————

Every time Shirley repeats her anguished question about hope, I receive it as a blow to the gut. She undoes me completely with this. It's an ongoing lashing. I don't know when the next blow will fall – but I do know it will.

How can she need to even ask such a question? I agonise.

She does ask it again and again. Foreboding fills me – fear wrenches at my gut. What's worse is that it feels as if she wants me to agree that there really isn't hope – because then she'll feel justified to do whatever.

Then, almost as if answering her own question, Shirley repeats, "There really isn't any hope, is there? What's the point? What's the point of going on?"

This is beyond terrible. Oh, how much I want to hold her – as I did when she was little – to make it better. But she's in her late thirties now. And what's more, I am always, it seems, six thousand unforgiving miles away.

———————

Satan evokes the voices that best express hopelessness. Often, in the dark hours of the night, Shirley prays fervently that God would "please, please" take her.

"I'm… so… disappointed… when I'm still here the next morning," she confides, "so, so disappointed."

As she reads Crabb's book, Shirley is struck by his claim that occasionally all the pain and terror of existence coalesce. Then it is that agony penetrates so deeply that it crowds out the possibility of gladness. The darkness that results is so impenetrable as to exclude the possibility of light. The only option left is to wail.

CHAPTER TWENTY

Desperate Measures

*"Very early in her life, I realised Shirley's emotions
spin round in an endless whirlpool."*

AS 2013 BEGINS, I REALISE THINGS ARE OMINOUSLY WORSE.
Now Shirley is quite irrational at times. This has never happened before, as
far as I am aware. And it frightens me to the core. Reason, couched in intense
love, is the way we connect with normal, functional people, I believe. James
1:18a says, "He chose to give us birth through the word of truth." But if
Shirley has become so mentally unstable that she can no longer respond to
reason, what is left? How do I keep in touch with her? Exactly what do I
do?

"Mum, you are the only one who's always there for me," she says.

This loads me with more responsibility, at a time when I'm increasingly aware that I'm fast running out of ways of being able to help anymore.

My child is seriously mentally ill, in need of a powerful intervention. God may choose for it to be a psychiatric intervention, I know, but something needs to be done, and soon! I know we're very close to the point beyond which I can't reach her. For her to get beyond that – beyond lost – terrifies me. What frightens me more than ever before is that normal interventions won't work – and that I have nothing else. It means the lifeline I try to hold out to her goes limp.

Very early in her life, I realised Shirley's emotions spin round in an endless whirlpool. To go there – while it might connect us, soothe her and reassure her of my love – is to enter her endless turmoil with no way out. So, beyond my frantic praying, I'm left feebly seeking a rational response – in case I can still reach her.

To acknowledge now that my brilliant, beautiful daughter has become irrational – is actually psychotic – spells ultimate disaster. I don't know that this is what the situation is. I only know it cannot get more serious. So, hopeless though this now seems, again I simply must do something. I cannot stop trying.

What's driving me now is my beyond-frantic need to rescue my child and the knowledge that she is lost unless God intervenes. It's going to require something miraculous from him, but there's no psychosis that can stop him. The snag, however, is that in this emotional frenzy of my own, I don't wait as God wants me to.

I grieve that Shirley's lost her grip on reality to a significant extent; and how she must ache – not to be part of the Sunday worship team anymore, no longer to help with counselling or with the prayer teams.

Over the years, I've always tried to hold back from too much control, even though she can't control her life. Still, I've kept encouraging Shirley to make her own choices. *Doing that will empower her,* I've reasoned, *and enable her to run her own life.*

Now she herself says, "I can't do this anymore. I need someone to take care of me."

This is crisis – and my cue. Now I have no choice but to really muscle in. I confide in my doctor. He says that, from what he can tell, Shirley's very depressed and needs medical help. He thinks it probable there's a psychological problem that's shadowing her life and leading to despair. That's my gut feeling too. I so badly want Shirls back on medication. A long time ago, I reluctantly made peace with the idea that Shirley needs to take pills – permanently. It was horribly hard to accept. But I came to understand that life, for her, is awful without it. In fact, it is not really doable. I'm desperate enough to play with fire. So I bring up the subject of antidepressants.

Shirley puts me in my place. "Last time I went to the doctor about depression, he was very, very reluctant to give me pills. 'This is the third time, Shirley,' he said. 'The last time was only six months ago. I'll give you something now, but if you need to come back again, we'll have to do a psychiatric assessment – okay?' So I can't go back, Mum. It'll get on to my medical record. Which won't help when I need to apply for jobs. No, I'm going to do it through counselling with Phyllis – you need to know we've discussed it already."

What I can see is her history of depression and black holes. There have been three or four episodes since her divorce, two years on Prozac, and more. I'm finding it hard to see much progress, certainly not through counselling alone. So her going for counselling, on its own, doesn't do much to convince me that this the full answer.

In spite of what Shirley says, I try many times to persuade her. I know that to do this is to risk any relationship I have with her – really fragile at best. Is it worth risking a complete breakdown between us? I mull it over for hours and hours. In the end, I decide the crisis is so extreme, it's worth the risk. I love her far too much not even to try.

My heart in my mouth, I email:

> *Sweetheart, you've tried to do without pills before – for long periods – and it's been so hard. It also hasn't really worked.*

Silence follows my email. Days go by. So I write another:

> *A number of times you've shared with me you have never been happy. That's torn my heart. That's what it does to me – I can only guess what it does to you. This thing's pretty pervasive, isn't it? It's destroying your happiness. It's making you more and more desperate.*

> *Since this is the situation, we have to ask why. I firmly believe it's because of a problem that's always been there. But it can be dealt with. I'm sure of it. You can be freed up.*

I know what I'm asking is huge. It involves overcoming great fear. Here she is, already terrified by what life seems to be showing her about herself, and I'm asking her to take on more, this time what I believe will be excessively bad news; something so big and so deep. But – God help me – I have to do this. Because I believe, all things considered, that's the only chance she has.

My strategy – *oh, God, how awful that I should need a strategy* – becomes to smooth the path for Shirley as much as possible. To do that, I choose to trivialise the situation. I try for us to treat the whole alarming issue like a normal, unthreatening, day-to-day matter. I think that if I make light of it, she might find it less terrifying – feel lighter about it too. I'm sickened that it should be so – and deeply reluctant. But I just have to try something, even if it has only the very remotest chance of working. There just has to be a fix.

The normal way would be to share and connect – to be honest and real. But I know, through talking with Shirley, that she can't respond to that. So, perhaps unforgivably, I resort to coercion. The ends seem – to me, at any rate – to justify the means in such an extreme case.

I'm not doing any of this without praying. I'm pleading with God, "Please, Lord – you are the only answer. I believe that with my whole heart." But I do what I have decided.

So much for my faith.

You can come out into the sunshine and play among the daisies, you know.

I write that to make it seem easy. Silly? Absurd? Totally insensitive?
How else will I ever persuade her?
More silence. Sadly, I try once again.

I hear your anguish when you say no guy'll look at you if he knows you're on pills. You tell me Dylan actually said that. Then the same Dylan comments on how miserable you've been – without pills.

I'm trying to reason her into it. For me, it's been an excruciating journey to come to accept she needs pills – but I play it down for her, thinking that if I don't do that, she'll never do it.

How beyond excruciating – massive – it must be for her. Very sadly, I'm not honest with her and I don't tell her I have no idea of how frightening this is. So, once more, I make light of it.

I know you're always a delight on mild medication. If you'd been on something, Dylan would never have needed to make a comment like that in the first place!

Pain-filled silence once again.

You have all that it takes, because you're so attractive – physically and otherwise.

Probably because Shirley finds me totally insensitive, she doesn't reply. But instead of heeding her silence, I choose to go on:

A psychiatric assessment's not necessarily a bad thing, you know. Knowing exactly what the situation is will put you in a position to deal with it.

I'm trying to lower the hurdle as much as possible. My love and anguish for her – and need to rescue her – push me hard.

If they say there's no problem, how cool to have it confirmed! Then you don't have to wonder ever again. On the other hand, if there is a problem, it's possible to do the right thing about it and free you up, once and for all.

Silence. I know that this is not good. So, after waiting for a long time for a reply, I write once again.

Use that very pretty head of yours and not feelings. You stand at the crossroads of making the very decisions that can change your future experience of life radically. Are you going to put this problem in its place? Or are you going to allow it to continue to wreak havoc in your life?

This time Shirley responds with a phone call. "Mum, stop trying to put me in a box! You think I'm mental. You're always trying to diagnose and label me! How do you think I feel when my own mother's doing this?"

My ears sting from the boxing. I knew that the risk was enormous. But I'm still incredibly sad that it has turned out like this.

And then, out of the blue, a little email arrives:

Hey Mum, I just wanted to say that I love you so much! Differences of opinion aside…

It's precious – possibly pretty superficial, but we're still talking. This is at least something. How very relieved I am. There is quite an increase in the emotional distance between us. But I'm left hoping that, in time, things can be mended.

Nats, a close friend, says God gave her Galatians 4:19 for me. "Paul says, 'My dear children, for whom I am again in the pains of childbirth until Christ is formed in you...' That's your role, Ma." She hugs me. "You're birthing her all over again."

If God is doing that, what more could I want?

Chapter Twenty-One

Suicide

"Shirley arrives home, beside herself."

EVERY TIME DURING 2012 THAT I SUGGEST COMING FOR A VISIT, Shirley flatly refuses. Brian and I debate the wisdom of me booking a flight and simply arriving on her doorstep. We are desperate enough. What holds us back? My respect for her boundaries is part of it. And right now, she's so very fragile. How can we do anything that might just push her over the edge? How deeply I feel my near-absolute ignorance about mental issues. We find ourselves hesitating, feeling more anxious day by day.

At the beginning of 2013, Mana has a dream about Shirley. Mana is part of our church small group and one of the intercessors who pray for Shirley. She asks to come and see me.

"Sure," I say, wondering what can be so serious she can't tell me over the phone. The waiting fills my mind with anxious thoughts, so I'm really glad when she arrives.

She cuts the small talk short. She knows this is hard for both of us. "I'm so sorry to say I dreamt that Shirley had died, and that Brian phoned to tell us. He said, 'But you'll be comforted to know that it wasn't suicide.'"

Some time ago – when the spectre of suicide suggested itself – I flatly denied the possibility and buried my head in the sand. As things went more and more pear-shaped, I was forced to acknowledge the possibility – occasionally and only fleetingly. God knows, I've always considered suicide the worst thing a parent could have to cope with – that and rape.

What makes possible suicide ten times worse for me during these dark days? It's the thought of what Shirley would suffer, when she's suffered so much already.

But right now, as Mana talks to me, I do not focus on suicide. I focus on – and reject – the possibility of Shirley dying. *Shirley's going to die? Impossible! Shirley's not going to die! That's quite absurd.* I remind myself that I did pray "whatever it takes" for her to come into a relationship with Jesus. I was that desperate. But I didn't ever think too much about what "whatever" could mean.

Once again, I don't get it. It's a step too far to even countenance something like this. I don't understand that God wants me to know that Shirley is going to die. And that he wants to comfort me – that it won't be suicide. God knows how much I dread that. So, sadly, the loving comfort he's offering goes clean over my head.

Instead, I busily create an interpretation of Mana's dream that suits me. Perhaps, at last, Shirley's going to make a fresh new start? Death to her past? A new birth? Open a new and exciting chapter fully healed, after all our praying? This I can live with. So I move on and forget the whole thing.

One desperate, lonely night, at the end of 2012, Shirley arrives home, beside herself. She opens the door with a struggle, drops all she's holding and slams it shut. Then she lets rip. She screams and screams. She screams out despair. She screams out hopelessness. She screams out the years of relentless anguish.

In the kitchen, she gropes for the switch of the downlights. Dishes stand all over the countertops. She grabs the nearest thing – an empty tumbler – and smashes it into the wall. Shards of glass scatter. Still frenzied, she picks up what remains of it – and slashes wildly at her wrist.

At the sight of blood, something gives way deep inside her. The storm subsides, its fury spent. She crumples, folds, sinks into a heap. Then, in a daze, she wraps a dishcloth around her arm and goes back to the lounge, where she collapses in a chair.

Shock, horror, fear, anguish, turmoil flood over her.

At last she comes to herself. "What have I done?" The words escape her lips in a sickened groan. *"What... have... I... done?"*

The next morning, Shirley phones. I can immediately tell by her voice that this is bigger than anything ever before. And I just know – I know before she says a thing – that she's either tried to end it all or got very close. I think, *overdose of pills.*

I can't imagine what she's been through to actually do this – she has such a sweet, sensitive nature – and what it's been like since she did it. I sense that right now she's utterly horrified. And she's so overcome that she can't begin to talk about it. I realise she's locked it up in a place no one may enter at this time. So I do not try to force my way in.

I also sense that this crisis is so huge that I can't afford to fail her. I can't afford to be anything less than extremely direct in my response. This is not the time to preach, or lecture, or any such stuff. Words – pathetically – are all I have. So I do the one thing left to me: I speak truth.

"My darling, you've tried so many things," I hear myself say, knowing that my words need to punch deep. I also know that if they are to reach her, they need to be coated with all the love I have and, more importantly, the love God has for her. "I can't think of anything much you haven't tried, to escape your pain. You've even asked God to take you. And now you've tried this. And this hasn't worked either. Where does that leave you now? All you have left – there's one thing left – is to give yourself to God. There really is nothing else, is there?"

I'm surprised at my frankness. *Where did that come from?* I ask myself. This is either over-the-top – or from God.

She's calm and quiet when she puts the phone down again. But by this point, I'm reduced to pulp.

Thoughts swirl through my brain. My darling, I know how you've embraced wonderful truths from Crabb – and others. Yet, in the same year that you drink in what Crabb has to say, you hit rock bottom. You end up in the deepest depression. And go one step further and attempt suicide. How – just how – did you get from there to this? I honestly don't know. I've always feared this. I can only imagine what went with every step that brought Shirley to this point. *Was your dismay at coming back to a dysfunctional life – your words – after the Red Sea holiday so complete?* I know that's when something snapped. That was probably a big part of it – added to a long past filled with pain.

What were the hours really like for Shirley from the time she did it? Each one was surely thick with darkness. Perhaps she sat lost forever in profound darkness. Perhaps she attended to her arm. Or even went to the hospital. Who knows what she must have suffered – her twisting, tortured thoughts? To a spirit as tender and delicate as Shirley's, how dark the pit must have been, how difficult the struggle and daunting the trauma of it all. And how huge the struggle being played out in the battle for her life.

Much, much later, Nick tells me the few details he has. He's the only one with whom she's ever shared them. When he tells me what she actually did – himself so overcome as to be able to give me only a very sketchy picture – grief paralyses me for three days.

What, then, must it have done to her?

CHAPTER TWENTY-TWO

When the Crunch Comes

"Katy believes that Shirley is such incredibly good, easy company when she's in a good place."

THE DAY SHIRLEY GETS THE CANCER NEWS – 14 JUNE 2013 – SHE doesn't want to be alone. Nick drives her home after the consultancy. His hugs and gentle words soothe and encourage her. But once he's gone, she knows clouds of darkness are just waiting in the wings. So she picks up the phone.

"Hi Katy," she says, relieved when Katy answers. "Listen, could you come over? I wouldn't ask, but I really need you."

All sorts of alarm bells ring. As soon as Katy's got four-year-old Amelia to bed, she gets in the car. When Katy sees Shirley's face, she hugs her enthusiastically.

Katy believes that Shirley is such incredibly good, easy company when she's in a good place. Then she's so open, spontaneous and lovable that you just want to hug her. But for quite some time now, Katy's known a different Shirley. And she's tried to be there for her.

One of the things that worries Katy is Shirley's yo-yo relationship with God. One moment, she walks and talks with him; the next, she cuts off all contact. One minute, Shirls says, "I've been finding it a lot easier to involve God in the details of my life and so I feel very peaceful." The next minute, she's angry and dismisses him for letting her down all over again.

At a conference, Katy felt God say, "Take special care of Shirley. Love her; be there for her." And that's exactly what Katy's done – taken God's directive to heart. It's helped her to be extremely kind whenever Shirley phones – sometimes in the middle of the night.

Now they talk for quite some time. Shirley needs that – and Katy listens willingly. Numbed by shock herself, she tries hard to respond appropriately and gently. It feels the most natural thing in the world to pray, and so they do. And there's something about the peace they feel that smacks of joy. Impossible? And yet it is, most remarkably, what they feel.

As Katy drives home, she says to herself over and over again, *Shirley of all people – she's got cancer? How's she ever going to cope? She'll never cope with this.*

Now when Shirley's heard the worst news and is in the biggest trouble ever, she faces a dilemma. Men have certainly let her down – repeatedly. They don't, or can't, give her what she thinks she needs. Disappointment after disappointment in each one marks the course of her life. *But what about God?* Shirley wonders. *Has he really let me down too? And – more than that – what about now that I have cancer? Will he fail me in this?* She knows her Bible quite well. But is that all there is? Or is there something more? Is God a living person? If he is, she can enjoy the wonderful dynamic of constantly meeting him face to face.

Her mind continues to comb out tangles of deception. But what she needs right now is not argument but relationship.

"I come to the garden alone," she hums, "while the dew is still on the roses... And he walks with me, and he talks with me..."[8]

---

[8] Words and music by C. Austen Miles in 1813

What Shirley does know is that her diary's the trustworthy companion that has never failed her. A lot of the time, writing in it is actually rather like talking to God. He seems to be in almost every entry, one way or another. That means God was there when her desire was to carve out a career for herself. And so on. And that means he's here now. She becomes the 'secretary' to their 'meetings', jotting down 'minutes' after every encounter. They stroll together as Shirley jots down the deepest – and changing – desires of her heart.

Jesus follows up, when they talk about desires, with an invitation. "Come to me with an open mind and heart," he says. "Allow me to plant my desires within you."

———————————

Shirley's progress is real. It's bumpy and torrid, but it's growing. She began 2012 by telling God:

You make all things work together for my good.

Next, she wrote:

My Lord knows the way through the wilderness, all I have to do is to follow.

She completed that entry by scribbling:

Hmm, what do we need / do I need? Fellowship with God – which addresses loneliness (me). We have nothing else!

Safety – fear of the future. Thank you, Lord, for rescuing me from my mistakes/entrapment.

Help me to wait, trust and know that you are God.

As the year progresses, Shirley loses ground some of the time and gains it at others. One moment she can't believe God cares about her – *oh, he's there alright, but he's distant and disinterested;* the next moment, she's thinking:

God won't provide anything other than more pain, and he isn't trustworthy.

Later she pleads:

I'm afraid of more pain: dear God, please let me rest!

She doesn't know it, but at such times she's assuming God is not distant but very hands-on.

Next, she's fighting, flailing and unable to be still and allow God to comfort her. That's when she ends up "feeling like I have no roots, been listening to crappy voices telling me that I've messed everything up and that my life has no meaning and no worth". That's also when hot tears blot the page.

Somewhere along the line, Shirley scribbles:

Hmm – problem with sleepiness, distractions this morning – cup of torment time?

She scratches through the kitchen drawer that's stuffed with a mishmash of medicines, until she finds her Nurofen. She swallows several pills – and waits for answers that don't come.

Tried to relax and spend time with God – distracted, tired. This seems to happen a lot.

My challenge: resist the desire to self-medicate, distract, control – and trust God with the well-being of my soul. Help me to wait, trust and know that you are God.

Suddenly there's a sharp tap-tap of the knocker on her front door. Shirley jumps up, glad of the interruption.

"Oh, Shirls," says Katy, "I've escaped for the morning! Amelia's gone to a friend and suddenly I have time on my hands – so I couldn't think of a better thing to do than come and spend it with you. Do you mind?"

She thrusts a packet of yummy doughnuts into Shirley's hands.

Delighted, Shirley makes coffee. It takes her a while to find clean mugs.

"How are you?" Katy asks – always so caring – and curls up on the couch to listen.

"Do you really want to know? This could take a long time!" Shirley giggles – her special giggle – which makes Katy smile too. "You ask how I am. Right now, numb, confused, frightened, struggling to believe any of this cancer thing is true. If you ask where I am, in terms of my life, that's a whole different ball game. The best place from which to answer that is from my diary."

It's always nearby and Shirley flips it open.

"'19 September' – Hmm, that's 2012 – so that goes back a bit. 'Jesus – most constant companion and guide ever. Can be yours at all times and in all circumstances.' Then, let me see... '20 September: Lord, please give me the strength to focus on you before everything else. Practise saying I trust you in every circumstance.' Still need to move to that place where I am passionately in love with God."

Katy starts to respond, but Shirley stops her.

"Let's add one more. '25 September 2012: leave the sorrows of the past behind. Made in the image of God, your identity, your joy and your purpose are completely wrapped up in your relationship with God.' That was then. What do you think? How am I now?"

"Hmm." Katy's pensive as she bites into her doughnut. "I bet there's an awful lot more in there that will make good reading," she teases.

Serious again, they flip through more entries.

"You know what, Shirls? I can see progress. You've put down what was in your head. But you're not leaving it there – you're applying what you know, and that's real progress."

"I don't follow."

"You know in your head that Jesus – a very wonderful Jesus – is with you in every circumstance. So what do you do? You start asking him for his help! And not just any help – help with your relationship with him. Which you now seem to value a great deal."

"I have changed – a bit. Hmm. But the snag remains to hold on to the new things, new beliefs. I still keep blowing hot and cold."

"Amen to that!" Katy smiles at her very warmly. "But he's in this with you, you know. And he's busy with you. So hand over – he's the key to success and not you. He is making progress with you – I'm seeing you blow more and more hot, and less and less cold."

The conversation moves on to a new colour in nail varnish, shower gel that has a wonderful scent, scarves at half-price in Sainsbury's and other such feminine concerns.

Katy's right, though – there's an awful lot of interesting stuff in Shirley's diary. For example, she chronicles another gem from Crabb. He claims that the outcome of brokenness and repentance is the conviction we can't change without abandoning ourselves to the Spirit. Shirley adds:

> *Whatever happens, God is in control of what matters most. Ask the Spirit to penetrate to the exact centre of my heart, find the empty hole, and fill it with God's love.*

This is where the rubber has always hit the road for Shirley. She notes:

> *God says:*

> *'For love of you I left my Father's side. I came to you – you ran from me, you fled from me, you didn't want to hear my name. For love of*

you I was covered in spit, punched and beaten. For love of you I stay with you and hold you every day of your life – Jesus' (The Message).[9]

How do I abandon myself to you?

'Seek me first.'

Lord, I come to you, just as I am.

Smudges on the diary page reveal some crying – some considerable crying. For her the issue is becoming:

> *In the circumstances that come up in my life, am I so undergirded by the love of God that I can let him take me through them?*

The minutes of Shirley's strolls with God fill more and more pages. Sometimes the smudges are coffee and not tears. Just once, it's Marmite.

A really big mistake has been trying to work her life out for herself. Another, she admits, has been to live utterly selfishly. As she looks back, she can see the failures and not much else.

But at times, as she keeps company with God, he blesses her with special encouragements. It's in such gentle fellowship with him that she comes to consider she might be okay. She begins to list things to be thankful for – especially realising that, in his eyes, there's nothing wrong with her. And, at long last, she sporadically knows some satisfaction of the yearning that has perpetually parched her soul. Every now and then she gets to slake her thirst for him just a little more.

There's an amazing print in Shirley's bedroom. It's the crucified Jesus on the cross. But the perspective is from above and almost behind the aching Christ. It is Jesus looking at the world. From her bed, she takes in his focus – on her, and on the needy world below, throbbing with its personal pain. What was she thinking when she chose this print for her room? How did she make that choice? Was it the influence of God? Surely it was!

At some point, she's taken the trouble to gold-frame Psalm 16 from verse 5. It sits on the dresser at the foot of her bed. Is this the influence of God on her too?

---

[9] Shirley's own paraphrase of a passage from The Message

> *Lord, you have assigned me my portion and my cup; you make my lot secure.*
>
> *The boundary lines have fallen for me in pleasant places ...*
>
> *I keep my eyes always on the Lord. With him at my right hand, I will not be shaken ...*
>
> *You fill me with joy in your presence, with eternal pleasures at your right hand.*
>
> *Psalm 16:5-11*

On Facebook, Shirley writes:

> *Every day, I have choices to make. There are good ones and bad ones. The big one is: Do I believe God loves me?*

Here it is again – her biggest – the one big realisation she needs for what lies ahead.

Now, when the crunch comes and Shirley has cancer, the strolls in the garden, walking and talking with Jesus, bear fruit. God has been knocking for a lifetime – her lifetime. Now it is cancer that turns the key.

And now nothing can restrain God's love – on hold for so long. The most plaintive words of Jesus are the heart-stopping question: "Do you love me?" When Shirley answers yes, how different her Gethsemane becomes from what it might have been.

She says of this terrifying Gethsemane:

> *I was filled with pure, pure disbelief. Hmm... no... disbelief isn't the right word... I did believe what was happening to me. But I think I had no concept of what that was actually going to mean.*

She talks and cries. She looks back over her life. And, very haltingly and tentatively, she faces what she can understand of the future. This moves her on towards facing her Gethsemane choices – mainly in the small hours of the morning.

Then she phones.

"Mum," she says, stunning me, "now it's time to cut my c**p." The words are heavily pregnant with resolve.

Really? She's thinking that? She's never, ever called her struggles "c**p" before – never!

Amazingly, Shirley says it again. With impressive resolve, she declares even more firmly, "I'm going to cut my c**p and do it with God, Mum."

My cry to God becomes, "What now? How can I help Shirley now?" The mantra of my life has been to help her. On 28 November 2012, I record in my diary God's gentle but clear advice: "Now you can cut the umbilical cord."

I'm totally shocked. To no longer need to compensate for what was missing will set me free.

"I can't do that," I respond. "She'll sink!" I know that will bring on the disaster I've worked so hard and long to prevent.

But God insists. "What I needed you to do in the past I no longer need you to do. That's over now. Trust me."

I struggle to get my mind around this. I'm not called upon to 'parent' anymore? And I don't have to help her do cancer?

I can see that, right from the start, Shirley takes the cancer in hand. Amazingly? No, *miraculously* – there's no doubt about that.

So I do actually – very gently – cut the umbilical cord. It happens so unobtrusively that even I don't notice I'm doing it. God gives me time. Months later, I begin to recognise that what I'm feeling is relief – a huge burden lifted. But it is only with hindsight that I get to understand that this is what I've done.

God makes it clear that, from now on, I'm to keep quiet. Others will do what I was doing – point the way. That's not my job anymore. When I get to England, I'm to see to everyone's needs, and to love and encourage them. I'm to do the driving, to organise, manage the household, book appointments, make coffee, clean house, do the flowers, feed the cats, do the washing, answer the phone, comfort, encourage, shop, fetch meds – and pray.

CHAPTER TWENTY-THREE

Bed Fifty-Six

"I am so grateful to have Nick with me again."

JUST THREE DAYS AFTER THE WORST DAY OF HER LIFE, SHIRLEY finds herself in the Churchill Hospital in Oxford. The strangeness of it all traumatises her. The shock makes her recollections vivid and precise.

"I am taken into a four-bed ward by a sister and plonked on a bed and abandoned," she recalls. "It feels so weird. I feel so absolutely lost, as lost as you can get." A gentle smile plays round the corners of her mouth. "I am so grateful to have Nick with me again. I say to the next person who comes along, 'Can you tell me what's going to happen, because I've never been to hospital before and I don't have a clue how this works?'" She chuckles a little. "The only thing the nurse says is that so-and-so will be along shortly.

Hmm… I think that the first thing you learn about hospitals is that 'shortly' is a special type of time called 'hospital time'. Everything goes according to hospital time… And you are just kind of helpless."

It's only seventy hours since Shirley received the results of the PET scan from Prof. Kumar. She rearranges the transparent plastic pipe from her drip. At times the wiring from her earphones threatens to ensnare the tube from Fred – the aluminium drip stand and monitor beside her bed – into the central line in her chest. This line was inserted – really painfully – only a very few hours ago.

"So there I am, feeling really helpless…" She nods her head a few times as she remembers. "Kind of caught up in the drift of all these things that have to happen. Next, they plug a bright-red drug into me. It's a mixture of two chemo drugs that they call the Red Devil. I did wonder why – but not for long."

She checks to see if the two-drug cocktail is flowing smoothly. It invades her chest slowly, red drop by slow red drop. A semi-opaque orange bag covers the bag on the stand. It warns all staff that this drip is highly toxic and may only be handled by a cancer nurse.

"Next I'm wheeled into a side room. There I'm left to my own devices to kind of collect myself, if there's any collecting to do. It's a very, very strange experience. I remember thinking, *I really have no idea what's happening to me. I do know this is very scary. It's actually very, very bad. So many people are so upset. I must say, I still feel kind of numb. This must be just a blip. It can't be anything else. I'll get over it… and then life will be back to normal.*"

Back in South Africa, I am aware that they are pouring the most awful poison, drop by stealthy drop, into my beautiful girl. And I can, and must, do nothing about it. That one thought fills the whole day. The resignation I feel is like quicksand. Even though I'm not there to watch, it's as if every drop of chemo methodically pounds both her body and my soul, like a Chinese torture. So, for us both, it becomes a very long, very wretched day.

––––––––––

In the meantime, Nick has been busy.

We've set up a dedicated group page on Facebook, so that we can support our lovely Shirley, making sure that she's never without witty banter, Hello magazines, iPod tracks, chuckles, grapes and cat stories.

The idea is also to be able to organise status updates, transport to and from the hospital, visitors, a meal train and other practical things that crop up.

> *Let's make sure that our Miss Glameron is not overwhelmed with our humour, help and hospitality, but has friends with her when needed.*

These friends deluge her with Bible verses, prayers, flowers, hugs and kisses. Shirley responds:

> *I am so loved. How very humbling!! X*

Her busy thumbs communicate her response via iPad and iPhone.

> *Ahem, one request: For all my brilliant organisation, I forgot to bring a towel! Could someone bring me one – during the next few days?*

Not surprisingly, her packing has been some sort of chaos – and she's not had too much idea of what to take to hospital.

Rather like crickets chirping at night, the monitors in the different wards beep and buzz beside many beds. To avoid infection, there are many single-bed wards for cancer patients.

As drips approach empty, the beeps intensify and become necessarily urgent. "Mayday, Mayday," they shrill.

Doors swing on dry hinges. And feet scurry to and fro.

Along cluttered corridors, pale patients slowly push the obstinate drip stands to which they are tethered. Like supermarket trolleys, some of these devices have a mind of their own. And the maze of food trolleys, medicine lockers, laptop stands, bins, buckets and other pieces of equipment form a unique obstacle course.

Some pasty-faced, others rather yellow, the shaky sick do find their way back to bed, amazingly. There, visitors murmur and bend over ailing loved ones.

Doctors, nurses and trainees consult in small groups in the disinfected passageways. Lively Polish chatter comes and goes as the cleaners sweep and wash the grey floors.

Once again, the menu offers cottage pie and not much else. Shirley emphatically rejects the pie – it's one of her pet hates. She also refuses most of the other options. In her opinion, hospital food, somewhat like hospital time, is something very strange.

Turning to her diary for comfort, Shirley writes:

> *A very hard day. Am finding it very hard not to hate everything about Bed fifty-six, Oncology Ward! I've been upset by the seemingly haphazard nature of everything today. Also have been upset by the insertion of my brand-new central line.*

Typically, Shirley doesn't dwell on what it feels like to go through all this. What does distress her is the possibility of scarring in the middle of her chest.

She turns to her diary again.

> *I feel like normal life is over for ever and I've entered some weird – mostly horrible – universe. I want my old life back! This is very hard... feels like a mountain to climb. How could this have happened?*

She wrestles her pillows. And gets to thinking about her old life. *I was so busy – too busy – like everybody my age. Before all this happened, I was under quite a lot of pressure at work. I ran around, travelled a lot. I have to say, I spent an awful amount of time thinking about, and planning, my holidays – scuba diving, skiing, you name it – because I love action adventure holidays and kind of being on the go and being out there... yeah.*

A smile plays round the corners of her mouth. Then a cloud blots out the sun. A dark, dismal sensation envelops Shirley. Sadly, her mood changes. It's not new. And, as in the past, it lingers. She recognises it – this is monstrous fear. She knows it far too well. While the circumstances are unbelievably different, the feeling is as awful as ever. Fear rises, writhes, cowers and fingers her heart. Then it slinks briefly into the shadows. For now, it cowers there, but never really goes away.

Then God steps in. With perfect timing.

Shirley writes in her diary:

> *God hugged me. Have been moved to a great private room with a lovely view – and they started the chemo twelve hours early. Amazing. I'm feeling peace again.*

She's pensive for a moment or two. After another short while, she adds:

> *When we ask God for something, He doesn't necessarily give what we ask, but He does give opportunity. Evan Almighty[10] asked God for patience. Instead, God gave him the opportunity to learn it. I*

---

[10] Lead character in the movie *Evan Almighty*, 2007.

asked God for the ability to learn / for the knowledge that he loves me...?

She closes her diary for a moment, tugs her pillows this way and that – again – and looks out through the window to her right. She finds the sunset beyond a row of summer-green trees especially beautiful. "What a beautiful sunset – I feel such love," she scribbles.

The silence that follows is warm and comforting. She basks in peace for a while. Finally, just before she closes her much loved companion for the night, she writes:

Thank you, God, for my sunset too. Like Mary, I am holding things in my heart; I am holding all these things.

Chapter Twenty-Four

Taking Up the Battle

"Tonia keeps the prayer lines buzzing."

TIME TO MOBILISE THE TROOPS. "SHHHHHHIRLEY'S SECRET Helpers" – set up by Nick on Facebook – buzzes with life. The first post is about the present status. The good news is that no pain meds were necessary during Shirley's first night in hospital. And Shirls is to go home on Wednesday or, at the latest, Thursday night. A detailed schedule of the next two chemo cycles appears. Updates to follow, Nick promises.

Next, the group page describes the plans that need to be put into place. The idea is to try to meet every need that pops up, as soon as it does.

Nick smiles next time he writes. He knows Shirls is going to enjoy this.

NewsFLASH! S's internet connection in the hospital is rubbish. I'll install her dongle this evening (no medication required)!

Tonia – asked in her pastoral capacity by Greyfriars Church to care for Shirley – loses no time either:

I've created a meal train for Shirley Cameron. This will simplify the process of giving and receiving meals and more. Be the first to contribute!

Tonia also keeps the prayer lines buzzing:

Heard from Shirley this morning. Her leg is quite swollen and it feels like WWIII is going on. Please pray that this is not serious. Shirls also said not to be offended if she doesn't reply to texts, etc. as she is finding it very difficult to concentrate.

The doctors have warned that, once home, Shirley will be very vulnerable to infection. So another text appears:

Cleaner needed (volunteer or paid) to give S's house a quick blitz. Anybody who knows a cleaner/can organise? Please post your offers and suggestions.

Nor do the doctors want Shirley left on her own. Nick steps up to the mark:

Shirley will have completed the first chemo session by 7 p.m. this eve.

Katy Lyne is visiting her and will be bringing her back to mine for Night 1.

Tonia Elliott is picking her up tomorrow midday from mine to take her back to base camp in Wokingham and get her settled in back home.

Helen Dibley is with her for Night 2.

ALL: Offers of meals (and frozen meals for back-up), cleaning, visiting, support, shopping, TLC and potential transportation can commence!

Nick's relieved when he has the weekend sorted out. Stuart and Johno will be with her on Saturday and Sunday. But she needs more sleepover/day/meal support extending into the next week. Then she goes back for Session 2. He ends:

Hello all. Saw Shirley tonight and she's in good form and very positive and happy. Not in pain and sleeping well. Napping in the day too. Appreciating all the love she is receiving.

———————————

The Secret Helpers meld into an amazing band of friends. At first, like everyone else, they are paralysed by the news. Together, they pour out their distress, cry, hug, and deluge her with love. Gaynor, in particular, is traumatised to think she's on a Greek island enjoying a fabulous holiday while Shirley is in hospital on a drip receiving chemo.

Shirley experiences not only her own shock but theirs too. Their distress bruises her heart. She doesn't want anyone hurting on her behalf. In fact, she's a bit embarrassed at so much attention. But she's also deeply touched that her 'peeps' care so much.

They step up their efforts. They do what they can to help, love, encourage and take up the challenge alongside her. Others are drawn in. Katy and Gaynor organise meetings as a group to worship and pray. The battle for Shirley's life gathers momentum.

———————————

Nick remembers:

Once we got over the initial shock, we started to get word out to nearest and dearest. We recruited a band of prayers to go before her. This grew and grew, right across the world. Every detail – to inform regarding surgery, treatment, side-effects and required support – was relayed constantly through the wonders of social media.

———————————

On Wednesday evening, 19 June, Katy drives Shirley back from Oxford to Nick's cottage in Shiplake. The girls talk very little on the way.

As they drive, Shirley's thoughts retrace each day in the hospital. She shudders again over the insertion of the central line. The possibility of disfigurement appals her. For now, she's determined to make sure the line stays out of sight. The next invasion, she remembers, was the chemo. The Red Devil trespassed sinister drop by sinister drop. Tears escape from the corners of her crushed soul. *How can I possibly do this?* she cries. *Oh, oh, oh, God.*

Then God tells her to stand; tomorrow they will take the next step together. She searches for any little sign of encouragement. They *did* start twelve hours early; and nine hours in, she still didn't feel any side-effects. So she praises God.

Shirley thinks about yesterday. She was less alert then – especially from mid-afternoon into evening. Now, for the first time, she knows the horror of chemo-induced queasiness. For hours and hours, she feels horribly ill, but at least she sleeps well. Her thoughts turn to things to come and she stresses out about what lies ahead – like losing her hair. The rollercoaster ride that is cancer treatment has begun.

———————————

Later, tucked up warm and snug in bed at Nick's, Shirley relaxes. They sip hot chicken soup together. It's good to do something so normal.

"Hey, you," Nick says when all the soup is gone, "what did it feel like – being in hospital and all? I mean to say – so you're plugged into the chemo and the chemo is running into your veins; what was going through your head?"

"Hmm," Shirley sniffs. "I think at that stage I still didn't have the foggiest as to what was happening to me. Hmm... I had no idea of now... or of the future. I did google 'chemo', you know."

"Oh?" This takes Nick by surprise.

"I discovered that the drugs going into me are quite a weird cocktail." She half-chuckles. "Hmm... I think people who do research on chemo drugs must be slightly 'out there' because, apparently, some of these drugs are derived from fungus and mushrooms. So, I mean... who goes around inventing drugs from fungus? But anyway, I am to have three drugs in total. I am to have a few days in hospital... hmm... and then time at home to recover before I come back for more. The idea is to do this every two weeks... for six months."

"But what's it like being on a cancer ward?" Nick's really intrigued.

"You are surrounded by other people who are sick, very sick, and there you are... within forty-eight hours of having the results of your PET scan. It really wasn't nice, Nick. The people are so sick... the atmosphere so seriously heavy and sombre. I was lucky in that... most of the time... I was able to be in a private room off on the side. But it also meant that I had a lot of time... a lot of time to myself to think and... hmm... *too* much time, I think."

"Oh, Shirls," Nick's face creases with concern. "What kind of thoughts?"

"Frightened thoughts, scared thoughts... hmm."

Her laugh – really only half a laugh – fades quickly.

"Fear was one of the terrible, terrible things to deal with. It's been with me forever, for so long anyway... for other reasons, as you know. Now it just came... settled in and didn't plan to leave."

Nick pats her arm for a long moment. He picks up the tray and goes downstairs to clean and tidy up.

———————

Shirley can't remember what it was she wrote down in her diary that morning. Not surprising, with such a woozy head. She pages through. Ah, here it is:

19 June 2013: I'm feeling peaceful again. God loves me!!

Love the version of Isaiah 43 in The Message: 'I am God, your personal God, the Holy One of Israel, your saviour. I paid a huge price for you... That's how much you mean to me. That's how much I love you. I'd sell off the whole world to get you back, trade creation just for you.'

Nick had a word for me: God is going to use this experience to renew my mind. Whoop!!

Maybe 'renewing my mind' means understanding once and for all that I am loved – utterly and completely – by an awesome God???

For a start, I remember the beautiful sunset from my window he gave me.

Shirley's so comfortable now that sleep overtakes her like the softest down. Her diary slides to the floor. Nick sneaks in, muttering at the creaking staircase. He looks around and takes it all in. Feeling encouraged, he turns out the light and tiptoes downstairs.

CHAPTER TWENTY-FIVE

Back Home

"Shirley, hair cropped very short in preparation for it falling out..."

FIRST SHIRLEY – INDEPENDENT AS ALWAYS – AND THEN TONIA struggle to open the front door. Cats in abundance tumble out in welcome. Shirley's so glad to see them – and to be home again. But she's also glad to lie down.

For now, Tonia plumps up pillows and cushions and settles her on the leather couch in the lounge. Shirley cuddles the fluffy blanket to her chest. Her eyes, heavy and still pretty cloudy, close in relief.

Tonia grabs the opportunity and reports:

Hello gang. Shirls is back in her own house with her lovely brood of pussy cats that all seem very friendly! None of them thought I was the wicked witch of the North and got their claws out, so that's good! She was very tired, but in good spirits. She has asked that there is only one visitor a day. Between me and her, we will try to make that happen.

The first few days home are pretty horrendous. Much of the time, it's all a blur.

Shirley tells Jo, "I have this very overwhelming struggle with fear. What I feel is a constant burden... and I'm so heavy and weary. It's just... it's like losing your mind... not being able to think... hmm... to concentrate on anything. I think the longest I can do is an episode of *Friends* on TV... and then I have to nap again."

"Oh, Shirls," Jo says, a catch in her voice. "Oh, I'm so sorry."

Shirley's diary entries are brief.

21 June: Clearer moments, bad eyes. Very tired. Napped mostly. Struggling to concentrate.

22 June: Napped most of the evening. Eyesight not great. Head clear though.

23 June: Clear head, only one nap, eyesight better.

24 June: Feeling strong. No nap today and clear head.

Shirley's thumbs lie idle. For quite some time, there are no texts – not even one. So when Shirley does get back to texting, there's relief all round.

Dear amazing friends and helpers, I have a special prayer request today. I believe that the meds are going to dramatically reduce the tumour in my leg, if not shrink it altogether before surgery. Can you join me praying this in? As you know, the leg is giving me some hassles at the moment, so it feels like some offensive prayer is in order...

Nick continues to organise.

Increasing pain in the leg means someone must fetch the new pain meds prescribed. Shirley needs to be taken back to Oxford to test kidney function. It could take four hours.

Any peeps able to help?

And on and on and on. Nothing is too much trouble. Rami cleans house. And Nick helps Shirley stop the sale of the house – already in process, and not a good idea right now.

"I'm cooking Persian tonight," Rami promises, "and will make enough for freezer meals."

The days slide into each other. Eight days after the first deadly chemo drops course through Shirley, she knows she's in big trouble. Throughout the day, the developing stomach pain worsens. They've laid it on heavily that she could so easily pick up an infection. At one point, she realises she's taking her temperature nearly every half hour. Bouts of vomiting and diarrhoea alternate with pain that defies all but considerable morphine. Rami, who has arranged to stay on a few days, drives Shirley to A & E, where they spend much of the night.

Shirley waits on a trolley in a windy passage. She clings on with sheer guts, as no pain relief is possible until the cause of her suffering is diagnosed.

Once in the ward, they push and prod, question and frown, and take bloods. Rami sits beside her, wiping her forehead, and gently stroking her hair. How sweet that is to her during those long, anxious hours.

The docs decide, at last, it's huge inflammation caused by the chemo.

When she gets back home during the afternoon of the next day, her stomach is still really tender. And she's very tired. In no time at all, Shirley opts out. Rami arranges her iPad, phone, Sarah Young devotional, diary, thermometer and a bowl next to her. The cats – who have been nowhere to be seen – appear. One by one, they slink cautiously back on to the bed beside the sleeping Shirls.

"Oh, Mum," Shirley says, "Rami's been amazing. Nothing's been too much trouble – even the horrid bits. She's cleaned up and cooked and then insisted on praying with me."

I'm deeply, deeply grateful – and glad my ticket is booked to fly to Shirls.

"Oh, Mum," she goes on, "you'll enjoy this. The cats have chosen a special spot on the bed beside me where they always snooze. One time, when we prayed, Rami buried her nose into that very spot – and began to sneeze and sneeze and sneeze. Guess who's very allergic to cats? I tried not to giggle... but just couldn't help it in the end."

Tonia reports:

Saw the lovely Shirley earlier today. Her stomach is much better than it was. She managed to eat something too, so that's wonderful. I am going next Tuesday afternoon with Pauline K to help with the housework and then again with Dan – our pastor – on Thursday afternoon. She also has lots of food, so thank you one and all. Thank you, Lord, for answering our prayers.

Shirley chips in:

Stomach better. More energy. Pain in leg excruciating, though. I've also lost ten pounds in a week, which is a bit concerning – need to be careful.

She also reveals her heart:

Today I'm scared that it is not God's plan for me to get well. I'm not able to accept that. God will need to do a lot of work in my heart to make this okay.

I feel so helpless.

I believe God will do whatever is best for me. However, this may turn out to be very different from what I hope and long for.

Be careful! God does care about what I want. My prayers do make a difference: 'The fervent prayer of a righteous man avails much.'[11]

A day later, Gaynor hooks up with Shirley for lunch. She tells the Helpers it's to "talk about boys and nails and God and make-up and cats". The idea is "to hit a pub garden – weather permitting".

Tonia responds:

Fab. Have a great time – talk more about cats than men. Much more straightforward!

Since it certainly is pub weather, they sit in the garden. And they do talk about most things under the sun. When they get to God, Shirley, hair cropped very short in preparation for it falling out, says, "Do you know what? I do believe God loves me desperately – he cares about my feelings and desires, and he really hears my prayers. He really, really does hear me." She nods her head.

"Now that's a change!" Gaynor dimples at Shirley.

---

[11] NKJV

In round robins, as well as texts, Shirley shares her heart:

> *Been finding things tough – over the past few days. One time I went to church, I was horrified to feel so alienated from all there.*
>
> *They don't know how good their lives are. I am facing death at thirty-eight.*
>
> *I realise how much I'm having to cope with, and what a shock it's been. Had a good talk to Phyllis (my counsellor) yesterday: she reminded me that – in an emergency – one does what has to be done. You put emotions aside to some extent, but, in due course, you have to process them.*
>
> *I've had the emergency – but now, with these protracted waits at home, I'm starting to process some stuff. I'm also grieving, having lost a great deal (although, as I've said before, some of the things I've 'lost' can stay that way!)*
>
> *It is hard – but I just have to feel what I feel – and keep my eyes fixed on the hope I have in Christ. Disaster has struck, but God is here, and he will make all things new and bring a better hope.*

The day after Jo's wedding, she writes:

> *I've been struggling mentally and emotionally as some of the reality of what has happened to me has begun to sink in. I've been struggling with fear. I've been feeling incredibly frustrated with how little energy I have and how little I can do, compared to my old self. This really isn't something one can prepare for, so I have to learn all sorts of things in order to cope. There are certain truths I do my best to cling to – when things get really dark.*
>
> *I believe God is good and loves me massively, and so he won't allow me to be overwhelmed. He's with me every step, protecting me and ensuring the best outcome. I also believe there's a reason I'm still here, and so comfort myself by looking forward to a good (long) future. (I have quite a few plans!!)*
>
> *Keep trying 'to suffer well'. Surrender to the Prince of Peace is the goal … Involves surrendering to this situation, and whatever God has planned for my future, even if that is death. Looking for reasons.*
>
> *On the positive side, I was well enough to go to a close friend's wedding yesterday. To everyone's amazement, I lasted till the very*

end! I'm an extrovert, so I must have absorbed loads of energy from being with my friends. ☺

She pauses for a moment to relive the lovely event. Greyfriars church was full front to back, Jo stunning in her bridal dress, Colin dashing in his tails. Nick and Shirley sat side by side a couple of rows from the front. She chuckles as she remembers Jo in her jeans the week before going up and down the stairs over and over again to 'wear in' her wedding shoes.

Shirley took Nick's hand and squeezed it tightly. He turned to see soft tears cascading down her face. She was so happy for her much loved friend and so sad that she might never stand in a wedding dress again. He put his arm around her waist, drew her close and she rested her head on his shoulder.

She also remembers the magical moments of friendship, laughter and revelry with Nick and Laura at the reception. This took place in the grounds of a beautiful English country mansion, surrounded by moats and lakes, and drenched in summer sun.

Someone took a picture of the three of them. And that was when she said to Nick, "It's moments like this when life in all its fragility and uncertainness means so much and it all comes from those that love me — isn't God good?"

Now she smiles as she gets back to writing:

❋ *Had such a lovely day yesterday!! Jesus, you are so beautiful. Your love for me is so lavish. You are for me and fighting for me – in any circumstance. You will save my life and deliver me. I believe in your promises! I love you.*

She copies out her encouragements and paraphrases Isaiah 43 and Zechariah 8:13:

I will not allow you to be overwhelmed/crushed. If you trust me and acknowledge me, I will make your path straight. Do not be afraid but let your hands be strong.

It's like finding treasure when God tells her:

"Don't panic, I'm with you. I'll hold you steady; keep a firm grip on you." (Isaiah 41:10, The Message).

Many times, she declares her faith. The spin-off is that it strengthens the hope in her.

> *Yeah – the cancer in me has already been defeated. It has no power over me – other than what God allows. It cannot win!*

The Secret Helpers are impressed.

> *Wow – now there are some faith statements alright. Good for you, Shirls. Amen to that. We also believe and stand with you, you know.*

More encouragement flows in from all sorts of places. Shirley pages through the book of promises sent by her dad. *No better time than now to look at these! Now – where's my diary?* Obediently it crawls out from under the blankets.

> *Promise: When you call for help, I will answer.*

> *I care about your pain and suffering.*

> *I have prepared a place for you where there is no more death, sickness, or sorrow.*

Laura reminds Shirley that the one who perseveres under trial will receive the crown of life.[12] "Oh, Shirls," she says, "it's your victory that is truly at stake in this situation, not your health."

Nick keeps popping in. He tells the eager page:

> *Was on good form tonight was the Camerrooooon :-) Taking great sympathy in my youthful hair loss as she so stylishly, bravely, with humour and God-endowed beauty, watches hers start to recede. Thankfully, she will regain hers, and can change style and colour with an eclectic range of follicle fashion wear. In the meantime, though, I will remain a slaphead! Knock us dandy, Shirls, you ARE the girl :-) Psalm 20. X*

Chic little headscarves – ordered online – arrive in good time.

When Shirley turns to Nick later, it's a different story. "Oh, Nick, I'm upset about my hair! It most definitely is coming out. I realise how much comfort and confidence I get from my looks. And I realise how much pleasure I get from…"

One look at her face, and he immediately becomes serious.

---

[12] See James 1:12.

"I feel upset that, with my chest tube and baldness, I'm becoming a freak. I'm so afraid people will see only my illness and not me."

"Oh, Shirley, Shirley," he murmurs, stroking her hand.

After Nick leaves, Shirley picks up her diary.

> *Realise – if I live and accept bald me, that's a big/good start. Am also afraid that my hair won't grow back well – need to pray. Felt good to have a cry this morning, although I did wonder if I would be able to stop!*

A day later, she writes:

> *Hair fell out totally today – kinda glad to get it over with, too. If nothing else, it was itchy! I feel very vulnerable ... like I don't want anyone to see me this way. It's tough. Had another good cry. Feels hard not to be defined by cancer ... when it is invading every area of my life.*

> *Leg is very sore: phoned hospital and they recommended more morphine! Turns out I can still take a lot more than I have been taking ... So I wasn't shy with my morphine consumption but now I have a woozy head.*

> *Swings and roundabouts!*

> *Mum is here! So lovely to see her and get a real Mum hug!*

Chapter Twenty-Six

Changes

*"I'm surprised at how quickly I get used to the bald head ...
But it takes Shirley a whole lot longer."*

A GREAT DEAL NEEDS TO BE DONE. THERE ARE ONLY EIGHTEEN days between the time Brian and I get back from the Kruger Park and the day I fly to the UK.

We know my visa allows me only six months in the UK at a time. So, for this first visit, we plan for a three-month stay – July, August and September. This makes it possible to take care of Shirls for most of the chemo; and takes the pressure off those doing the driving – from Reading to Oxford and back – for consultations, scans and fortnightly hospitalisation.

I particularly need to be there for her for the leg op. And before I come home, she needs to have recovered enough to be able to fend for herself. That's when Loren, her 'bestie' from Stellenbosch, plans to visit for two weeks and take on the nursing.

Shock and unbelief dog me through these days. I know I'm going to be away for Brian's birthday in August – the first time in our marriage. I buy and wrap new shirts. I pen an encouraging and loving card. Then I bury the parcel deep in a bottom drawer. I plan to tell him about it on the day. And I plan to send an email to a whole bunch of people asking them all to phone and email to wish him happy birthday. I can't think of anything else to do to make it easier – I wish I could.

I also manage to cook and freeze a considerable supply of meals. These are favourites – with detailed instructions on how to prepare, and little smiley faces every now and then to surprise and cheer him up. I give him practice in cooking rice and peas.

Numb and traumatised, I'm anxious over what I'm going to forget, so packing is a challenge. I need to be able to do summer, autumn and hints of winter for the odd, unexpected days. This feels so strange – so different from the holiday-thing.

I also need to find a few pressies for Shirls that will really express my heart.

I've built a great relationship with Jenny, our tenant-friend Nats' eight-year-old daughter. It began when she was not yet three. Playing games, combing and putting my hair in bunches, making up stories, play dough, and all the things grannies do, have made us real friends.

I know she's going to get very sad. So I buy a whole lot of little gifts, put them in gift packets and pin large, smiley faces to them. Then I put all of them into a large packet to give her at the airport. Her instructions will be to open one on the days she misses me and feels sad.

The morning I arrive at Heathrow, John is there to meet me. I can't tell you how glad I am to see him. Soon we're on the highway, John providing commentary on the considerable (according to him) antics of the traffic. I struggle to chat. Fresh waves of shock and disbelief wash over me. What, for goodness' sake, am I doing here?

Truth to say, from then on, most of the time I'm in England, I'm beleaguered by a profound sense of unreality.

It's so good to hug my darling girl. She looks so pale to me – and strange, with such short, dull hair. I pull out the crocheted prayer shawl, bright with stripes of colour, stuffed into my case at the last minute. It arrived from America literally an hour before I had to leave for the airport.

Shirley looks very puzzled, so I explain. "It's from Cathy, who studied with me. Once the ladies of her church in Virginia Beach knew your story, they prayed over you by name – then made this for you. Every time you pull the shawl over your shoulders, they want you to feel God's love and their prayers for you. They would love it to bring you blessing to overcome what lies ahead – together with warmth and security."

Thoughtfully, they sent one each for Brian and me too.

We sip coffee together – Shirley has huge Manhattan mugs bought in New York. At the same time, she pulls her large, navy-blue handbag towards her.

"Mum, let me show you this," she says. "This is the book they gave me to keep on hand – at all times. If there's any crisis... I collapse or something... all the numbers you need to phone are in here, on the back page."

I stare at her aghast. I take the red book very hesitantly, almost as if I expect it to sting.

There's a chart of possible symptoms. Anything red means dial 999, then dial the number given and press green. Immediately. Any doubts of any sort, phone the twenty-four-hour helpline. Where will I find it? Oh, it's in the navy-blue bag. Where does that live? Right here, next to Shirley, at the end of the couch.

All of this terrifies me beyond measure. My brain goes rigid with horror. What if we do have a crisis – and I don't remember something? My head's so numbed with shock these dizzily traumatic days, I'm really scared that I will get it seriously wrong.

While still in Cape Town, I began compiling a little book. I put in anything I might need to refer to at any time. It's even got recipes in it – and plenty of Bible verses. I need to know how to cook bobotie, butternut soup and milk tart – so that I can prepare nice things. And there are verses of Scripture that I think might help – not just Shirley, but me too.

Now, in Wokingham, I feverishly add more and more. I diarise appointments, consultations, chemo sessions, bloods, telephone numbers, scans and X-rays in Oxford. I put in dates with friends, visits from the district and Macmillan nurses, prayer sessions, physio, gardeners and cleaners, you name it.

I'm anxious to have it all at my fingertips as soon as possible. I know I won't feel secure until I have every phone number and name, just in case. I need to know where Boots is. And where to park, if I need to go anywhere in a hurry.

I set up the kitchen table as my 'office'. This is my 'control centre' for the months to come. There my little book, the meds and thermometer and, in time, the hypertension monitor come to lie tidily side by side.

Shirley and I talk about this and that. I can't help staring at her enormous upper right thigh. I try not to let her notice.

Three cats come in from their favourite places – one from the windowsill, one down the staircase and one from the kitchen table. Respectfully, they wait to be introduced.

Then, to my surprise, Shirley crawls into my arms. And my heart swells with love for her.

"I'm really very sick, Mum," she says.

It's a joy to hold her – and a shock to hear what she's saying.

"Oh, Mum." Tears muffle her soft voice.

I'm overcome with emotion. We wait until we recover.

Then she says, "I need all the help I can get. For one, I need to get the doctors on my side... so that they also fight with all they've got. Mum, unless I have a miracle... I'm a gonner."

I admire her courage. She's right, of course – but I battle to even say these things.

"And you must believe I'm going to be healed. I have to have someone in my family believe it... I can't have negativity around me."

I so want to believe and not let her down. So day by day, I declare my faith. And I begin to look at what's happening – to see if there's any sign that God intends to heal. How I long to recognise something – *anything* – miraculous that only God could have done. And I do see that – and I'm excited by it – in the signs of spiritual victory.

There's more chitter-chatter between us about the neighbours and Secret Helpers – who have taken her breath away. Then she says, "I don't know if I can do this." Her deep understanding of the extent of the challenge connects us heart to heart. And it helps me grasp reality a bit better.

"Shirls," I say, "you've handled this all so honestly and bravely. So it looks like you can. And the way you are doing this – being honest and real and facing the worst possibility – is making it that much easier for the rest of us. You've so courageously brought it all out into the open. It's no longer a dark thing in the closet that's eating us up but we can't talk about."

While I unpack, Shirley showers. She's been putting this off for as long as she can. She knows that this is when her hair will finally all come out.

"When I'm done, will you please shave my head?" she asks. "The prof says it's the best thing – otherwise, when it begins to grow again, it's uneven."

Will I *what?* I try to take all this in too, as I open and close drawers.

Water splashes continuously in the bathroom. Apparently, it needs to be a very *long* shower. No wonder. When she finally calls me into the bathroom, she sits cowed, bare-headed, naked, totally exposed and utterly vulnerable. I catch my breath.

Oh, God; oh, oh, God, I whisper in my heart.

It seems that new horror awaits us around every corner. Neither of us can say a single word.

With razor and soapy cream, I set to work. What kind of ghoulish activity is this? The real sting in it is that I feel it's such an outlandish thing to do – on the first day of your stay, to shave your thirty-eight-year-old daughter's head because cancer has reduced her to a hairless state! How weird – *beyond* weird – is all that?

I'm petrified I might nick her pale, exposed crown and hurt her. More and more loose – almost spongy – shaved skin appears. Every stroke across that soft, pink flesh freaks me out. I feel the cancer ravaging her, bit... by bit... by bit. It has set out to pillage and plunder – and it doesn't hold back.

But I keep calm. She's so amazingly brave – how can I not be brave too? I have to do this with no fuss. Otherwise, I will let her, myself and all of us down.

At first, every time I see her bald head, it 'freaks me out' afresh. I have to turn away. This monstrous cancer steadily puts me through more and more that palsies my soul. Each new horror recedes to make room for the next. I'm surprised at how quickly I get used to the bald head, though – and her need to cover up with a scarf.

But it takes Shirley a whole lot longer.

CHAPTER TWENTY-SEVEN

Out on a Limb

"I've built a great relationship with Jenny..."

I FEEL SO FAR OUT ON A LIMB AS I GET USED TO A STRANGE BED-room and shower – Shirley's housemate Johno's – and not having much communication with home until we get my laptop sorted out. *What if my stomach plays up and I want my doctor? What if...?* I'm frightened. Actually, I feel out on a limb pretty much the whole time we're facing cancer.

The BMW is a strange new experience, as are the endless roundabouts – and the way the English drive. I manage to stall on the highway which, apparently, is quite an achievement. How thankful I am that Shirley very sweetly says nothing at all.

That first weekend, we barbecue some lamb chops. As I bite into mine, my front tooth splits. That leaves me with a glaring gap (and with too much else on my plate to do anything about it) for the full first three months with her. I'm terribly self-conscious and mortified. It's not as if I wasn't feeling so far out of my comfort zone, so lost, so challenged already...

One evening, Chris kindly invites me to meet her at Showcase Cinemas to watch ballet. I love it – but get hopelessly lost on my way home. Roundabout after roundabout appears menacingly across my way. I end up in a housing estate, thinking I will have to spend the night there – in the car.

At last, after many calls to Shirls on a borrowed cell phone, I manage to retrace my 'steps' to the cinema and take the correct turn. I feel very foolish as I finally open the door. I'm so thankful Shirley welcomes me warmly and doesn't say a thing this time either. *Mortified* – again!

Shirley's office and other friends take her out to the pub. At those times, I feel so alone. I sit in the backyard for hours, anxious, until I hear her open the front door. So many times, I just long to hold her. I just don't want her out of my sight.

Every day, first thing, Brian texts me. I learn to look forward to that more and more, as soon as I open my eyes. Every evening, Skype – once we get it working – also links us.

Thankfully, in these ways, 'home' and everyone in it comes a little nearer. Every contact with the people I know strengthens me. Phone calls from my sister-in-law Lynn become, and remain, a lifeline. And daily texts from Faye.

I remember that a long time ago, in December 2005, I journaled:

> *Shirley and I had a wonderful quiet time together. She had come for Christmas. And it was Christmas Eve. We sat in the double bed and prayed quietly for over an hour. Then she said, 'Thank you, my friend.'*

But the question is, after years of more water under the bridge, what is our relationship now? It's been years that we've each lived in our own space. Now we need to live in the same space for a full three months at a time – and under a deeply intimidating cloud.

Over the years, for so much of the time, I've felt I'm treading on eggshells. And this feeling stays with me. Just what did our relationship become after I pushed so hard for Shirley to take antidepressants permanently? I do know God wants Mrs Fix-it out of action – the umbilical cord cut – unless Shirley's control of the cancer falters. It's what Mrs Fix-it has always wanted. So for now, she packs her bags and leaves.

But right at the start, I do something wrong with the toilet rolls. Shirley says firmly, "I don't do that. Everyone runs their own home their own way." Of course, it's right that she's in control. So, a little amused, I undo my mistake.

I plan to be more careful and hold back. At this point, I'm a guest. Shirley's in control. She decides what we will buy, cook and eat. I'm sad already, because I know that this won't last if the cancer progresses. It will loot and rob her of more and more control of her life.

Shirley comments on the cancer's scorched-earth policy: "I'm not grieving for the life I've lost; just for the horrible things that are happening to me now."

What lies ahead for me is to wait well. I need to discern when to do more – only when she can do less. The challenge is to know if, when, where and how much. I want to get this right – to distress her as little as possible. And I want her to feel safe – safer and safer – with me.

Nick calls in to see how it's going. I get him coffee and Shirley some cranberry-ginger tea. As usual, to intrude as little as possible, I slip upstairs. I'm thinking that keeping out of the way will help to make life feel just a little more normal for her. That's also why I go out for many walks. I get to enjoy the winding lanes, no matter what they're wearing: leafy green, autumn, or the daffodils and primulas in the gardens in spring.

"How are you doing?" Nick asks as he sits on the couch beside her.

"Oh, Nick," she says, "I'm a grumpy girl! It's having Mum around all the time. I think we still need to settle into this new 'normal'."

"Oh? What do you think the problem is?"

"Mum's so uncertain of herself at times. That leaves me feeling like I'm the bad guy, bossing her around."

"Have you said anything to her?"

"No – and I won't. But we do need to find peace and acceptance of each other."

―――――――――

Shirley does a number of kind things for me that I find so thoughtful. There's a map book of Oxford waiting, so that I can find my way around during the spells she's in hospital. She's arranged that for my first trip to Oxford, Katy will drive, to help me adjust to the highway. In the back seat, Amelia and I play with Tiny Tim the tortoise – and I do end up feeling much better.

For my laptop, Shirley buys a soft, white bag covered in large green, blue and cerise circles. "Because it's bright and bubbly, just like you," she chuckles.

Her considerateness touches me. Soon I am able to email the world:

> *I am very grateful to S that my laptop is fixed! I have missed you all so much. Now you can talk to me – as much as you like. And I can talk to you – I hope not more than you would like! I can Skype again. I feel connected, instead of feeling trapped by so much silence.*

"Oh, Thy," Brian shares during one of our late-afternoon Skypes, "Jenny's had such a meltdown over your not being here."

"Poor poppet... What happened?"

"They had a Grandparents' Day at school and she couldn't take you and me."

I'm so disappointed – and not just for her. We're the granny and grandpa she adopted as hers when she was three. My busy head knows it's impossibly cold comfort, but I suggest sending her to school with a large photo of us.

When we Skype again, Brian says, "Jen cried and cried last night because she's missing you so much."

Oh dear. Oh, oh dear. How miserable this makes me! I do wish I could do something about it.

Then he says, "I had a bit of a sore throat. So I took some Nurofen. Then I wrapped myself up in a blanket and had the happy hugger on my lap. But I was still cold. Bed was the only place to get warm."

"Aww, I'm so sorry, Pet."

"Please give S my special love," and he ends off.

More oh-dear-oh-dear...

When we don't Skype, we email:

> *It's quite something to have been ripped out of my comfort zone. I've even had to learn how to unlock the cantankerous front door! Thankfully, driving is getting a bit easier.*

> *We girls know times of peace and times full of pain and tears. I marvel at the reality and tangibility of the peace I know every day.*

I'm glad Brian and Honey take a walk every day. (For a moment I picture the golden Labrador tightly curled up at his feet.) I wonder if the meals I've cooked taste okay. I feel for him. This whole thing is proving grim beyond measure for all of us.

"You are carrying part of the load and are a vital part of all this," I write. "I'm also missing our lovely walks along Muizenberg beach and Sea Point, and long to wiggle my toes in the sand."

CHAPTER TWENTY-EIGHT

The Blimp

"I don't like my hairless look!"

"HI, ALL!" NICK POSTS. "THEY'VE FOUND A BLOOD CLOT IN THE knee. Please pray that with the additional help of the medication – yet more! – it shall not be! And that Shirley's spirits will again be lifted up."

She has to inject herself every day, which nettles her. Every evening she puts it off – I know she does – but at last she sneaks off into the kitchen. She screws up the courage to stab her stomach. She's so miffed at times that she yelps and roars.

Two days follow when Shirley falls deeply quiet and becomes very withdrawn. Then it dawns on me: she is going back to hospital on Monday, this time without her hair. In the safety of her diary's pages, she confides:

I don't like my hairless look! I feel ugly and weird. Call me G.I. Jane. I will need to work hard to feel good again about how I look. Tried looking for some biblical comfort:

1 Peter 3:4: "Rather, it should be that of your inner self, the unfading beauty of a gentle and quiet spirit, which is of great worth in God's sight."

She doesn't like the headscarves – and never wears the orange one. She goes back to the oncology ward wearing her prettiest one to hide the plunder of her head.

At this time, Shirley makes one of the saddest entries in her diary. It reveals her devastation. And it's deeply honest:

I miss my hair.

She texts:

Checked in and good to go for Round 2. Am back in Room 8, which made me cry – bad memories. So I moved the drawing pins on the board around – trying to make it different – somehow – from last time.

Mum told me that she will be praying most of the time the drug is going in – how wonderful! I feel really humbled and blessed.

Apparently this round – fifty hours – won't addle my brain like the last lot, so I should be able to do lots of reading/writing/watching, etc. Have a great weekend everyone, and love to Gaynor and Tonia – have a fab holiday, ladies!! X

Soon Shirley's tethered to 'Fred'[13]. She lies lost in thought. In those rare periods of real quietness, when the staff's busy with everyone else, she goes over it all again and again. She can still hardly believe it, let alone handle it. But every now and then, she does – just a very little. Then confusion and fear sweep back in.

As always, Shirley goes to her diary to share her deepest and most private thoughts.

The overwhelming struggle with fear the first time I was here, the heaviness, the weariness and huge burden have come back to haunt me. It's gut-wrenching fear – that's what it is.

---

[13] the aluminium drip stand and monitor

NB – Core idea: If God loves me, I have no need to fear. God's Word states that he only wants the best for me – and his love is huge, therefore his care for me will be huge. At times felt tangible/physical presence of God in the room – comforting, bringing peace and hope.

The door bursts open. Shirley pulls a face. It's time to select what she wants for dinner. That done very quickly, she continues:

Encouragement to keep praying and asking God to save my life: James 5:16: "The prayer of a righteous man is powerful and effective."

In days gone by, she pleaded with God to take her life. Now she's fervently asking him to save it.

Shirley's worship leader Eileen bursts through the door, carrying packets and parcels aplenty. Shirley comes alive. Eileen writes later:

Our Shirls is being a total trooper. Asked her what to pray for. Seems we need to tackle the meds – to make the blood clot disappear. Then pain management, as the leg's very sore – which does mean the chemo's doing its work – which is good. Also pray that there's no damage to her hearing – a possibility.

And for peace – to find stillness, and meet with God, in the midst of all the hospital craziness. It's pretty busy with nurses in and out, machines beeping away, etc.!

Katie Rose, another member of the Secret Helpers, responds:

Ava and I are praying – and kicking the cancer's butt far, far away.

Shirley remembers the lunch at the George[14], when Ava sat on her lap. The baby girl tugged at her scarf; nerve-racking in case it came off, but so much fun for Ava.

A while later, Shirley's consultant, who is also one of her oncologists, also bursts through the door. "Hi, Shirley. I followed up for you, as I promised. I'm sorry, but the fertility clinic says that it is too late to harvest and store your eggs for a possible future pregnancy. The amount of chemo you have already had has probably damaged any eggs you may have. And you may be infertile after all this anyway – okay?" Claire smiles, sad to bring more bad news. She doesn't linger, but her kindness and gentleness does.

Shirley turns to her diary:

---

[14] a local pub on the river Thames

Wow, just found out about damage done already – that my periods might not come back after this. So I might be infertile. Quite a biggie.

I'll say! How tragic it feels to me that, under such incessant bombardment, Shirley doesn't really have the time or the capacity to grieve and mourn something as huge as this. Cancer strikes again and again – relentlessly, savagely, allowing Shirley no time to catch her breath between blows. I can't help remembering, with a lump in my throat, the beautiful little Beatrix Potter set Shirley has stored away in a cupboard, with so much hope, for her children. Once, she showed me this very beautiful set of Beatrix Potter figures together with the author's books. She'd bought Flopsy, Mopsy, Cotton-tail and Peter in his blue jacket for her children. She'd stored them, for the time being, in a top cupboard.

Now, in hospital, every time she's up, Shirley looks in the mirror. She's trying to get used to the scarves. But she's also disturbed to see something else. Her whole body is swelling.

She's had the Methotrexate. Now, as usual, they're washing any traces of it out because if any of it lingers, it can do serious damage. Throughout the chemo, the docs carefully watch Shirley's heart and kidneys. Now, instead of passing water, she's swelling up like a blimp.

Her sense of horror – mine too – grows as the swelling increases. It's about what's actually happening to her body, never mind her appearance.

The consternation spreads to doctors, nurses and consultants. They pump in diuretics. They encourage Shirley to walk as much as possible. As I walk along behind her, I stare – freshly traumatised – at the new love-handles down her sides.

While some staff giggle about her "blimping" (Shirley amongst them) I can see that this is very serious. The scale records a weight increase of over twelve kilos. I gather the threat to her heart and kidneys is considerable.

Nick posts a photo to Secret Helpers:

I thought a pic for those who can't get to see Shirley could connect you.

We all need to know what she has to contend with. She asks that you please do not share this photo beyond this group.

Shirley, we love you. We care hugely for you. Every fibre of your God-sewn being is covered in prayer.

Shirley winces with the pain of the further ruin of her body. But touched, she responds:

They won't let me go until I deflate! Go figure. I'll also need a blood transfusion as I'm now anaemic. Good news, though, is that I then get next week off – to chill and recover, before we start again. Let's pray that they can get this fluid out and the anaemia vanishes. X

This means Shirley's got to stay longer – a big deal for her – and she's so disappointed. So that night, because I have already said goodbye to my host and brought everything with me in the boot of the faithful BMW, I sleep on a mattress kindly provided by the hospital, beside Shirley. Nurses come and go while I cuddle into blanket and pillow. Even the aircon is set to fight infection. That means cold currents swirling across the floor. So it's 'mighty cold down there while the west winds blow'.

At last there's a breakthrough. The diuretics start to work and Shirley has a very busy night. What's really nice is that the mattress is an escape for her from her hospital bed, and we relax and chat on it all next day.

Once she's deflated enough, we drive home. Very relieved, Shirley texts everybody:

So loving being home – and being able to see my ankles and wrists!! And did I mention that I'm no longer a blimp?? Lotsa love X

Flowers arrive and friends gather round. "I feel pretty good – much better than after Round 1 of chemo," she tells them.

I make tea and cut the cake Caroline has baked.

Always sensitive to Shirley's feelings, Katy wants to know, "How was it *really,* Shirls?"

"It was hard…" Shirley swallows. "Very hard." She swallows again. "First, I was really stoned with morphine – and then swelling and swelling…"

"So now they've cancelled a session of chemo?" Laura's concerned. "How do you feel about that?"

"I feel certain that whatever chemo I'm getting is enough. God won't have me fret about a session being cancelled. And I'm so grateful that I don't need to be in… again… this next week."

Shirley smiles, then sips her tea.

CHAPTER TWENTY-NINE

Shirley's Heart

*"Shirley grins as she reads, and hugs the fluffy
stuffed-toy lungs..."*

"HUNDREDS OF THOUSANDS STAND WAVING AND CHEERING me on. I know some of the faces – but the rest are from heaven. They all believe and want to encourage and uplift me. I'm overwhelmed. I feel such love and support; the unity of purpose is amazing – all agreed, and all literally roaring for my success." Shirley shares, then falls silent, entranced and with her hands upturned, ready for blessing.

Katy has arranged this unique meeting. Everyone is touched and has a profound sense of God's presence.

Shirley continues to share, from the heart. "I believe that my God is who he says he is, that he's walking beside me in every situation, that he's faithful and bringing out the best in me, even in these circumstances."

The picture she has seen lingers – and she basks in blessedness. Then God gives her another.

"I see a lion walking ahead of me. It's Aslan. He's bringing me strength and courage. He's the source of my perseverance and victory, even though the journey is dark. I have cried today, though. I want to have a full life. I want so much to have a second chance to live – I don't want this to be cut short. *Oh, Father, hear my prayer. I love you so much.*"

It was only a day or two ago that Katy texted:

> *I've been really challenged by the story of Joshua and the walls of Jericho recently – we need to keep marching round Shirley with our songs of praise. This is a spiritual battle, and we need to keep fighting with our prayer and praises!*

> *Just a reminder that we'll be meeting at Shirley's on Monday evening – 8 p.m. – to lift her up in prayer before her op on Wed. Let us know if you can make it! The more the merrier! X*

So in this meeting, we worship and pray as fervently as we can. Katy, deeply allergic to cats, sneezes her way through, but won't be put off. I am ominously aware of Shirley's lungs – a dark shadow – as we pray.

Gaynor pours out her heart, putting into words what's in ours. "Lord, look after our Shirley. We care about her so much; and you care about her a zillion times more than all of us clubbed together. Wow! Hold her in your mighty hands…"

"What a wonderful hug from God, Mum," Shirley says later.

Shirley continues to open her heart in round robins, Secret Helpers, visits, texts and chats with all of us, but never as much as in her precious diary where she often walks with God:

> *The consultant's happy with the leg – yay! He also said that – given the type of tumour I have – it's amazing that I'm not in more pain. He's given me funky purple morphine pills, as he doesn't want me to be in any pain whatsoever – I like the sound of that!*

> *Mum's been feeling an overwhelming sense of God's love for me – how wonderful! She felt this strongly… when I was anxious about hospital, and before they plugged me into the drip. To her, this is*

God affirming that he is going to use the chemo to fix, minister to, and bless my body. Sounds amazing!!

A while ago, I spoke to Chris about the cross not being personal to me. Well, one of the things I've realised is that Jesus took it all on... the sins of the world, plus all our suffering, pain, and disease. Therefore, Jesus took on and defeated my tumour!! I am so incredibly grateful... and finally able to respond by saying, "I love you, Lord." Wow.

Shirley turns from her diary to texting.

Encouragements this week: no pain... and my leg is visibly less swollen. I'm managing on far less morphine... the chemo is certainly doing something! I was told that I would definitely get painful sores in my mouth this time round... nothing... praise God!

It means so much to have you all standing with me and holding my arms up when I can't. Prayer please: I start next week again with the chemo drug that wiped me out so completely. I really want to pray that the drug continues to do a fantastic job on the tumour, and that I manage to sleep lots and stay strong through it.

I've been a bit anaemic and wobbly the last couple of days. Please could you pray for my general well-being?

Shirley's delighted whenever she has something positive to share:

Such good news at the doctor's today. I had a scan of my lungs – the difference is remarkable!!! Some of the nodules seem to have disappeared completely, and the rest have all shrunk massively. Praise God!! The consultant was really pleased. I'm pretty emotional, celebrating with a dark chocolate magnum, and a bucket of rosé wine... Xxx

And she's tickled pink by the responses on Facebook:

What fantastic news, Glameron!! See, 19 July was always going to be a good day!! Enjoy that rosé!!!! Suzy X

Oh, Shirley – that's just made me cry! Praise our amazing God!!! Katy Xxxx

That's amazing, Shirley!! Praise God! Katie Rose Xxx

So, so greatttttt!!! So pleased, excited, thankfulllllll, yayyyyyy. Greg

> *Well, that's it – I've gone completely (tears rolling down my cheeks). I am so pleased, Shirley – I knew you could do it. Those fluffy, pink-and-blue lungs must have worked a treat with the visualising. I couldn't be happier for you. Woooo hoooooo!!! Andrea*

Shirley grins as she reads, and hugs the fluffy stuffed-toy lungs Andrea's talking about. She ordered them online from a company that supplies organs of every kind – fluffy, furry ones – for the sick to cuddle and pray over.

Shirley opens up more:

> *Yesterday (20 July), at the hospital, the prof decided to do another scan of my lungs to check progress. I went into meltdown – just felt incapable of handling bad news, discouragement, whatever.*

> *In the end it took about 45 mins. I had prayed so hard, cried, prayed more... I was just about calm... it had been a proper meltdown though!*

> *Felt stressed and frustrated today (21 July) because of all the things I'm not doing... if that makes sense. Feel like I'm wasting this time...*

But she's very glad – and very quick – to be able to go back later to giving good news:

> *The screen showed a really big change. The prof was very pleased. The lesions in my right lung seem virtually gone; in the left, the large lesion has shrunk massively, and the others are much smaller. It's real – I have to keep pinching myself – the chemo's really working. What an incredible answer to prayer!!*

> *Mum and I cried afterwards, I phoned Nick, he cried... wish I could just sear the lung images into my brain to keep reminding myself...*

> *It's so incredible to see such visible answers to prayer so soon!! God is all over me, renewing and restoring my life – I want to know how he wants me to live for him in the future – time to get asking!!*

> *Today Mum and I are going out for steak, yay. Small simple things to look forward to!*

Circumstances keep changing. They buffet her heart – like a soccer ball at the mercy of the players.

> *A team of eight ran Race-for-Life today to support me. I was going to run with them, but – when the time came – I was just too ill. They*

showed pictures at the evening service at Greyfriars. Carol even had a picture of me on her back!

In all honesty, this made me feel a bit weird – how did I go from being normal and healthy to someone people run races for? Another cancer patient? Seems unbelievable.

So wonderful at church last night to be surrounded by friends and to be chased out by JT dimming the lights… what a prayer time we had too! I'm convinced these tumours are living on borrowed time.

To think I felt really anxious about going to church – but I didn't want everyone staring. Seeing friends – and just being in church – so compensated for the people who might stare and gossip.

More and more pours from Shirley's full heart:

Frustrating. Painful day yesterday (1 August). Tried to go out (shopping and books) and got all fainty again. Also shivered most of the day. I was upset.

Talked through with Mum my fears about going back to hospital. I think I'm feeling better about it, just need to focus on the good that the chemo is doing in my body. Hopefully – in years to come – this will all seem like a bad dream.

Am wondering whether I'm being real about my feelings – I haven't cried a great deal. I do know I feel so much. What I don't know – much of the time – is what I feel.

This is such a horrible, sad thing – and a happy ending is by no means guaranteed… It's happened so fast too…

Am I burying things in order to cope and not being real? Or am I taking time to catch up with my processing?

If I start to cry about all this, where will it end? Will it end? I don't know the answers – over to you, Lord!

Father, will you teach me the lessons I need for my future? Will you help me work the future out?

God never lets go of Shirley's heart. Chris sees a picture of a beautiful handbag. It's full of dirt and personalised rubbish. As she watches, the bag turns over and all the rubbish falls out. She's struck by how beautiful and clean it now is on the inside. Another time, she sees a very different picture, but it says the same thing. She sees a chrysalis, with its wings wound tight.

As she watches, the wings begin slowly to unfurl. They uncrinkle and – at last – stretch out fully in the sun. A beautiful butterfly replaces the indifferent brown body. Not long and it can fly!

CHAPTER THIRTY

New Normal

"The cats scamper over everything;
and drink water, sitting in the basin under the dripping tap."

I GET OUT OF SHIRLEY'S BEAMER FEELING PRETTY SMUG. IT'S A good parking place, down a quiet side street. Neat, complaisant cottages nestle in leafy green gardens – all rather nice.

Finding parking in the hospital grounds next-door is a nightmare. Most of the time there isn't any. And when there is, it's very expensive for us – on top of hospital stays, consultations, scans and X-rays. So, why not simply park nearby – and slip through the gap provided in the fence? Finding parking in Oxford itself – let alone the hospital grounds – is also like finding hen's teeth. Hence, this feels like quite an achievement. I come back hours later, after spending the day with Shirls in hospital, to find I have a parking ticket. I really should have seen the no-parking sign. For a South African to finance with the tottering rand, it's a hefty fine – thirty-five pounds. Once again, my self-confidence is under fire.

Compassionately, the hospital chaplain, Margaret, sends me deep into the bowels of the old hospital. A smiling clerk, who according to Margaret is also a Christian, issues me with a free pass for future parking. This kindness and many others from the pretty, petite Scottish lady with the short, softly curly grey hair comforts me.

Every morning, I trundle my pull-along over rough pavements from the parking area to the Oncology Ward. At the sight of Shirley, my heart always lifts. Just being with her soothes me. We do a little catch-up before I settle into my corner out of the way. Listening to music, reading, praying and writing emails break the tedium of the day.

So do my many walks. The corridors take me past private rooms, each occupied by a cancer-pallid, usually older sufferer. There's something so sad about the fact that the rooms (and the general wards on the other side too) rapidly empty and fill all the time. I love to chat, but this is a sombre place and chatting doesn't happen often. Oncology wards have a gloom of their own.

The corridors create a large square. At each corner, a Day Room welcomes patients – briefly out of bed on parole – and their families. My favourite Day Room provides tea, coffee and iced water. I can't recall how many times I page through the magazines and read the notices – the same with every visit – and try out all the chairs. The apple-green cushions, fuchsia-pink couch and the TV with shelves of videos of *Friends* underneath make it a great haven – for Shirley, for me, for many of us.

At set times, a pungent, brown-gravy smell assails our noses. Cottage pie arrives so often that Shirley makes her own plans. There's nothing much else on the daily menus that she can stomach, so she brings her own food – little red, round Babybel cheeses; granola bars; sweet, pumpkin-yellow tangerines; bacon-flavoured biscuits; juices; apples and berries. I find a Spar up the road from the hospital, where I buy pineapple slices, watermelon, strawberries and grapes. If I can find cherries, I'm delighted, because I know she will be too.

I'm so thankful for the fridge in the Day Room shared by the patients, where I stash my Tesco two-for-the-price-of-one meals. And for the microwave. I visit WHSmith for ploughman's prawn-mayonnaise, and tuna-and-sweetcorn sandwiches. Shirley becomes passionate about orange juice, so I move loads of freight upstairs to her ward.

I never walk past the wigs and scarves on sale without being chilled by their significance. Sometimes, in the foyer of the Churchill Hospital, I queue for coffee – and listen to a volunteer playing an oddly out-of-place grand piano between the wheelchairs.

On the way to the chapel, buried deep in the old wartime section, old, gunmetal-grey rubber doors gently slap my arms from either side. At last! Beautiful, stained-glass windows cast puddles of colour on the floor around me. And peace into my soul.

Visitors have a long way to come – from Reading and Wokingham – but they just keep coming. Sheena comes by train and bus. Suzy arrives with lots of gifts – even food for Shirley's visitors! Flowers fill the empty spaces.

Again and again, friends and workmates lift Shirley's spirits. They always bring her to life. As always, she makes little of her pain and discomfort, and adds many a chuckle to the conversation. As a result, she sends her visitors away enriched.

Friday consultations, Tuesday X-rays and Thursday scans are another story.

I grow to dread driving home on Friday afternoons. The traffic's heavy, and I'm so tired I don't drive well. Shirley guides me round the countless roundabouts. And just when I think I'm getting the hang of it, she says, "Now this one works opposite to all the others, Mum." *Really? Why?*

At one stage, at the beginning of her chemo, Shirley was sure she was going to be too "wiped out" to guide my driving. So she arranged for us to follow Gaynor. Unfortunately, we lost her in the traffic – early on. Then, when we eventually found here again, I began to think, "I'm really enjoying this. It's fast – and a special type of dodgem!"

Every evening, at about half-past six, I set out for my lodgings. The half hour before I go is always bitterly hard. I find it heartbreaking to leave Shirley. So I have to prepare myself to go. Eventually, armed with my map, I drive off through the traffic.

On my very first night, I take a mixture of right and wrong turns. At one point, I drive up a little farm road, and meet a delightful family of rabbits at the top. Fortunately, the farmer knows the area. So I do get to my host, down beside a tributary of the Thames – although embarrassingly late for dinner. Exhausted though I am, I politely fish around for topics of conversation. I'm so grateful to them for having me – but it is heaven to fall into bed at last.

Next time we stay in Oxford, I meet a couple we have been put in touch with – the Brockies. "How was Shirley today?" Jan asks, opening the door for me.

She's there to do that many evenings, because they kindly let me stay very many times. She always gleans more from my face than my words. Before dinner, I often feed my tired soul by sitting in their amazing garden. I love the squirrels gathering walnuts under a splendid, spreading old tree. And it's especially beautiful there when Jan's hanging baskets are at their best – dripping fuchsias and petunias.

They're a family of six. Once Jan's husband Andy gets back from his daily trip to London, we sit down to one of Jan's super meals. It's a special treat for me; everyone chats, and I enjoy being part of a family. Their last holiday was in Ullapool which, according to Sam, was about lobsters and steaks. We take turns to do dishes, then I say goodnight and get down to emails and Skype.

"Sam wants to know why you're doing this, Thy," Jan asks one day, "and whether I'd do this for him, if the need arose." She folds laundry as she talks. "'What do *you* think, Sam? Of course I would!' was what I said."

I smile as I sip my coffee. Of course I do this. Like Jan, I can't dream of doing otherwise. Apart from the practical side of being there to drive, there's always the hope that somehow my being present – encouraging and listening – will help. Shirley likes me quietly there with her – with my toys. I know it's not possible for me to be anywhere else now.

––––––––––

On my first two of three visits, we spend roughly six months alternating between Oxford and Wokingham. These are the days when I watch the trees – in both places – go from new-green through full-green, eventually to yellow and then red.

I'm in Oxford often enough to trace the construction, from floor to roof level, of a unique, very modern building – across the road from Shirley's ward. The cranes meticulously swing the strangely shaped wooden panels and beams into place. Sometimes, they swing uncertainly in the wind and just hang there – much like the outcome of all we (but mostly Shirley) are going through.

This, for me, is the new normal.

Shirley's new normal is very different. The chemo regimen prescribed for her is extremely tough – two cycles of it back to back. Usually it's given to teenagers, who are younger and stronger. Often it necessitates a blood transfusion. But she does so well that the doctors persist. She does admit,

"Seems like a bit of a mountain at the moment. But I'll do whatever the doctors think is necessary."

By the middle of August, Shirley is close to being pain-free. The doctors want her off morphine as soon as possible.

"How much are you taking?" her consultant, Claire, asks.

"Oh, I don't know," Shirley replies. "I just take a swig every now and then."

Claire's deep brown eyes grow really big.

As always, fear crowds in. It comes, lingers or flits temporarily away. But it's especially active every second week, when Shirley's back in hospital. The two days before find her swaddled in what comforts her. On one occasion, she posts:

> *This feels like a silly thing – in the greater scheme of things – but it's a big deal to me. Last time, I found it very tough being cooped up. So I'm feeling anxious – how will I fill the time? Courage and patience needed! Also, any ideas for things to do – that aren't too mentally taxing? Thank you! X*

Now, back in bed for another round of chemo, she can't find her diary. Then it peeps out from under the dull, bland-blue hospital blanket. And she pounces.

> *Red drug, ho hum!*

She knows that means she's tethered to Fred for five days – maybe more, if she becomes anaemic.

> *Have been wobbly today. I know the chemo is necessary/helpful, but I'm not massively looking forward to being really ill – and feeling so weak and wobbly, as a result.*

This time in hospital, after the blimping before, we're all especially anxious. But thankfully, Shirley picks up only about five kilos.

> *Been feeling afraid that I won't get well. I'm clinging to this today (27 July): Let me paraphrase Zephaniah 3:15: "In the midst of disaster – the Lord is here" (Zephaniah 3:15).*

> *I am in the midst of disaster – but the Lord, the mighty one of Israel, is here! (Therefore all will be well, therefore I can rest and be at peace.)*

All day long, we watch the door to Shirley's ward open and close. They come to clean, to medicate, to change beds, fill in charts, change drips, fetch pee, dispense medicine, take blood pressure, consult and sometimes just to chat. The loss of dignity gets to her at first. She can't even pee without someone wanting to measure and comment on it.

Shirley often asks the nurses, "How was your day?"

That she's so kind blesses me. She appreciates one male nurse who's especially gentle. And she giggles over "the flirty one" who knows how handsome he is. We both love Dawn, who is South African – with an authentic accent to prove it.

Once the chemo starts, Shirley's eyesight dims and her brain becomes fuzzy. She listens to music, texts a lot and emails a bit. Concentration plummets to an all-time low. She dozes for hours – or pulls out the little black-faced sheep she's knitting for Amelia. She works on the poppies and green fields of her tapestry. Or reads Winnie the Pooh – at three o'clock in the morning. Stitch by stitch, Shirley makes her way through each round of hospital life.

On one of our many walks along the corridors, we discover a rooftop garden with a pagoda. We love to pray there when we're alone. In season, the flowers enchant us. Every plant – climber and shrub – boasts blooms that are a shade of blue. It becomes one of the nearest things to escape that Shirley can find.

Being tethered makes Shirley more and more frantic. Sad for her, I watch the tension build up steadily. She gets to a point where she's so uncomfortable, she contorts her mattress into a bent, twisted thing. Just when it seems she'll explode, it's over – one more time. But it's all taking so, so long – this mix of chemo, pain, frustration, fear and faith.

Free at last, we drive home, stopping only for petrol – and to buy chicken pieces and prawn cocktail for supper. We have one thing in mind: bed. We bundle through the entrance hall and up the steps. We dump bags and coats and things. Shirley stops only to undress. Next moment, she's cuddled under her duvet. Once there, cats invade, so glad she's back. I bring whatever she thinks she'll eat – often only tea – before she passes out.

Two or three grey days follow, depending on the effect of the chemo. When Shirley begins to feel better, she also begins to chat a bit – to this one and that. And I feel less desolate.

Hi everyone, I've been very tired since getting out of hospital on Wed. But, otherwise, I'm doing okay. If anything, I'm a little bored – but it's hard to plan anything at the moment, as I have to be very careful of infection this next week. I can't even go to Tesco – or church, or a pub. It's a good problem to have, though! This last stint in hospital really flew by, and I didn't feel half as bad as previously – a real answer to prayer.

There can be no doubt that the chemo's really taking effect – my leg is significantly less swollen (I can see dimples on my knee again!). Even better, I'm in virtually no pain. After months of nursing an achy leg, I can't tell you how good this feels!

Shirley buys herself a box of shell-shaped Belgian chocolates and me a box of Lindt balls. Only afterwards do I realise this is a little ceremony to say a teary goodbye to chocolate. At one stage, thanks to the chemo, Shirley craved chocolate milk, but that has to go too. All her Easter eggs, including the bunny I buy her every year, go to Caroline's children. And so the cancer, true to form, continues to invade her life and to pillage and plunder.

Even the shopping changes. We buy fewer and fewer Sainsbury's cooked chickens, boxes of ready-made soup – no more salmon – as Shirley loses ground. And more and more often, I do the shopping on my own – a clear sign that the new normal is beginning to change.

"Wait, let me read that again." Shirley gropes for the place in her Bible, then copies the words into her faithful diary:

"I will not die, but live, and proclaim what the Lord has done."
(Psalm 118:17)

I'm going to take heart and believe that God wants me to live, that there will be no more disasters, and that God will give me a great story to tell. Hmm. These past few days, I've been very, very afraid regarding my lungs – and not very well.

Nick's response to Shirley's needs is to take her a hot-off-the-press issue of *The Fireman*. He tells Katy, "It's packed with news, sizzling stories of heroic bravery, and loads of photos of your favourite hunks in action. That should keep Shirls distracted for an hour or so."

It does help – but then Shirls writes:

My faith is so teeny and small; I have such a long way to go. I even started questioning God's kindness and good intentions towards me – Father, I am sorry.

"No, Shelley-cat," I yell. "How did you get in here?"

Every time we're home, the battle begins. That's because, as part of the new normal, the threat of infection puts the kitchen out of bounds.

When I first arrived in Wokingham, someone said to me, very reasonably, "Of course, the cats must go."

But I know they have always been such companions to Shirley – especially at those times when her life has been so dark. And she really loves them. For me, already so sad she is losing so much, this was unthinkable. So I said, "No – not now, not yet."

I'm not sorry – the 'moggies' lift my mood when they line up one behind the other to take turns at the cat feeder. But they do infuriate me. I diligently disinfect the tabletops, taps and sink and they – just as diligently? – undo all my hard work. They scamper over everything; and drink water, sitting in the basin under the dripping tap.

Shirley, often absent-mindedly, strokes now one cat and now another, as they cuddle against her legs. We both try to wash our hands every time – but to stop the stroking is out of the question.

While Shirley's tenant, Johno, is still with us (he will leave in September), I come down in the mornings to the overpowering smell of the bacon, eggs, sausage, tomato and whatever else he depends on to get him through a day's work. Shirley can't handle it, so I close the interleading glass door, fling the back door open, and let the smell out – and the cold in. Nowadays, when I cook my omelette, it's always with the door open.

No omelettes for Shirley. She does best on cereals. But she's eating. Before her op, the doctors want her to top up on protein to replace muscle. She loves the juices I concoct – sometimes twice a day – from carrots, cucumber, celery, broccoli, spinach and ginger. I add either an orange or an apple and top it all off with ice. In time, twice a day becomes once a day – and then, not at all.

Flowers keep coming so that at times we have five or six bowls. They are like the breath of God, topping up our war-torn souls with beauty. For more than eleven months, Shirley is lovingly swathed in wonderful colour. Because bacteria are a no-no, on my three visits I check every day that there are no slimy stems in brown water – no places for bacteria to lurk – and no cat fur anywhere.

Kindness flows over us unabated. Katy gives me lifts to morning service. And Stuart and Lindsay bring me home. Caroline brings fruit cake – many times. Gail collects gifts from our family and friends – to help pay for all the flights backwards and forwards – twelve in all for Brian and me.

Gail also makes supper for me! One night, Shirley's morphine-induced woozy head puts her straight to bed and I feel so alone downstairs. We've just done the harrowing drive home, so it's the most wonderful, warm, tasty supper ever for a deeply weary soul.

CHAPTER THIRTY-ONE

Grief

"Shirley looks stunning in the long,
golden-blonde wig she chooses."

NOW SHIRLEY'S IN PAIN OF ONE SORT OR ANOTHER EVERY day. But it's only when it gets close to unbearable that she calls for help and I phone the doctor.

"All lines are busy," says a mechanical voice. "Please hold – you are number five in the queue."

Most times, the doctor comes pretty quickly. He prescribes new pain killers, injections – and more morphine. Even before I can fetch the meds, relief of a kind floods over Shirley.

We grieve over so many things. Grieving is a big part of our new normal. One day, Shirley opens her old upright piano and runs her fingers over the keys. For a while, her beloved music just pours from her soul. Head bowed, I drink it in. I so want to make sure I remember this, because I just know I'll never hear it again.

Then, quite deliberately, she closes the lid and bids another treasure goodbye. I know she also knows. Here it is again: loss. Another great loss for her, for both of us.

When I first arrived, Shirley asked me to pray with faith and believe she would be healed. Ever since then, I've been asking God to communicate to me what I am to believe about her healing. I don't have any problem with believing – just with what it is I am to believe. I remember Abraham who believed in the seed he was to have – descendants as many as the stars – but only after God had told him it would be so.

These are the days when I wait, anxiously, for *something*, a sign of miraculous intervention for Shirley. So far, nothing. Or, at least, I haven't seen anything.

First thing every morning, I creak down the stairs to fetch a mug of coffee. I worry about the noise. Not so Wilf. He shows his delight that someone's awake by coiling in and out between my legs, proud tail flying high.

Back under my white duvet, I begin a precious hour with God. Together with my own stuff, I pray for Shirley, especially the things with which I know she's struggling ("Will God heal me or take me home? I know I must trust, but I can't shake off my huge fear. I so badly want to live for God full out. I feel so useless, and sidelined.") So often she can't feel God near. And her faith yo-yos – a bit like it did in the past.

Emails, Skype and texts become a part of my new normal.

I keep up with my round robins.

> *Praise God for the improvement in the lungs, Shirley coping with chemo – for four friends who fast and pray for her every day. Praise God for the peace we have – and the sense of God's presence here. When we've felt fear, God has given us times of closeness that are hard to describe. Praise God for her longing to shine for her Lord.*

> *Every time S asks to pray, I try to memorise our prayers as precious treasure to keep. I long to make sure I store it all.*

Nats encourages:

> *Relax into Abba, who holds you so tenderly.*

179

Faye and Lynn send me hugs from South Africa, and Claudia from Atlanta, Georgia.

Brian writes:

> *Hullo sweetheart. I am working away at my jigsaw. I woke at about 4.30 a.m. and used the time to pray for you – and especially for S. Missing you badly and loving you lots.*

I respond:

> *I know – I hope we will each say one day: "But I learnt such a lot from God." If we can, we will have been at the receiving end of a lot of grace.*

> *I'm sitting outside in the backyard at 8 p.m. with the cats – because it's so hot.*

> *I am lonely too – it's quite something for us all to have our comfort zones ripped up. You know what? I'm so glad you are missing me!*

Each new normal is a necessary but extremely devastating one – cruelly demanding, and it spares no quarter.

Brian writes:

> *Jenny's very quiet. My sweetheart, I was really distressed talking to you last night. You seemed so exhausted. I understand – but it was not good to see. I wish I was with you to carry some of the load.*

I'm quick to write back:

> *Please buy a large Aero for Jenny and tell her it's from Ma, and that every bubble says, "Ma loves you, Boo."*

> *And please don't be distressed. Getting used to so much and having to learn so much – even how to lock the front door! – is now over. I am amazingly strengthened, and Jesus is always here.*

Shirley's email to Brian thanking him for what he's doing, though so far away, is such a comfort to him.

One afternoon, just before the leg op, we sit on the bank of the Thames, swinging our legs at Sonning Lock. Misgivings and dread mess with Shirley's mind. I haven't the foggiest idea – not the foggiest – what to say. All that comes to me is to listen, put my arms round her and hug her.

I tell God that I'm totally out of my depth, that this is impossible. Then he reminds me of the words, "My grace is sufficient for you." And I imagine him saying, "Now just what part of that didn't you understand?"

That shuts me up – ever so gently but firmly. I journal:

"He gives strength to the weary and increases the power of the weak"
(Isaiah 40:29).

God helps me to celebrate progress. I see the changes in Shirley – in spite of the cancer looting more and more – and the progress in my own stubborn heart.

"Maybe I'll buy a goldfish today," Shirley says as I hand her a huge mug of tea.

When her head's not fuzzy, we manage a number of errands. She's already got me to pot favourite plants – her olive tree and perfectly shaped little maple tree for starters – ready for the planned move to London. I do wonder about that but choose to say nothing. Now it's goldfish? What a lovely idea!

To herself, Shirley says, *I feel safe – functioning in the world of little things makes me happy.*

So we go to Homebase and buy 'Derek' and 'Dorothy'. Thankfully, we can put them straight into Jo's fish tank. I learn very quickly how to clean it – after syphoning green, slimy water into my mouth just once.

When we get home after another outing, Shirley and I discover she's locked the house keys inside. I look at her and she looks at me. We both know that she has a key hidden in her locked backyard, under a stone.

Next, I look at her leg. That settles it. I drag a dustbin up to the back gate. Once on top of the wooden fence, I swing my legs down on the other side. I have no idea how this is going to turn out. I slither – until my foot catches a crossbar. Deeply thankful, I jump the rest of the way. And nothing breaks!

We giggle as we imagine what a watching neighbour – if there were one – would make of all this.

While Shirley can, we visit some favourite places. We drive to Wargrave and stop in at the George. We meander along the Thames to Henley, while Shirley remembers lazy regattas in Nick's boat.

Chris introduces us to Dinton Pastures, close to Sandy Lane. She wants to quieten Shirley's heart with stillness and beauty. We take in the swans along the shores of the lake. We have tea in the garden.

Chris also wants to help with the boredom. So she pops in one evening with a bag full of nail varnish. We chat and giggle, and talk a little about heaven, as Chris paints our nails.

"Oh, Mum," Shirley moans, "I look so weird with all my eyelashes and my eyebrows gone."

She does, but I don't tell her that. Instead, I say, "Then what about doing the very most you can with eye make-up?"

It's Suzy, not me, who drives us to Crowthorne to choose a wig at Beesley Wigs.

This is such fun; it takes a long time. The slim assistant brings now one, now another. We comment – and giggle sometimes. Soon everybody in the shop is helping too. After a while, they realise what Shirley really wants. She looks stunning in the long, golden-blonde creation she chooses. However, she does admit to me later, "I don't like anything artificial."

While Shirley settles up, I read a card pinned to the counter. With feminine flourish, the writer thanks the establishment for restoring her self-confidence. This, in fact, is what they do for Shirley too.

All the way home, the girls chatter and laugh and make (to my mind) a special kind of music. Quiet in the backseat, I love it, because this is just what Shirley needs.

And when Nick comes to visit, he tries the wig on, looking quite fetching in it and making Shirley laugh.

Every time Shirley gets back from hospital, she has to inject herself for five days, to build up her white corpuscles again. She hates it, but she never complains.

Once a week, a district nurse arrives. He irrigates her central line to guard against it blocking. He's young and very handsome, with large blue eyes. So he brightens our day.

When Shirley can't concentrate, she watches TV. Many times, she takes my hand. Less often, she crawls up on to my shoulder for a little while. As I hold her, I do all I can to make sure I remember forever how wonderful this feels.

At times, when I see Shirley begin to struggle and become depressed, I know what will help, and pray for friends to encourage her.

Katy pops in to natter. One time, she talks about joy – and Shirley's mood lifts. Laura, all the way from Bradford, sits cross-legged as she shares the message God has given her for Shirley. Gaynor confides – and they uplift each other. Chris leans close – and leaves Shirley smiling again. This is what

God told me: friends would minister to, comfort and encourage her. How glad it all makes me.

One afternoon, Kim, Ant and Mark visit. They're all close friends. Mark is Shirley's ex-husband, and it's a gathering of South Africans. The afternoon slides into easy laughter and fun. When they leave, Kim gives me a look that speaks volumes; it says, "Thy, she's going… to die! This is too awful. And I hate, hate, hate it." Kim's not the only one. Many times, I see this in the eyes of others.

Dan and Tonia bring communion. Tonia writes:

What an inspiration. We sang – I have to say, Shirley's voice is still angelic. The presence of God was awesome. So was the peace.

Upstairs, shrieks rend the air. Jo and Katy are sitting on Shirley's bed, each cradling a warm 'cuppa' I've just made. I hear "woohoo" and tear up the stairs. Shirley's standing in a pair of jeans – zipped up – for the first time in months. She's been reduced by the watermelon-leg to wearing long skirts – granted, always with style. Only recently, she's messaged the good news that she can bend her knee again. And she's started to walk, not hobble.

Tried a small exercise routine in bed today to loosen up my muscles. Ooh, ooh. Next step – one foot out of bed! Maybe… tomorrow (30 July)?

Now this. She's out of bed – and in her jeans! No wonder we celebrate.

"Wow, Shirls," says Jo. "What an answer to prayer! Now, what else must we pray for?"

"I'm struggling with my appetite," she admits, "and a very sensitive stomach. My consultants don't want me to lose more weight before my surgery. And please keep praying that these tumours shrink and disappear; they have no place in my body!"

"Amen." Jo beats the air for emphasis.

"Sure thing," Katy says, and reaches out tenderly and squeezes Shirley's hand.

While new normals are temporary and keep changing, the peace certainly never leaves. But all these losses leave us with an old, pre-cancer normal we can now barely remember. For Shirley, it's a continuing struggle with fear. And pain. And loss. For me, it's grief and a struggle to accept that all this is real and true. For Brian, it's a struggle to juggle work, loneliness, and anguish. But for all of us, it also becomes a growing intimacy with God.

CHAPTER THIRTY-TWO

D-Day

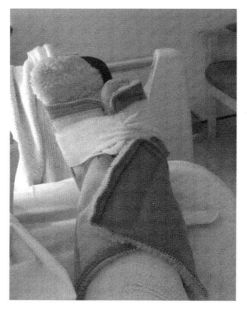

"They had to take out two-thirds of my femur."

ON MONDAY NIGHT, THE NIGHT BEFORE WE GO TO THE
Nuffield Hospital in Oxford for the op, Shirley lies looking up at the stars
studding the night sky. Her bedroom curtains, patterned with twisting,
chocolate-coloured stems, are half-open. The theme she has chosen for her
bedroom is "wildness and wet", but she's not thinking of Gerard Manley
Hopkins' poem, *God's Grandeur*, right now. She's been awake for hours –
again – as she often is. And again, she's processing a great deal, especially
what lies ahead.

Shirley's always found night – the middle of the night – the hardest time.
"There's something about it… It's just horrible," she told me a while ago.

"There have been times when it's just been awful... lying awake in the hospital, listening to all the sounds and all the beeps. Yeah... and not being able to sleep... and having all sorts of thoughts rushing through your head."

She yawns and stretches. And looks at her watch. And groans. It's only 1.30 a.m. – an infinitely long time to wait. Tomorrow, in the Nuffield – not the Churchill Hospital this time as the proposed treatment is not oncological but osteopathic – they will prep her for the operation on Wednesday.

She remembers explaining to Nick, "The idea behind the high levels of chemo was to blast the tumour in my leg. They wanted to kill as much of it as possible. So they hit me as hard as they could with everything they had."

"They certainly did that!" Nick's response was vehement.

"They have to take out two-thirds of my femur. Then they replace it with a metal rod. And then they will put a shaft up the rest of my femur to keep it in place. Next, they'll replace my knee... but I do get to keep my kneecap. The last thing is to put a shaft down inside my tibia to keep my leg in place... sort of at the lower end."

Like clouds across the sky, dark grey shades of fear slide in and settle in her stomach. *I'm quite blown away. What about the things I love doing? All of that needs two working legs! What am I going to do if I don't have two working legs! I did ask about skiing again... They said "ye-es" but seemed pretty evasive on that one. I'm so scared... It's all just such a big deal... terrifying.*

At last, Tuesday dawns. We each pack for what is probably going to be two weeks. We supply Mark and Amanda from next door with a mountain of cat food.

Shirley's been particularly quiet for two days – more so than usual – so I expect a silent trip. That's what she needs right now.

We struggle to find parking in the grounds of the Nuffield Hospital; then trundle Shirley's things through the pink, central rotunda. First thing are MRI and PET scans. Then Shirley has to have her central line removed. They don't want anything artificial in her body as this could lead to infection. Usually she doesn't cry out, so when she does this time, I cringe. That can only mean it's very, very painful. *Oh, Shirley, how much more must you suffer?*

Shirley is sad and pale as we make our way to the ward.

Ward F, Room 7 has a view of a little courtyard below. As the day wears by, the grip of anxiety tightens relentlessly. *Will I wake up in ICU? Will there be pipes everywhere? What about pain? When will they get me up? What about physio? How normal will the leg be afterwards? When will the chemo start again? What about my lungs – while there's no chemo?*

Katy texts:

> *I saw Shirls earlier – she was calm but, understandably, nervous. Hopefully she'll have the op in the morning, so she won't have to wait around too long. Praying for you, Shirls!*

Shirley plugs in her earphones. She's looking for *Oceans* by Hillsong. What strikes her so deeply about this song is that it describes being called out and being alone with God in what is completely unknown. It is a place where fear surrounds but God never fails, a place where trust increases and which extends her, way beyond anything she has known before. *Oh, please, please, Lord, away from fear; far away, and into faith.*

Flowers flood in. Nick does an impressive arrangement himself: bright sunflowers, no less. A beautifully soft, pink gerbera from someone else takes up prime position – in the front, in the middle – in its creamy-coloured vase. Chris and John's arrangement blossoms behind it, also with cheery yellow sunflowers. Roses from Tonia complete the display.

I create my usual nest, pulling a hospital chair to one side. Distress throttles back the praying, but every now and then, I do manage a bit. Every day, I enjoy the canteen downstairs. I discover that all you can get on Sundays is bacon and eggs, which I really like – even for Sunday lunch. Nursing staff come and go. The activity around Shirley speeds up – and then they wheel her out. All I see in my mind for hours afterwards is her ashen face. She's speechless with fear.

Nick brings everyone up to speed:

> *The surgeon has said that they have to get close to some major nerves, so there's a small risk of nerve damage, which will result in a dropped foot. As well as everything else – thank you! Please pray specifically about this. Will post operation time when I know, but she's third in line – so circa midday.*

Katy texts me:

> *Thy, would you like me to come and sit with you?*

I'm so touched by her thoughtfulness and kindness. But no, I decide, I'll do best on my own. And I need to be alone with God.

Through the endless afternoon, I sit quietly in my nest, beside the large, empty space that was Shirley's bed. Vicky, the Macmillan nurse caring for her, pops in to talk a little. I'm so happy to see her – and so glad she thinks of me.

"Oh Thy," she says, "I was amazed to see how scared Shirley was. She's usually so chatty and friendly. But she couldn't get a word out."

In many ways, the time slips by quickly. In others, it feels as if it can only plod along – grinding minute by grinding minute. I think we have become pretty experienced with the really slow ones. We feel them one by one as we wait for drips to empty, or sit in waiting rooms, or wait for consultations, or medication. But somehow, the minutes of this day are just that much more sluggish.

My thoughts range far and wide. I long to understand what God is doing. I believe he's glorifying himself. I want others to know. I keep thinking that when Shirley is well again, she will have such a song to sing with her lovely voice, such a testimony to share. I picture her in lots of places leading worship and telling her story again and again – glorifying God, as she longs to do.

Surely, that's the future God has in store for her?

On 4 September, Honey wakes Brian and demands her breakfast very early – as usual. He tries to fall asleep again but – no way! Today he has to deliver two reports – one as general secretary and the other as treasurer – to the Annual General Synod of his church. That makes today his most important challenge.

But his focus is very much elsewhere; the fact that he's stuck in South Africa, while doctors operate on his only daughter in the Nuffield in Oxford, bites deep. So in a daze, he goes through the motions. He tucks into a hurried bowl of muesli. Next, he picks up his papers, hoping he has everything he needs. He wonders how he's ever going to cope – and hopes there'll be few questions from the floor. Shock and trauma walk with him through the day. Numbness wraps around him.

My heart's really sore for him. I write:

Well, my sweetie pie, I have always been there to support you through Synod week. I'm so sorry that it has to be so different this year. And that the day for which you carry the most responsibility has to be the day of S's op.

Please keep your cell phone on. God, give us the courage to focus – and do what we each have to do.

At last, nearly five hours later, I have news and text from Shirley's ward.

Just spoken to S. Four-hour op. Doc says she has done really well. Lost a lot of blood and will stay in recovery overnight. Is alert and pain-free. Tumour successfully removed – praise God.

What strikes me is how relieved Shirley sounds in the Recovery Room – weak and woozy, but so very relieved. I'm intensely glad for her. And share the relief.

"I'm still so mad, Monica."

The pretty young nurse in the recovery room looks up from filling in a chart.

"He borrows my car – and then he takes another girl out in it! Can you believe it?"

"No! You're kidding me, right?" replies the redhead next to her, busily rolling bandages.

Shirley's head pops up. She's been awake and alert for a while now, but at this point she's suddenly wide awake, and deeply interested in anything and everything going on around her.

"Oh, Mum," she tells me on her mobile, "it was better than an episode of *Friends*!"

"What happened next?" I ask. "Do tell."

"It's a long story," she says, "and I felt for her, especially as he apparently scraped the car. Mum, I feel really good. I'm properly awake with no pain at all – how wonderful is that? I hope they'll let me come back to the ward a.s.a.p." Then she adds, "I'm getting quite bored. Every time something happens that seems remotely interesting, my head pops up – like the heroes in *Meercat Manor*."

We laugh at the picture.

It's a very long time before they bring Shirley back to her ward. We love it when the Australian doctor who assisted at the op drops by and drawls, "That was one seriously unhappy tumour!" He's very confident – delighted that they got it all and that there's no chance of a dropped foot.

Vicky, and others in Shirley's medical team, happily report:

We've got our Shirley back!

A nurse bursts in on us. Her busy hands fumble with a packet of elasticised stockings – to prevent blood clots. To put them on for Shirley, she flings back the blanket. And stares. Shirley's right leg is huge: heavily bandaged and in a plastic cast. *Surely not? How can I put...* Flustered, she does the other leg; but dumps the other stocking, still in the packet, in the basin. And flees. Shirls and I look at each other and burst out laughing.

Another stern, older nurse – a sister, I think – opens the door, outrage on her face. She points at the jug I found in the kitchen for new flowers and says, through tight lips, "That's our milk jug, you know."

Oops! I am so sorry – sorry enough for her to show me where the spare vases are. Sorry enough (but smiling to myself) to put things right.

Nick texts Shirley's earnestly waiting Secret Helpers:

> *Though wires and tubes appear from many places, this afternoon (5 September) Shirley was radiant. I confess, my update was written with a lump in the throat – and grateful tears (butch man-tears of course!). God's hand is so clearly over Shirley. He hears us. He cares so-o-o much. And our praying draws us all closer to him.*

> *Go figure – the pic (inserted) is of the new leg which – even this afternoon – has toes happily wiggling!*

Nick suggests that over the next fourteen days, "visits, flowers, chocolate, entertaining reading and news from the outside world" will be most welcome. He just can't help himself and posts again:

> *Miss Shirley C bright and chatty – no more drips, except morphine. So no knowledge whatsoever as to what she's chatting about – but she's blissfully happy. Moving leg quite a bit more. Complete removal of tumour improves her ongoing prognosis – Yay :-))*

As I sit in my corner, I notice that today all Shirley's gorgeous flowers, on the windowsill beside her, are bathed in bright sunlight.

The day after the op, Shirley's consultant visits her. Claire's very pleased. But what she says next fells Shirley and me with one deft blow. She walks out unaware of what she's just done, but Shirley and I look at each other appalled.

"She doesn't believe she can heal me, Mum!"

Unintentionally, Claire has just revealed that her efforts have always been to win Shirley more time – never to heal her.

That's par for the course with stage 3 and 4 cancer. But we didn't realise that. We hadn't got the message – not really – until now. So the real picture bludgeons us.

Shirley starts to cry. And continues crying, ever so quietly, for two days.

I cry silently alongside her. Sometimes I watch a slow tear or two course down her cheek. Other times, I can't bear to and I turn away. I feel my complete helplessness again. All I can do is to grieve through the long hours – and wait for our crying to stop. Once again, cancer reveals its grip. It contorts our hopes.

A whole lot later, when God steps in, we are in shreds.

In spite of Claire's chilling revelation, Shirley chooses, after a slow, silent, heartbreaking struggle, not to be overcome by it. She chooses to hope and trust. I marvel at such faith. "Mum," she says, once she can function again, "I need to be positive for everyone's sake."

I marvel, too, that under these circumstances she's concerned about others. She feels responsible to keep our spirits up!

She courageously shares with her friends the progress she's making. Only five days after the op, she tells them:

> *Hey everyone, brilliant progress. I just managed to stand up beside the bed – using a heavy-duty, Zimmer-frame thingummy – but who's counting?*

A day later she writes:

> *Second standing attempt today – successful, but very, very sore. Hoping the pain will ease soon... Apparently I'm going to be taking a few steps later!*

Brian replies from South Africa:

> *Yippee! One small step for (wo)mankind... and all that. Keep it up, sweetheart. You'll be running around anytime now. God bless. Dad.*

Shirley's thrilled when Suzy promises:

> *I will be visiting for an hour, or until Shirls can't bear anymore positivity and giggles from me!*

Afterwards she reports:

> *Shirls even sat on the side of the bed, while the physio wiggled her leg about. I've had a couple of teary moments – just because she's doing so well. She's in such a chipper mood – of course. Oh, and in*

typical Shirley style, she described last night's horrible pain as irritating. Think most of us would describe it as agony... X

Shirley texts:

Hi, can I ask for prayer – specifically, that the pain team gets my medication right. I reacted badly to this morphine, and they took me off continuous pain relief. So, during the night, I woke up in agony. I have a meeting with the pain team later – can you pray that they hit on a combination that works?

Facebook responds:

This had me in tears – again – for the faith and grace that Shirley and Thy show. It is very humbling. Katy

Tears here. Wow, Thy, maybe you'll be writing a book one day. Gaynor

Shirley Whirley – my beautiful, brave girl. I wish I could be there now to give you a huge hug. You are an inspiration. I miss your gentle presence. I thank God for your amazing friends and your Mum looking after you and – most of all – for the Ruach of God blowing on your life. Romans 8:28. Rami

Nick stands beside Shirley's bed looking at the leg. He finds himself thinking, *this is a moment in the journey that surpasses everything else so far.* He lays his hands ever so gently on the deeply bound limb. *I just know God is going to heal her. I feel a wave of certainty wash over me, like warm water.* Tears flow freely down his face, and on the way home, he can't stop crying, with such a sense of awesome wonder and thanks and – yes – even *surprise* at how God works, which leaves him speechless. As he cruises round the bends, he keeps thinking of the bicycles tied up outside the hospital. And in his mind's eye, he sees Shirley riding one again – *whoopee!*

It is high time I write home:

It's the third day after the op and Shirley's doing one of those very awkward bedbath efforts. At some point, if you're in hospital, you have to do them.

She's eating well. They've got her exercising every two to three hours. The surgeon says he's keeping her here for as long as it takes, for her to be 'safe' – his word, and I love it!

In no time at all, Suzy's back for a visit. And doesn't waste time before she reports back:

> *Mega-progress since last Saturday! Very chirpy. Moving the leg about like there's nothing wrong with it. Scar looks great. Very neat!!!*
>
> *And the best bit? Her hair has started growing back already – very cute and furry!!!*

Shirley's fingers are not to be outdone:

> *Found out today that ninety per cent of the leg tumour was dead – killed by the chemo! As I start again – at the end of the month – please can we pray that the last twenty per cent of cancer cells in my lungs are killed this time round?*
>
> *My wound has healed very well. But I can't bend the leg much (they removed thirty per cent of my quads). Still, the doctors are confident I'll regain full mobility – in time. Lots of answers to prayer... They told me my lungs are greatly improved, as well. Thank you for your ongoing love, prayers and support. Xxx*

Every day, Shirley really works in her physio sessions. She grits her teeth much of the time. A shaky step or two becomes walking with a frame – in little blue socks with suckers on the bottom to prevent falling – then crutches, which she finds key to being able to explore every passage and Day Room.

CHAPTER THIRTY-THREE

Recovery

"God has raised up an army around me."

WHEN THE DAY DAWNS FOR SHIRLEY TO GO HOME, I WANT SO badly for it to be a comfortable, pain-free journey. Before we came, I packed a couple of soft pillows to stuff the space under the rigid, plastic-encased limb. I wanted to keep it supported and straight.

Now it's raining. So, after several trips to pack Shirley's possessions into the boot, I'm very cold and very wet.

At last, it's all ready. I push a wheelchair – with umbrella attached – into her ward. The goodbyes and warm good wishes clingwrap our hearts.

I struggle – really struggle – to get Shirls into the car and comfortable. And out of the persistent rain. It blurs the road, confuses what I can see, and pushes my stress levels right over the top.

Shirley bravely grits her teeth. But I know she's not comfortable. I pull off the road, open her door and tug and pull. I know I don't really improve things. I also know the cold, wet rain's soaking my back and neck.

Pale and sore, Shirley holds on. She doesn't complain. My appreciation of how kind she is deepens, the further we go. It's raining hard, the traffic's heavy and frightening, and the leg throbs – but she doesn't even murmur.

At home, Shirley takes off her leg brace and pulls the crutches nearer. "I'm beginning to get the hang of this." Thanks to lots of ongoing physio – and her sheer guts – the leg's bending quite a lot. And the scar, pampered and greased with vitamin E oils, looks good. She feels well and thinks it's time to stop all the pain pills.

Late Sunday afternoon, when no one else is around, Shirley decides to take a bath. Luxuriating in the warm water is pure bliss, and worth the long, slow, halting hobble up the stairs.

Chloe-cat, curious, perches on the edge. I wait for the splash – but it never comes. "Pesky cat!" Shirley posts to her Secret Helpers.

I find myself cutting Shirley's toenails. It feels macabre. I'm thinking as I do it, "The last time I did this, you were a little girl."

"What do you see, looking back, Thy?"

Dan's question surprises me. The curate at Greyfriars and Tonia have come to break bread.

"Well, the op was a huge success. Vicky told me it was not possible to get a better result. She also said they were now prepared to consider applying for a very expensive drug. This is only given to patients whose lungs are cancer-free. But the improvement in Shirley's lungs has suggested they apply for this.

I think about his question as I pour more coffee.

"You know, Dan, we cried for two days when we realised that all they're doing is to try to win Shirley time. Then Shirley says to me, 'Mum, I surrender my life to God. If he does not plan to give me a long life, I am now okay with that.' What a huge journey – and what courage – for her to come to this point! I've been amazed to see her accept, little by little, some of the things she adamantly rejected before. It's a bit like God is feeding his plan for Shirley to her bit by bit. For me, in all the waiting (we've done so much of it), I've learnt how weak I am. Many times, God has made the impossible possible. Now I wait a little better. And peace – tangible and trustworthy – has not left me at any stage. We've all suffered – there's no doubt about that. But for me the question becomes: Have we suffered well?"

194

On 29 September, Shirley sends out a round robin:

My many milestones include the successful completion of my leg op, and the start of the next round of chemo tomorrow.

I thank God that the op was completely successful and my lungs are greatly improved. I should regain full mobility in the future, and the surgeons have declared my leg cancer-free!

I'm walking well without my brace, I feel great, and have no infection but only tiredness and lack of energy.

God has raised up an army around me. Wow! I feel overwhelmed. God has carried me so far, and he will continue to be faithful!

Please pray that the next round of chemo will wipe out the remaining twenty per cent of cancer in my lungs.

Thank him that unpleasant symptoms have been at a minimum and, in between treatments, I've been feeling strong.

Wonderfully, my leg is bending to about ninety per cent and I'm only using one crutch. Pray that the chemo won't now impede its rehabilitation. I need it to bend beyond ninety per cent to be able to ride a bike, among other things. And it would be nice to be able to cut my own toenails again.

I've received so much emotional and spiritual healing already. Pray that I may have many long, cancer-free years ahead.

Thank you so much for standing by me! Lots of love Xx

Somehow Jo, Katy, Laura and Gaynor all manage to perch on Shirley's double bed with her. Whenever they visit, Jo and Katy first make for the drawer in the kitchen where Shirley keeps antihistamines for her allergic friends. They sip coffee and fill Shirley in on what's going on in the world. Shirley loves this because without them she wouldn't have a clue about what was happening out there.

Then Gaynor asks, "How did you feel about the op?"

"I think I kind of... I don't think I dealt with that particularly well. I think I kind of went into a bit of a black hole. I just didn't speak to anybody for about two days and... hmm... just waited it out, really."

"Oh, Shirls," the girls respond together. "How awful!"

"Hmm... but once the operation was over... and I could see I had ten toes and my leg was okay... I felt in a very different place. I could see the surgeons were happy too. I felt very peaceful... and I felt that God really had his hand on me. That was a good time. I mean, obviously the leg was really uncomfortable and painful. I had lots of morphine... Maybe that was why I had such a good time!" she laughs. "I don't know!"

"So how do you feel now?" Katy flicks her long brown hair out of her eyes.

"I couldn't move the leg very much... obviously... and I had to learn to walk again, which was scary. At the same time... it was a bit of a challenge. I kind of quite enjoyed that." Shirley nods her head, completely covered now with soft brown down. She wondered once whether her hair would ever grow again – and now it has, and beautifully, thank God. "I think I definitely saw the learning-to-walk-again stage as something I could actually contribute to. Just lying in bed and having drugs poured into you? You know you just... you completely... nothing you can do makes a difference. But now here was something I could work at... and get my teeth into. It did feel like we had completed Phase 1" – she nods to emphasise what she's saying – "and turned a corner. Hmm... so yeah... all of that was a good time. I felt very safe... secure... well looked after. I had a lovely private room... my little sanctuary! The reassurance of having people praying was amazing. And so many of my friends filled my room with flowers from top to bottom. Hmm... yeah... it was a peaceful time."

"What did your oncologists actually tell you?" Jo stretches out to get more comfortable.

"The surgeon reckoned that they got the whole tumour. All the mechanical bits are working... they kind of fitted together, no problem. He said about ninety per cent of what they removed was already dead."

"Wow!" escapes from all the girls – more or less at the same time.

"Obviously, I never forget the cancer's in my chest. But it's logical that if the treatment worked in my leg, presumably it's also worked... or working... in my lungs."

"And what about..." Gaynor's very hesitant. "What about the future? How do you feel in the whole battle? Where's God in all this?"

"God is with me. I've never believed that the cancer came from God. I've always believed that it is something that he is using in my life... I am pretty sure that... right... you know it's been tough... but we have come so far... and now God is going to glorify himself. So we'll see restoration... we'll see healing. The end is in sight. At this point... doing physio and getting back on my feet... I feel quite bullish really. We've got through Phase 1 successfully… hmm… I think 'bullish' is a good word to use… I am feeling quite sort of… like, yeah, we are going to beat this thing. It's going to be okay!"

Katie Rose, Tom and Ava visit. Ava's moved on from tugging at Shirley's headscarf to exploring the world on two legs. Her eyes light up at the sight of a whole staircase leading to a wonderland upstairs. I follow up the stairs, ready to catch. Then I spend half an hour teaching her how to come back down. We turn around and slide on our bums. We're so pleased with ourselves, we do it again and again.

While we're so busy, Tom and Katie Rose are able to visit with Shirley. And Katie's eyes fill with tears.

Then Shirls tells Tom, "My love for Jesus is not just lip service; it's real."

CHAPTER THIRTY-FOUR

The Next Round

"I almost had to bust out of hospital, but I finally managed to escape!"
(Millennium Stadium, Cardiff.)

"IT WAS IMPOSSIBLY HARD – *IMPOSSIBLY* HARD – TO GET ON that plane yesterday."

My unpacking done, Brian and I sip our Savannas on our patio in the backyard.

"I thought you so badly wanted to come home?" I hear the disappointment in his voice.

"Of course! We planned this, didn't we? For me to be with Shirley from the beginning of July until a month after her op. Then for me to come home at the end of September and for Loren to take over and care for her for the first two weeks of October. Once Loren was there, I could picture Shirley coming to life and sparkling! And I so wanted Shirls to have a break from having me in her space all the time. Anyway, this is partly for me. I'm desperately tired and badly need a rest – some time to recover a bit, if possible. The two of us did talk through all the details, her walking was improving every day, and she really seemed okay with me coming home. 'I can order groceries from Tesco online, Mum,' she said, 'and I'll be driving soon.' So, on the strength of that, I felt okay too and went ahead. It's just that two weeks ago, Shirls seemed to get weaker and weaker. So, next thing, I'm full of misgivings. Have I made a horrible mistake to leave her? Can she cope?"

"Oh, Thy!"

"Make no mistake – it's been wonderful coming home! The garden's a feast; I love that you've planted flowers everywhere I look. The fridge and the freezer are bursting. You've done so much, and greatest of all are your bear hugs. And it's wonderful to see Nats and Jenny too. You're all very happy I'm back, except for Honey."

"Yeah – I notice!"

"She's still ignoring me completely. This proves… I don't know what." We chuckle cozily together. "Home, sweetie pie, is my space – and it's fantastic to be back in it. But 28 November, when I go back, will come up mega-fast. We do know I have to be there. Even more so because apparently the next round of chemo could bring on depression. And because it's Christmas. But thankfully, you'll join us for that."

"You don't know how glad I am!"

A little, gentle silence – and then Brian changes the subject.

"People have been amazing. I've had so many phone calls, so much prayer, so many invitations to dinner, and so many meals to take home – really totally amazing."

As we sip our drinks, we have so much to talk about.

———————

Thanks to Loren, two whole weeks of tempting meals, good chats and laughs roll by for Shirley. Loren's used her savings to take a turn looking after Shirls. She really gets her eating. She drives them to the George at Henley, to Sonning Lock, and to Sainsbury's when necessary.

Shirley's quite overwhelmed by this whole unselfish visit from her longstanding friend. "I'm feeling so good," she tells me.

Mum gone, the whole army step up a gear. For a start, everyone's fingers get busy on Secret Helpers. Shirley's overwhelmed by them all. And says so.

Apart from asking for the lifts she needs, Shirley feels free to share what's really worrying her.

> *Friday, 18 September, I have a clinic with the prof to decide what to do next – about my lungs; a biggee.*

She couldn't have chemo while her leg was healing. Now the lung tumours have seen the gap and taken it – menacingly.

"It's just the cancer delivering a shot across our bows, while it can," says Prof. Kumar.

"I'm scared," Shirley writes in a very brief text to all. Then a little later, she messages:

> *The tumours in my lungs haven't shrunk, but at least they've stopped growing. Now the doctors want to blast them with two new drugs a.s.a.p.*

Basically, she's in hospital every other week again, starting 30 September, for either four or five days at a time. Now she's getting an annoying cold – and asks for prayer:

> *I'm sure that all of this is under God's control – we will get there. Hope you're all having a brilliant weekend – love the sun today! X*

But two days later, it's a different story.

> *I'm feeling very scared about the new chemo tomorrow. Once again, I'm venturing into the unknown. Please could you pray? X*

In response, waves of love break gently over her:

> *Darling girl, you are in Jesus' hands. The Lord is bigger than all the meds and all the doctors. Jesus is in the room, Honey – right there with you!!! :) Jacqui*

> *Dear Shirls, being scared's okay, you're human, but he is God. This new chemo combo is just the next level of artillery. When David confronted Goliath, he was afraid too. But he conquered his giant – and so will you. You're so covered in prayer – as is the prof and his team. Nick X*

Later Nick types:

> *Hi all – dropped Shirley at the Churchill Hospital this morning (30 September) to kick off this next round of chemo. Please pray. She*

needs a lift home from hospital. Anyone able? I'm now away on hols diving for a few days. Tonia Elliott will be (Mother) Goose while Maverick plays in the water!

Gaynor, as always looking pretty and smiling, lifts Shirley's mood and fires up her own smiles:

Saw Shirley earlier looking glam and in good form as usual. Shirley, you are a blessing to all who visit.

Eileen comments as well:

Picked Shirley up last night, after her three days of chemo. Looked tired – which is to be expected – but, amazingly, walked to the car on her crutches! As always, she just loves it when we visit.

Shirley responds:

A few people keep telling me how well I'm doing. The truth is that I fight a daily battle against negative thoughts – that I won't get better, and that sickness and death is all there is left for me.

I do rebuke them but – each day – they come around again. I feel like a loser. I also feel afraid that even entertaining them is somehow going to prevent my healing and keep me captive.

I'm reaching out to all of you because you pray! But also – maybe – you can help me get beyond this familiar place of struggle, to a place of greater faith and freedom. Love you! X

In response, bigger, more boisterous waves of love and compassion break over her:

You always bounce back!! You little tiger!! :) You are allowed to feel the full range of human emotions :) No matter what colour of the rainbow you choose to sit on, it's always a rainbow, a symbol of hope and God's promises. Jacqui

Hi, lovely. Not surprised you feel like that – but we will hold your arms up in prayer, while you rest as much as possible in God's. Tonia X

Oh my goodness – the last thing you are is a loser! You're a champion! I am praying, lovely Shirley, that you know God's truth and freedom for you. Lean into him, honey – he's your rock and your fortress. Katy Xxxx

Shirley, I love you for your honesty! Actually, we all struggle with these questions – but it's okay. If we didn't, why would we need a Saviour? I'll pop in soon. We'll pray, laugh and cry (and eat chips and chocs). Somehow I have this deep conviction that we will be together on a ski slope again one day soon. Rami

Suddenly, Shirley's in crisis. She sounds the alarm:

Guys, I am in trouble. Something incredibly nasty has happened to my back late afternoon / early evening – and I'm in agony. Have dosed myself up with painkillers, but can't move without shouting (poor neighbours!).

"Mum, I really don't know what to do," she tells me over the phone.

This is my worst nightmare. The whole time I'm away, I dread something like this happening. And now it has. Loren's come home to South Africa, and Shirley's on her own.

I've never had back problems before! Please pray… Am hoping I can drift off to sleep, but seems doubtful at this stage.

Alarm wafts through Secret Helpers, friends, prayer groups – and Brian and me. Then she tells us:

Feeling much better, let's pray it continues! Sorry if I alarmed everyone, but I was pretty alarmed myself. Think my neighbours are going to be looking at me funny for some time to come… X

She waits for the doc to visit.

So grateful – back pain almost completely gone – bar a few twinges. I have a newfound sympathy for people who struggle with bad backs – that was a nasty pain!!

It seems the pain was caused by a build-up of white corpuscles in the marrow, induced by the injections Shirley has to give herself after every chemo.

Shirley reports back on another consultation in Oxford.

Today's X-ray showed that the tumours have all responded to the chemo, and the largest one has completely disappeared! One tumour down, three to go. Whoop!! The prof is pleased, also that I'm keeping so fit and strong. He told me to keep eating – no problem there! X

Nick chips in:

More good news... The echo *echo echo echo* scan today showed no damage to the heart from the chemo... and... this next round of chemo is going to see the elimination of more tumours :)

Shirley's iPad tells her Wales and South Africa play in Cardiff on Friday night, 8 November. She begins to plan to be there.

It's been a long week in hospital. And usually they won't discharge her until certain tests show levels of contamination below cut-off. The levels are not quite what they ought to be. But Shirley pleads, promises – and pleads some more. So they let her go, with loads of meds and strict instructions.

Free at last – gloriously, abundantly free – she bundles her things together and hurries out before they can change their minds! Stuart drives her home, only stopping on the way to feed her – for which she is profoundly grateful.

When they arrive, her housemate Johno is waiting, keys in hand. As a fellow South African, he's just as keen as she is to watch the rugby. He strokes the Beamer to life and purrs them out of Wokingham and down the smooth highway towards Cardiff.

They find Rami ready too and pick her up from her Cardiff home. Shirley tells Rami, "I almost had to bust out of hospital, but I finally managed to escape!"

It's difficult to find parking *at all*, let alone near the Millennium Stadium. Johno and Rami look at each other alarmed. It's a long walk. But, nothing daunted, Shirley sets off – no crutch because she doesn't want people staring.

"Oh, Mum," – she sounds so excited over the phone – "it was fantastic. Take a look at my pics." She sends us the pics as selfies, with texts on her phone. They show her in her wig, blue scarf and warm black jacket – looking pale and in pain but so happy.

Later she admits reluctantly that the walk was almost too much. But she also confesses, "Something profound has happened to me – and going to rugby was the catalyst. I've realised that I've been living like a sick person, in fear of my illness, and subject to all the warnings and dire predictions of the doctors. I'm not having it anymore! I've decided that I'm going to change identity – live like a well person, and pick up the things I love doing, as far as is humanly possible.

I'm not sure how and why this shift has happened, other than a really profound prayer session I had with the wonderful ladies from the Oxford Vineyard prayer ministry team last week. Amazing that

Carol, who leads them, comes from Cape Town! All I know is that I feel restored, new and invigorated. Praise God! "For God did not give us a spirit of fear, but of power, love and a sound mind" (2 Timothy 1:7).[15]

One week later, Shirley's sitting in her car in the hospital car park, after a three-hour wait to see doctors. She's bravely driven herself through for this consultation. How badly she hoped to get some definite answers about future treatment. But the doctors aren't prepared to plan beyond the next few weeks – and the next scan. She's bitterly disappointed.

There is also a spot on her leg. It turns out to be post-operative inflammation, but that doesn't help either.

She phones me. "Hi, Mum," she says.

Oh dear. Past memories crowd in and squeeze my heart. She just cries and cries. As always, I'm drawn into her pain. I turn to putty.

Patiently, I wait. And listen. And wait. Then she drives home, and texts me once she's safe and sound. But I'm a traumatised mess.

I share in my next round robin:

I can hear in Shirley's voice that she's taking strain with these long days in hospital, chained to the drip. We're all taking strain. For a start, going back again is particularly hard. Then, as the days drag on, she feels more and more frantic and confined. Thankfully, she has few side-effects, the worst being an occasional woozy head and tiredness.

I stop writing, sigh and think for a while. Then I continue.

In the last five months, Shirley has been in hospital ten times. The good news is that she is very close to the Lord.

The blessings continue to flow. For one, Brian and I have received the most amazing gift of over thirty thousand rand for air tickets.

It was good to have a number of you – who live close enough to Cape Town – for coffee this Saturday to celebrate God's grace together. Thank you for praying and supporting us all.

---

[15] KJV

How wonderful it would be if the last of the lung tumours were gone by Christmas! What a Christmas present! Please pray.

Smiling and chatting, Katy perches on the edge of Shirley's double bed. She's thankful that, for the moment, there isn't a single cat in sight. That's when Nick pops in too.

Shirley finds it so good to confide in these two. "Do you know what's really tough? At this point, there's no end in sight... And being in hospital every time is getting more and more difficult. I know that I should be glad for the ongoing treatment. But I feel so weary... *downhearted...* that's the word, I guess."

"Oh, honey, I just can't imagine what you're going through," Katy almost whispers.

Nick wanders over to the window, not knowing what to say.

"Today I read Isaiah 53:3-5," Shirley says, "and was reminded that Jesus bore all my suffering and sickness on the cross. So he did that... which comforts me no end. I am so comforted to know that Jesus has gone before me. He walks beside me, having been there, done this, and got the T-shirt for suffering... long before me." Shirley takes first Katy's hand and then Nick's, as he comes close again. "I keep thanking God that I feel so strong in between treatments – and that I thoroughly enjoy my weeks at home."

"I hear you. Talking about 'enjoying', let's go down to the pub for a drink."

The girls don't waste any time to get ready.

Much later Nick reports:

So. The smile radiant, the hairdo a knockout, the legs... Well, the young lads at the next table were checking them out. What more to say? The banter so-o-o Miss Glameron!

While Nick natters on Secret Helpers, Shirley sends a round robin:

Hello, I am so grateful for a very encouraging chat with the docs today. I shared with them that I'm finding the current week-on-week-off regime very hard. They made me feel like a person, not a victim, in all of this. I can do the chemo ahead now with a lighter heart.

And did I mention that Mum arrives from South Africa in less than a week? I can't wait to see her. When Mum left in October, managing without her seemed impossible, but step by step God has taken care of me. How wonderful is that!

CHAPTER THIRTY-FIVE

Christmas

"Shirley's well enough to cook. And she loves it…"

THE TWO MONTHS BACK HOME ARE ALL ABOUT REST, CON-
necting, and recharging my batteries. And constantly supporting Shirley –
long distance, for now. I love being back in my own space. I know Shirls has
enjoyed having hers back too. I know it's been scary for her but feel that, all
in all, it's been a good thing for us both.

For me, packing has become routine. But I do have to make room for
Christmas presents. What do we buy for Shirley? Brian and I find a lovely
long dress. We buy it, taking a step of faith that she'll be able to wear it in
May when the bluebells crowd the fields.

At the flea market in Hout Bay, we find two delightfully curious wooden meercats standing on tiptoe. They appeal immediately, because they remind us of Shirley in the recovery room after the op. And she loves meercats.

This time, it isn't so hard to say goodbye. Brian is joining us in the UK in two weeks, on 13 December, and will stay until after Christmas.

Meantime, Shirley is feeling good. So, really hopeful, she wants to know, "Is anyone around to play this week? Have lots of free time before Mum arrives on Friday…"

December in the UK is a fairytale world. Offset by the darkness and wet, London sparkles with lights. Little trees in the windows and garlands on the doors drive back the grey cold. The days are short and crisp. Christmas is everywhere – and I love it.

In Shirley's hallway, coats, scarves and caps compete for coat hooks. Trainers and boots cluster on the floor below. We hunt for what we need from the pile. Then we savour the fresh, cold air. And our cheeks tingle and glow.

In the gentle gloom, little lights – Christmas garb – twinkle in the windows. We shop for a new Christmas tree. We can't find an angel, but we capture a delicate golden star. Last year, Shirley was so cross with God and threw her tree out. Now she loves him, nestles close and can't get enough of him.

Shirley shops online for presents. Every now and then she calls out, "Oh, Mum, look at this. Whisky glasses will be great for Nick, don't you think?"

As a present to herself – why not? – she buys some beautiful tops, full of character, from FatFace.

I delight in Shirley's delight. I try to save and store up every precious moment. I'm living with the hope that there will be many more Christmases. But at the same time, I'm trying to savour and treasure every single memory I can.

What adds to my pleasure is giving the little presents I have brought with me. And I cherish Shirley's pleasure, nearly every day, when the 'postie' arrives with a newly bought online parcel. Her lifetime of 'parcel-pleasure', developed from babyhood, surfaces powerfully. I'm also programmed like that, and feel my excitement stir too as she rips the paper off.

From her many floppy bags, Shirley unearths "Shirley's Creative Creations", as Gaynor calls them – little gifts, stitched or knitted in hospital. She feels a special pride in them as she wraps them. On Christmas Day, I discover that I'm to have the tapestry with poppies.

She composes messages with real Shirley-care for the special people in her life. I put her parcels under her tree, as she directs. And she takes a couple of pics.

On 1 December, a wet, rainy night, I drive Shirley to Holy Trinity Brompton in London. Very quickly, we forget the nightmare of finding parking because the message is "fabulous", in Shirley's words. Full of God's presence, we drive home, talking excitedly all the way.

That night, in her treasured diary, she summarises:

> *"When moving mountains by faith, don't focus on the size of your mountain, but focus on the size of the Mountain Mover." Fabulous sermon at HTB[16] tonight. I went up for prayer as the pastor felt that someone had a pain/problem in their chest. Let's move some mountains...*

She also texts about what lies ahead:

> *Off to hospital tomorrow for another week – potentially the third last treatment in this cycle. Can I ask for prayers...? Also, for the decisions that need to be made in January, when the chemo ends. If I'm not clear by then, of course! Still believing in my miracle.*

A few days later, Shirley's communicating again:

> *Hello, a reminder that you're invited to Christmassy eats and drinks, at my place, on Wednesday, 11 December, from 7.30 p.m. This is just a small way of saying an incredibly huge thank you for all your love and support. Hope you can make it!*

So that night, in the soft lights from Shirley's tree, we tuck in to wine, cheese and biscuits.

Next day, Shirley attends her office party at a hotel near Heathrow, and the following morning fetches her dad from the airport. She has always loved driving, and by now, thanks to all her hard work with the physio, her leg is bending a full ninety degrees. She takes a back way home. Brian is so specially delighted that she's been the one to fetch him.

Once home, he's quick to unpack. But on his way downstairs, he stops in his tracks. Shirley's swept her wig off her head and hung it over the end of the stair railing. This completely unhinges him. Harsh, cruel reality

---

[16] Holy Trinity Brompton church in London

bludgeons his heart. Now, for the first time, much that he's known in theory becomes reality. He's stepped much more deeply into our most awful reality, almost at the same time he stepped off the plane.

————————————

Brian hardly has time to catch his breath before the next trip to Oxford. While we drive through on Monday morning, 16 December, Shirley writes a round robin.

> *Today there are just nine days to Christmas. My family is here – Dad arrived on Friday, so we'll be having Christmas together!*
>
> *Please could you pray that I bounce back well from the last chemo in hospital? And that the cancer doesn't flare up, after the chemo stops?*
>
> *I've been quite up and down emotionally, so I really see God's mercy in the treatment break coming up. Right now, I'm weary and impatient.*
>
> *Fear continues to be my battleground but, along with you all, I want to declare that I do have a good future and that God has done, and will continue to do, wonderful things. Watch this space! Loads of love to you all, and a very happy Christmas.*

We park, carry Shirley's belongings into the oncology ward, and watch her settle into a private room once again. I show Brian our favourite pink-and-green Day Room – and we stash our freezer meals in the back of the fridge.

By the time we get back to Shirley, she's hooked up to Fred – for the last time. This is the end of the ten chemo sessions which began on 17 June. It's steadily been getting harder but, amazingly, she has done it all with courage and grace.

What makes this last visit more difficult is the new, strange chemo drug. She just never knows how she'll handle a change like this.

Soon it's time for Brian and me to find our lodgings. In the gathering darkness, the map Shirley bought me pilots us through rain and mist. We have some takeaways, and then knock on the door of Di Wilkinson, a Christian woman we have been put in touch with.

It's fun to help Di hang the charming Christmas balls I've brought her, lovingly knitted for her by her mother, Denny, in Cape Town. And, I have to say, it's wonderful to fall into an amazingly comfortable bed in Di's beautiful home.

Each day, Brian and I sit with Shirls, or Brian sits in the Day Room, each with our iPads. I'm glad that Brian can experience what our trips to Oxford have been like.

One afternoon, we explore Oxford using a hop-on hop-off bus and take blurry photos as we go. The street decorations depict bicycles, which we think are perfect as Oxford has so many of them.

With every previous spell in hospital, Shirley was busy – with crafts, reading, texting and watching movies. This time, she just lies in bed. I see the difference and grow so sad. It means that she's had enough and with every new onslaught from the chemo drugs, her body is losing strength. It really is high time to stop.

After the last three sessions of chemo, the X-rays show that only one tumour of note is now visible. Claire's so excited that when she tracks us down to the pink-and-green Day Room, she wheels in her laptop to show us.

"We're going to cancel your last session, Shirley," the encouraged consultant says. "Actually," Claire smiles, "you've already had all the benefit you can have from your treatment. In your first three or four sessions, the drugs will have taken maximum effect. Now we need to give your body – and mind and spirit – a chance to recover. So, go home and have a lovely Christmas."

Throughout all the hardship of her treatment, Shirley has never complained. I remember that on our last trip in the car without oxygen, we waited for an hour and a half in the parking lot for medicines. Nick was inside trying to do a miracle – and I was in the car beside Shirley, growing increasingly alarmed. I could see she was so sick – feeling so terrible – but she did not utter a single word of complaint.

Now – at last – Shirley can write:

> It's been gruelling, but it's over. Thanks again for your support! Xx
>
> First and foremost, I'm grateful for the healing – but my lungs aren't completely clear yet. One tumour, in particular, on my right lung has not budged – yet! So, please can we ask God for more – more of his goodness, grace and healing?

Like excited children let out of school for the holiday break, we head for home. Now for Christmas! But Shirley needs to recover from the chemo first.

One of the things I manage while she rests is a round robin:

Dear friends, as I sit down to write to you, I am heavy-hearted. Shirley has come away from this last round of chemo very, very wacked.

She crawled into my arms in front of the TV last night. And just stayed there. And then, later, asked me to tuck her into bed, like a little girl.

I know that in a day or two's time, she will be much better. For now, we keep everything scrupulously clean. We feed cats and do the shopping. Twice a day, we feed Margaret, Dorothy, Fred and Derek, the goldfish.

By 23 December, my birthday, Shirley's recovered quite a bit. She makes a yummy chocolate slab cake for me. It's supposed to roll up like a Swiss roll but has other ideas. It's absolutely delicious.

Now that she's up and about again, we all perk up. In the evening, she drives us to a pub she loves for dinner.

Shirley's well enough to cook. And she loves it – especially the new recipes she's found. To see all this makes me glad – for her and in myself. My battered heart gently rejoices.

Not only has Shirley planned the birthday, but she's got Christmas sorted out as well. Apart from the chocolate cake on Monday, she plans to put together a cranberry cheesecake trifle on Tuesday for Christmas dinner. Meanwhile, a duck waits meekly in her freezer.

She has Brian and me shred the red cabbage and peel potatoes. She's always wanted a sprout tree, so we bring a large one home, play with it, take pics, and lop off all the sprouts, also for her Christmas feast.

In between all this, Shirley delivers presents. And we make several trips to Sainsbury's. Outside the front door, Nick and I have built a ramp of bricks, covered by a plank, to make it easier for her. But soon, much of the time she manages without even a crutch. We also visit Homebase for Brian to buy me a Christmas present. To my delight, I come away with two fat little robins with very red breasts. As South Africans, we revel in the beauty of the decorations for sale in the UK – in colour, more red ones than anything else – and glowing and tinkling under a variety of warm lights.

At one point recently, Shirley said that she's lost her courage. I wonder about that. It certainly doesn't look like it to me. In fact, all this activity strikes me as rather amazing and brave.

I feel the need to write and share:

As Brian, Shirley and I celebrate together, in a way made much deeper and more meaningful by the experience of these six months, there's a deep gratitude for the love that we have seen, that is such a Saviour. And it is from this emotional place that we wish you, each one, a lovely Christmas and a preciously blessed new year. Thank you for all you have done for us and are still doing. How much we appreciate you!

Christmas Day begins with no ordinary breakfast. Shirley poaches eggs in rapidly boiling water on the stove. She serves them with salmon and other delightful trimmings.

The thankfulness that Brian and I share for a Christmas like this remains uppermost in our minds. It's like a soft blanket over us – warm and precious. There's a quiet joy in everything we do. It goes with us to the morning service in Greyfriars. Shirley and I sing together – just one more time.

Then there are Shirley's friends to meet and hug. And there's mulled wine, warm and fruity, smelling mostly of cinnamon, served with delicious mince pies.

For church, Shirley has put on her wig – a relief for Brian and me, exposed and vulnerable as we are to her bald head at home. Back home, she hangs the wig up on the stairs again and rolls up her sleeves to tackle dinner.

She sets Brian and me to work. In time, red cabbage, baked potatoes, Brussel sprouts and roast duck make our mouths water. These days, Shirley says she can't stop eating. So it's pure joy for her, as well as us, to tuck in. Cranberry cheesecake trifle appears next – made after several trips to find the cranberries. We talk, laugh a bit, text those we want to bless, watch TV and chill.

This is the best Christmas that Brian and I can remember in recent years. I feel as if I want to stop time somehow and live in the now forever. We feel the familiar peace that has come to stay. We are quiet, and together, and even happy, for now.

CHAPTER THIRTY-SIX

Future Plans

*"Gaynor invites us to visit
and do the bridges walk near her home in Reading."*

"HELLO, ALL YOU WONDERFUL PEOPLE," SHIRLEY CHIRPS IN her text of 2 January, "and a very happy New Year! The dark hospital days are over, but I still have a journey ahead of me. I feel that every day I have a choice: to live in fear and defeat, or to follow my dreams and live victoriously. Some days are much easier than others. Thankfully, God is always good – and doesn't hold the times I collapse in a heap against me! Loving you all, hoping you're all going to have a victorious 2014 too!"

Eight days earlier, on Boxing Day, Gaynor invited us to visit and do the bridges walk near her home in Reading.

"Oh, Mum," Shirley said, "I don't know if I can."

―――――――――――

Some in the group step it out, the children skipping, laughing and playing ahead. With true grit – and without crutches – trussed up in her royal-blue scarf, Shirley crosses bridge after bridge, biting back tears at times. But after she has successfully toughed it out, she feels quite chipper, and better prepared to face 2014 with some confidence.

Faithful as always to share her journey, Shirley writes:

> *The docs have said that once on oral chemo, I will be able to have a pretty normal life. All going well, I might even be able to go back to work. So that sounded... pretty cool.*

She chuckles.

> *Not the going back to work bit, but the just-having-a-normal-life part!*

> *It's a huge change... I can start going back to gym, my hair will start to grow... and I can go on holiday!*

> *The only thing I'm experiencing is tiredness and lack of energy.*

> *Mum is here until the end of January, so – at the moment – I plan to recover, relax and enjoy having her here, before tackling anything new.*

> *I do need to decide what to do about work. My company has been very supportive and given me all this time off from the time the chemo started. I want to do right by them, but my heart isn't in the job any more.*

> *I would love to get a job working for a Christian charity or organisation and/or using my counselling skills.*

She chokes up as she continues writing.

> *I haven't lived my life the way I ideally wanted to. So – now – I'm just so, so longing for the opportunity to do life again – and do it right, and do it for God.*

Tears now trickle.

> *Please – could you pray that God leads me into the right thing, and gives me much wisdom as I make decisions about the future?*

A few days later, Shirley texts:

> *I'm considering a trip to the healing rooms at Bethel in Redding, California for a week or so in Feb. Am wondering if any of you are free and would like to join me?*

Tonia asks when it would be and how much it would cost.

At her next consultation, Shirley reminds Claire, "I did ask you, 'What do they say, can I fly?'"

"Well, actually, the respiratory clinic says yes." Claire flicks her long, straight brown hair back from her face.

"I want to fly to South Africa and California."

"But what about insurance?" Claire asks.

"Oh, I just won't take any out," Shirley replies, completely disarming Claire with an impish grin.

Claire laughs, and then says, with a catch in her voice, "We will get you home to South Africa, I promise."

Shirley walks thoughtfully down Sandy Lane to a bench in the park – a good place to sit and think. *Here it is again... fear. For so many years now, this has been my struggle.*

In the weak wintry sun, two children play on the swings.

What does the future hold? In a way, the hospital routine was safe... the days ahead all predetermined and prescribed for me. That part of the journey seems to be over... at least, for now. What I do know for sure is that I don't want to waste a day of the life left to me. I want to use each day to serve God... Then I can't go back to my job. And I must find a Christian organisation that needs the love I have for Jesus... and where I can use the set of skills I have for him. I don't even know where to begin to look. Oh, why does everything have to be so complicated?

It doesn't take Shirley long to put together a list – a long one – for the immediate future. In addition to the February two-week worship conference in California, there's the Holy Trinity Brompton conference, and her precious friend Laura who works for Mercy Ministries has invited her to their conference in Bradford. Shirley wants to enrol with London University to further her studies in counselling. And start singing lessons again. And go back to leading a worship team at Greyfriars. She goes to see Dan about helping in the office at Greyfriars with her IT skills.

Shirley texts her Secret Helpers:

As you pray for mine, I'd love to pray for your mad, outrageous requests too! Just Messenger me and I'm on the case!

Chris comes up with a suggestion:

Why not join Still the Hunger, a newly established Greyfriars initiative in Reading?

"Oh, Mum, how wonderful – this is exactly what I want!"

She starts attending meetings straight away – but can't keep it up regularly because of the days when her strength fails.

"Hey, Nick," Shirley calls, as she bangs on the door of his cottage in Shiplake. "Here I am… at your service. Normally I'd ask for a glass of wine first, but not these days. I'm being so very good, you know. Not like someone else… How did you get to be lifted off a mountain top in a helicopter?"

Nick laughs. "Well… you know how it is… people like me…"

"People like you don't need to frighten the rest of us to death! But jokes aside, what happened?"

"I don't know, really. There we were, walking along a trail, and I suddenly felt very strange, slid to the ground and passed out. My friends couldn't bring me round so they phoned for help."

"Dramatic, I must say. What do the doctors say?"

"After lots of scans and things – you know about those – they just don't know. What they do know is that they don't want me to drive for six months…"

"Which is why I'm here: to drive you to Tesco. Otherwise we'll have to add starvation to your list of complaints!"

A couple of hours later, Shirley wrestles her reluctant front door open. She finds me in the kitchen. I can see distress on her face.

"Oh, Mum," she says, "Nick's challenged me to consider that… perhaps… God is not going to heal me. I wasn't ready for this. Not now."

The meltdown that follows is huge. I just stay with her through it, sad and aching, reaching out gingerly to her.

I cry out to God. I've come to know him as the only real comforter. Is this, in the end, what he wants Shirley to come to accept? Is it? Really?

In her diary Shirley compares every new blow to the echoing thunk of a shoe dropping to the ground.

In Oxford, Claire talks about possible options for the future. Right now, they want to give Shirley's body the chance to recover. One of the problems is anaemia. Another is a persistent tiredness that does not leave bones, flesh and soul untested.

The doctors encourage a good diet and plenty of rest. A couple from Greyfriars invite Shirley to come and stay with them. The idea is "no more chemo" and doing with her the diet they strongly recommend. This means everything raw, vegetable juices and no animal products.

She is really very touched by their kindness but decides instead to do her version of the diet at home herself, with my help. So, with the wry comment, "Luckily I like vegetables," she sets me the task of reading the two books they have lent us.

While Brian is with us, he helps with the juices, which form a major part of the diet. But it is Christmas! So we also eat mince pies and chocolate, and other 'delectables' from Tesco and Sainsbury's that we aren't able to ignore.

After Christmas, the diet begins in earnest. Brian, back in South Africa from 4 January, teases, "Phew! I managed to escape just in time."

I laugh, but actually I enjoy raw cauliflower and carrots, raw spinach salad and other recipes I find in the book. Every day, I prepare a smorgasbord of raw, healthy dishes for our lunch. I can always count on raw green beans to go down; Shirley loves those.

Brian plants beans in his summer garden. He knows how Shirley loves to pick and eat them – fresh and crispy. He hopes they'll be ready for when she visits us in March. *She never does.*

For Shirley, a big part of it all is to choke down huge quantities of powdered barley. She also snacks on apricot kernels from the fridge.

With the help of all the physio, she now walks without a limp. Most of the time, she does the driving. At Dinton Pastures, we walk right round the lake – Shirley with only one crutch. It's a day when the water captures so many lovely reflections: clouds and swans and overhanging trees. Each time we meet and compliment a gorgeous bundle of canine fluff, we collect appreciative smiles from its owner.

On another day, Shirley packs her swimming gear. At the gym, I settle down to read my e-book. Quite a while later, she comes back smiling. "I swam twenty-two lengths," she tells me, eyes glowing with triumph. "I had absolutely no problems – other than being unfit!"

As Shirley drives us to Oxford for another consultation, we chat about these check-ups.

"So many times, Mum, the news we get has been worse than it was the time before," Shirley says. "Now I'm beginning to dread these trips big time. Is that what's going to happen this time too?"

I know what she means – and feel it too.

After a long wait, and several plastic cups of cold water from the dispenser, Vicky ushers us in to see Claire.

Claire and Shirley make, and hold, eye contact.

"I'm so sorry, Shirley. The X-rays we got so excited about have been misleading. The scans, which are always more accurate, show that the tumours in your lungs have grown since November. There are two in particular that are *really* growing."

The colour drains from our faces. In November, the lung tumours had shrunk so much that the doctors were exploring the possibility of another drug, exorbitantly expensive at one hundred and twenty thousand pounds per session, given only to osteosarcoma patients whose lungs are clear. And now this?

Is it now, in terms of Crabb's analogy for life's tragic journey, that the other shoe drops?[17] Or have we not yet reached that point?

"We are discussing the options with the respiratory clinic." Claire's voice is soft. "These include two different types of radiotherapy, surgery and oral chemo. The trouble with the chemo pills, for as long as they are effective, is the possible side-effects. I have to say, these are really bad. They include very high blood pressure, nausea, stroke and damage to your heart. And your lungs could perforate, which will be fatal."

When Shirley drives us home, it's raining heavily. The windscreen wipers slosh the rain to and fro – like the profound misery we feel. Tears flood our eyes, blurring our vision more and turning the whole world coldly grey. We're cold and devastated, with a cold beyond what mere air-conditioning can address. We're so cold and we just let the tears flow. We are too deeply upset to talk – far too shattered right now.

At home, Shirley bundles up the stairs. She just drops everything and gets into bed. That's where she stays for the next two days. She doesn't eat, just drinks a little. When she can, after an agony of pain, she messages disconsolately:

Been a rubbish day. News from the doctors today wasn't great, plus I dropped and broke my phone!!

---

[17] *The Pressure's Off,* Waterbrook Press (Colorado Springs, 2002)

While all the focus has been on the operation on my leg, the tumours in my lungs, for want of a better word, have had a bit of a party and have developed quite a lot. We are pretty devastated, Mum and I.

I'll only hear next week what the docs recommend in terms of treatment, but most likely it will be pills (with side-effects).

I'm angry, sad, frustrated with the news, but am reminded that God gives us what we need when we need it, not when we think we need it ... my time for healing is not yet here.

So sad, though, that this horrible situation is causing so much pain to me and the people I love! Sucks.

Still very honest, she sends another message:

Very hard day today (18 January). Am heartbroken over yesterday's disappointing news. Today I'm not able to have hope. I'd really appreciate your prayers.

Jo responds:

We are standing with you, holding up your hands!!!!

To which Shirley replies:

Thank you. I feel that God is asking whether I'll still love and trust him even if I'm not healed... Very tough X

She sobs for a while and then reads another reply from Jo.

Very tough. But keep choosing him!!! He's always faithful, even when we don't know how or why... He always has been – and always will be!!!

All weekend long, I watch and wait. While an optometrist covers our eyes with lens after lens to improve our vision, lens after lens now falls across mine to deepen and deepen the grey.

I text Chris:

Today has been a nightmare. S heartbroken and without hope.

And Lynn:

S's agony heartbreaking. I am deeply distressed as well.

And Nats:

How grateful I am when you and others stand in the gap as I am so weak.

Lynn responds:

Thinking of how your mother heart is being wrenched.

God shows me a new thing – that I have come into a different partnership with him. I'm now also enrolled with him in his fellowship of sufferers. Now I qualify for that. For now, my way is plodding and heavy. I'm forging a way up his high mountain – such an arduous journey – and I am so weak. All he wants of me is to take the next step, clinging to his hand for strength and direction.

Disconsolately, I share my heart in a round robin:

We have talked a bit – very honestly – about the future. Shirley's finding it so hard to pick herself up – again.

She believes it's up to her to pick everyone else up too. She needs to put a brave face on it all so that they will too. But she's feeling so wiped out she's not sure she can.

We struggle so to still have hope. We have so many wonderful Scriptures, but need them to be effective right now in our hearts. I am asking God desperately for his power and grace and infilling as I have nothing of myself to give.

And Brian needs comfort, so far away. We really need a miracle from God, the sooner the better.

Shirley is so upset that her bad prognosis is causing others so much pain. She believes she is going to die – and would like to die now and get it all over with. She's worried about what will become of Wilf and Shelley-cat. (I remind her that Stuart has promised he will have them back – anytime.) She is worried her hair won't grow again and dreams about that. It isn't growing as fast as it did last time. God feels so far away. She has called out to him all day. Why doesn't he answer?

I feel at a complete loss, have no answers, am completely bankrupt. I keep crying out to God to use me somehow to help her. I pray through many of the long hours, in awe of God. To me, it seems he wants Shirley to surrender to him so completely that she will accept anything from his hand – even death. If so, then the question from God is, "Do you, my beloved Shirley, love and trust me enough for such a thing too?" It reminds me of

Abraham coming to the point of sacrificing his treasure. It is then that God stays his hand. Is Shirley to surrender all she holds dear – her treasure – completely?

I remember the meltdown just a few days ago, after what Nick asked: is God actually gradually helping her to face what, until now, has been totally unacceptable? Surely, if that is so, coming to that point is a huge spiritual leap – and takes a long, long time of the tenderest nurturing?

All weekend long, the struggle goes on. At first, Shirley just can't get out of bed. She's so very tired and has been battling for so incredibly long now to see the point of it all.

She texts:

Oh, Katy, I'm in such a rough place. I can't really find the energy to start fighting again – to pick myself up and be positive, and get going again.

Then, after several hours:

I don't understand why this setback has happened, or why any of this has happened, or why any specific thing has happened. Hmm... but it's really beginning to dawn on me... God actually loves me.

A few days later, a round robin follows the texts:

Mum and I have been hard hit by the news... shocked and disappointed, and finding it hard to focus. This weekend I visited some very dark places. I felt tested to the limit. The oral chemo that is probably next is weaker than the drugs I've been having so far, so it remains to be seen whether it will be able to keep the cancer in check.

Please could you pray that, although the doctors don't hold out much hope, we are able to have hope in God. Also pray for protection over me to prevent me from dwelling in very dark places. And pray for relief. I'm so very tired of the pain and uncertainty and long to know more of God's peace.

Texts arrive from all over thanks to so many very fast fingers. An army of friends empathises, encourages and prays.

When Sunday comes, and I crawl into bed behind her and just hold her, she says, "So... if God is not going to heal me... I'm okay with that, Mum."

Waiting to hear what the doctors are going to do is extremely hard. Shirley writes:

> *I thought the oral chemo tablet option was cut and dried. But when my case was discussed again, they decided more info was needed from the lung specialists. So they took my scans to analyse them again.*
>
> *I have a feeling they are considering surgery – two very big operations, first one lung, and then the other a month later. Please, could you pray for tomorrow's meeting – that God gives the team much wisdom as they decide on the best way forward. Thank you!! X*

CHAPTER THIRTY-SEVEN

God's Preparation

"Stow-on-the-Wold"
(Photograph taken on the common.)

IT TAKES TIME, BUT GOD PULLS SHIRLEY TO HER FEET AGAIN. And she makes sure holidays happen. One weekend, she drives us to Cardiff to stay with Rami. That night, we set out to attend a well-known healing meeting at Victory Church, Cwmbran. Rami tries to untangle a spaghetti-mix of wet highways and byways, but we just can't find the church. The disappointment sinks down over me. *Perhaps, if we found it, God would have healed her?* It's dark as we drive. I don't have a clue where we are. It's raining and I'm miserable. But I comfort myself that God knows what he's doing.

Once home again, the girls talk deep into the night, without sleepy me.

The next day, Rami takes us to explore the Millennium Centre and then we walk right round Cardiff Bay. It's a good five kilometres, but the distance doesn't seem to trouble Shirley. Once again, I am amazed by her sheer guts. She focuses on Rami's struggles to find work and pain over a boyfriend called Peter, and not on herself.

The next weekend, Shirley drives us to Donnington, near Stow-on-the-Wold in the Cotswolds, where she's booked a cottage for the weekend. I can see she's enjoying the driving and I'm glad. Just about the only thing that makes me glad these days is when I see something bringing Shirls pleasure.

When we get there, a feisty cock with flame-coloured plumes struts across, surrounded by several hens, clucking round him in admiration. They watch as we bump open the door of Woodbine Cottage – truly quaint, with sloping ceilings and a smoky fireplace.

I notice the title of a book on the aged bookshelf – *Not Without My Daughter* – and I'm destroyed.

We buy food and firewood and settle in to wait for Rami to join us. Shirley lights the fire and enjoys stoking it and watching it glow and flame. I watch her, glad again of anything that brings her pleasure – fleeting though it may be.

Over the next few days, we tramp footpath after footpath through the farm meadows past staring sheep. We plod up gentle spring-green rises, and along to the imposing old Manor House. Their potato and leek soup is the best it can be.

One time, I slip and slither down a muddy slope, try to get up, and slither some more. We go back to the cottage – me oozing chocolate mud from my jeans. I want them to go on without me but – no – after I change, we hunt up a warm little coffee shop in Stow-on-the-Wold with a friendly fire in the grate. Then we explore the shops.

Shirley sees me eyeing pillar-box-red Snoozies[18]. "Would you like some?" she asks and smiles warmly.

Would I? Of course!

---

[18] slippers

Next, we poke around in the Information Centre, Shirley looking at possible future walks. There we discover a Cricket Museum, of all things.

One night, Shirley and I drive to a meeting at Holy Trinity Brompton to hear a German evangelist speak on miracles and healing. When he prays for Shirley, she slips gently to the floor under the power of the Holy Spirit. And my heart is so full.

Later, Shirley goes over to ask him why some get healed and some don't. He's absolutely honest and says he doesn't know.

"Mum," she says when she gets back to me, "he just looked at me and his eyes filled with tears."

We drive home bubbling from our encounter with God. It's raining again but we don't notice. What I do notice is that Shirley's eyes are shining.

"Oh, Mum," she says. "Something's happened, for sure!"

Before bed, Shirley texts the Secret Helpers:

> *Been encouraged by a great talk on healing at HTB – wanted to share, as I think we've all been a bit discouraged recently. I've been reminded to go back to God's Word. In the Bible, it's clear that God is a healer and that he loves to heal. So, unless he shows me something different, I'm going to believe that this is what he wants for me.*
>
> *I don't know why many people aren't healed. All I can do is exercise simple faith and fix my eyes on God who is good, loving and powerful. Nothing is impossible for God! Let's keep believing for a miracle. Xx*

I send my own round robin:

> *Please pray about our exhaustion. And when we are sad and overcome.*
>
> *Brian and I thank God for so much abundant grace – time and time again. That's not a cliché – we really feel it washing over us.*
>
> *Thank you, Lord, for the army of believers you have raised up around S. When the need arises, there it is – incredible support – again and again and again.*
>
> *Pray that neither Shirley, Brian, nor any of us misses what God wants to give us, through it all.*

Shirley wrote this recently, in one of her round robins. I think it's so wonderful that I share it here with all of you: "May God help us – each one – to choose to focus upon a loveliness that can uplift us. That loveliness is the allure of his character and being, the sweetness of his dealings with us, and the permanence of our consequent state of blessedness."

Wow! I remember Chris's butterfly picture. Shirley's doing quite some flying, even now.

I pack up once again. After Christmas, I stayed on because the doctors warned us about depression after all the chemo. Instead, Shirley has had a month of being really well and pretty much on top of things again.

But now, when I'm about to go, I notice she's beginning to battle more and more to get up in the mornings. So I text Nick my concern. He comforts and encourages me. So I text again:

So much encouragement for a battered Thy! Thank you so much. Please, if possible, can S have company Wednesday p.m. – after she gets back from dropping me at the airport?

The day before I leave, Shirley suffers an enormous meltdown. She's very distressed all over again by the possibility that she's not going to be healed. So how can I possibly go tomorrow? But that night, at another Holy Trinity Brompton evening meeting, both Shirls and I are deeply blessed. And she slides to the floor as the Spirit of God ministers to her.

Every time God shows his hand is on her, I'm so comforted. To me, nothing is as important as that. It shows me again that she's safe, thanks to Abba Father. What relief! And my heart becomes a great deal easier.

Nevertheless, I am pulled this way and that – not gently – about going. Do I stay, or still fly on Wednesday?

Shirley improves enough to drive me to Heathrow. I'm somewhat comforted by her recovery, but the main encouragement to me is that God has touched her. Otherwise, as I tell Chris, my feelings are numb.

I fasten my seatbelt, smile at the lady who settles in next to me, and stare out into the night. A smooth take-off and we settle in for the flight. Soon I'm lost in thought. Heart and mind range over a whole lot of things. Shirley has such plans for the future. Only last night she talked about that.

"Mum," she said, "there are things I want so badly. I want a husband and a family... I want a job I really love where I can serve God... You know, there was a time when I gave up believing that God would give me the desires of my heart. The disappointment that always followed just hurt too much."

"Oh, Shirley," I said, "you have come a long way with God since then. Why not give him all your desires now – and all your future plans? He plans to prosper you, not to harm you. Let him grant them, or change them, or give you even better ones. He will make them perfect, in line with his will – different, perhaps, but always full of more blessing for you than you can imagine."

Three days after I get back to South Africa on 29 January, Shirley drives to Bradford for a weekend with Laura. It's cold despite the sunshine. Sheep dot the landscape while stone walls bisect it. She loves the Yorkshire Downs – drinks in the beauty all around her.

Her heart goes out to the ministry in Oxenhope in which Laura is involved. Mercy Ministries brings healing to young women, battered and bruised in all sorts of ways by life. Shirley would love to work there! Months ago, she showed me a pic of one of their artworks. This one was of Jesus carrying a limp, injured and devastated young woman. I think I know why it meant so much to her.

God uses Laura a great deal to bring Shirley comfort, encouragement and hope. They talk and talk. And Shirley ministers to Laura too. Then they go to Life Church, where Laura worships. God's presence is very real – they feel it and it thrills them as nothing else can. Many come to pray for Shirley. And she laughs and laughs.

It's always been one of my dearest wishes to see Shirley touched by the Holy Spirit. I once again remember that I asked, "Whatever it takes, Lord." Part of what I meant was, "Make her yours, Lord, totally and completely." Now I'm seeing that. God has let me see her blessed at HTB – and now this! How clumsy my human efforts to help her always were. How perfectly Abba Father has done, and is doing, this!

Shirley can't wait to update her Secret Helpers:

Been a wonderful week and I've been so blessed – I'd like to share with you!

I was so down a couple of weeks ago, but Katy prayed with me for joy... although it seemed impossible and unreachable at the time. When I was prayed for on Tuesday night at HTB – 28 January –

something happened, and now I can testify that it really is possible to have joy in suffering.

So, for the first time, the dark clouds and the heaviness I've been living with for so long are gone! I have complete faith that I will be okay, that God is on top of things and is working it out... and that I have a wonderful, amazing future.

I've had a new revelation of how loving, trustworthy and altogether wonderful God is, and my heart is singing.

Now – a few days later – I'm blessed right out of my socks all over again!

Had a wonderful prayer time today at Life Church in Bradford, and I just laughed and laughed. Celebrate with me... God is amazing!

Shirley sends me a warm little text:

Hello. Have had a lovely, blessed time. Looking forward to telling you all about it. Love you.

I reply:

Reaching out to you with a heart full of love. So, so glad you are so blessed! I think your miracle could be happening!

How he is loving you! Mum.

––––––

Shirley turns again to the close friend that is her diary:

"The longer you struggle with adverse circumstances, the darker the way before you appears, and the harder it is to imagine yourself walking along bright paths again" (Sarah Young, Jesus Today[19]).

I've realised that God really is bigger (greater, stronger, higher, healer, awesome power) than any circumstances. The victory he won on the cross was incredible – it covers all our earthly troubles, sin and disease – and we are free.

––––––

[19] Thomas Nelson (Nashville, Tennessee: 2012)

CHAPTER THIRTY-EIGHT

Losses and Gains

"Chloe-cat is a real nuisance as she likes to sit on me."

"SORRY TO HAVE MISSED YOUR CALL. WAS TRYING OUT MY new electric blanket and ended up having a long nap." Shirley smiles as she finishes the text.

Back in South Africa, I smile too.

She is due to go for a consultation tomorrow, 7 February, to discuss further treatment. The doctors have discussed her case at numerous meetings. Their focus is the immediate problem first, the two growing tumours.

For all of us, this is the 'biggie'.

Am okay about tomorrow. Will obviously be in touch as soon as I know anything. Could you also pray – have a weird pain in my back causing me a bit of grief.

It's really late in South Africa when Shirley phones. "Mum, the pain in my back is over the top. I am too scared to move – no, I can't move, it's too sore. What must I do?"

Tears trickle down my face.

She considers calling an ambulance, or her doctor, or toughing it out by staying quietly in bed. She knows she has some painkillers on the table beside her. There's no panic, just incredible courage. She decides on the painkillers.

How brave, how in control, how wise, I think, as I put down the phone. Nobody sleeps much that night.

Very sadly, but not unexpectedly, Shirley can't make it out of bed the next morning. She phones the doctor. He thinks it's a muscle spasm and prescribes drugs. Tonia kindly fetches them. Meanwhile Shirley brings everyone up to speed:

So I wasn't able to keep my appointment with the docs today... my back started hurting on Wednesday night. By last night it was total agony. Have spoken to my GP and he thinks it's a spasm – has prescribed muscle relaxants. Hopefully this will do the trick. So glad to have Tonia Elliott here looking after me.

I've asked Oxford to phone me on Monday to discuss my treatment. X

As the hours slip by, Shirley and I chatter – as much as our thumbs allow.

Shirley: Hello. Good day. Am warm and cozy – listening to music and reading. Managed to drive. Pain is much less, though I am still moving cautiously. How about you?

Me: Glad things improving. Lovely summer day here – starting with breakfast with friends.

Shirley: Getting there. Back complaints are no joke. Definitely improving though.

Me: My lentils are sprouting. Thought you'd love to know – Dad and I are on the diet you and I are trying. Praying that God keeps your heart and mind. Rebuking the tumours.

Shirley: Am planning to go to Greyfriars tomorrow evening – back permitting. Sun is shining at the moment, but will be blustery and stormy later.

Me: You are wonderful!

Oxford phones and Shirley sends the promised text.

Hello lovely peeps, really need to call on your help again as I'm more convinced than ever that we're in a battle.

We didn't get around to talking about long-term treatment options. It turns out that the back pain is pleurisy – fluid on the lung – caused by one of the tumours. I'm going to have to get the lung drained next Monday. Should be a simple outpatient procedure.

Once that has healed up, the doctors will decide what to do with me next! Please pray... the thief is seeking to rob and destroy, but in God we have abundant life!!

To me she writes:

Hello, love. Feeling cheerful. Procedure on Monday takes a few hours. When that heals, we'll look at treatment options again.

I reply:

Aw, what a struggle! Wish I was there! Wonderful to know Jesus has such tender, loving arms about you holding you in perfect love. Thinking of you all the time, darling girl. Praying, praying, praying... Lots of love, Mum.

Nick sums up:

Think not a problem to God, think God into the problem. Think not size of issue to God, think size of God compared to issue!

The next text we get from Shirley is grim. It's Friday again and she writes:

Hurts. Really hard to move or breathe. Lots of pain... Good job God sent an angel – Tonia Elliott – to take me to hospital right now! Please pray they can do the procedure today rather than wait till Monday.

It's raining and bitterly cold. And Oxfordshire is flooding.

Much later, Tonia writes:

Just to let you know they have prescribed pain relief for Shirley and will do the op on Monday. Please do keep praying.

Shirley writes:

Will be staying at Tonia's tonight and Sunday. She wants to keep an eye on me.

Nick reaches out to Brian and me, consoling us that Shirley's "being well loved and cared for by many". *Thank God.* Also, that they have given her morphine.

Since her pain has eased, Shirley's in a better place – for now.

I text:

Good that, when we can't pray, the Holy Spirit is always there interceding. Feeling huge pain – your pain. Hope you are experiencing God – feeling him holding you close. Praying with everything I've got. Just loving on you hugely, Mum.

I cry out to those who walk with me: to Sasja, that they start the procedure immediately; to Claudia, that Shirley will improve as she's so sick; and to many others.

For some time, Tonia and Dave have been house-sitting for friends. It's a modernised old mansion with a much-cherished garden. Catharine's hobbling about after a knee op, so Tonia takes her in. Next, she takes in Shirley – no arguments! And the house transforms into "Tonia's hospital".

One morning there's a knock at the door. Shirley opens and gapes. Chris is standing there wearing a neck brace. Her left arm is in a sling.

"Oh, Chris," Shirley gasps, and carefully helps her in. "What's happened to you?"

Catharine can't believe her eyes either. Nor can Tonia.

In the lounge, they carefully manoeuvre Chris into a comfortable chair. Then they sit on the edge of their seats, waiting to hear. Chris coolly removes the brace and the bandage and stuffs them in a plastic packet. Then she settles back, none the worse for wear. Everyone stares. Realisation dawns. And everyone packs up laughing.

"Well," says Chris defensively, "this is a hospital, isn't it? So I thought I needed to fit in!"

Later, knowing how I must be feeling, Chris emails:

I called in, and had a lovely time with them. It was a wonderful time of laughter – nothing heavy – it felt like being at college together, all girls together having fun. I feel fifty years younger! It seemed to me a very healthy environment for Shirls to be in – so wanted to write and let you know, and put your mind at rest, that she's being so well looked after.

But Monday, 17 February, brings more devastation. Claire says the enlarging tumours are causing the excruciating pain and discomfort. In their advance, they have collapsed part of Shirley's lower right lung. And they are compromising her breathing. Her liver has moved up into the thoracic cavity, adding to her suffering. Now largely unchecked, the cancer's gone rogue. It's ransacking with abandon.

I text Chris:

Really sad – but not unexpected. We are, nevertheless, so shaken. May God gently comfort us all. So glad of your prayers.

On her way back home from hospital, Shirley peers disconsolately through the rain-streaked window at the soaked fields around Oxford. Everything is cold and wet and dark. *Now what?* she asks herself, her peace shredded. *I have a collapsed lung – a collapsed lung?* She remembers the email from Still the Hunger, where she's been working once a week. They feel she's too ill to continue for now but want her back as soon as she's better. She's still grieving the loss – feeling such disappointment. But she knows they are right. The usual, endless streams of trucks labour past, but she doesn't notice. Can't notice. Her real focus, apart from the letter, is the fact that she couldn't have the procedure as planned. Bravely, she writes:

Ball now back with the oncologist, Claire, to determine next steps. Frustrating!! Xx

How do you respond to such a situation? Comfort your child? Have something to say? I'm so disappointed too. I guess, feebly, at how disappointed Shirley must be. I tell her that it's wonderful to know Jesus has such loving arms about her, holding her in perfect love; that I'm thinking all the time about my darling girl; that the Lord knows the way through the wilderness – even a wilderness such as this one; that I'm praying big time.

<u>Me</u>: *Thank you Jesus – you are right there with Shirls. Phone if and when you can. Love and hugs. Mum.*

<u>Shirley</u>: *Love you too.*

How incredibly precious, every time I hear from her and hear *that* from her.

Since the chemo finished in December, Shirley's been getting more and more anxious to hear what the doctors plan to do next. The sudden collapse of her lung puts all this on hold. Now she picks up again on the question of future treatment as she feels her future sway in the wind. She writes to Vicky, her gentle Macmillan nurse, on 18 February:

> *Yesterday was a bit of a curveball for me. As a result, I have a number of questions that really need to be cleared up as soon as possible.*
>
> *Firstly, how serious is my condition? (Collapsed lung, tumours causing pain, spots of fluid?) Is it safe for me to be at home? How is this condition treated?*
>
> *Secondly, I am now desperate to know what the next step is. I know this has been the subject of many debates since I had my PET scan on 10 January. However, the delay has been concerning me greatly, given how quickly the tumours grew in six weeks in September when I had my leg operation.*
>
> *Will it be possible to go back to work in the near or medium term?*
>
> *How do we expect this disease to progress? For example, how do I go about planning visits to South Africa to see friends and family? In your view, should I think about saying goodbyes?*

But – and there's a big but – Shirley's journey is not only one of loss, and deteriorating health, horrifying as that is. It is also one of gain. God nurtures her faith and dependence on him. Such gain is steady, impressive and continuous. Thanks to such grace, she's learning to fly.

Sometime later, Shirley tells me:

> *Getting kidnapped again around 5! Tonia insists I shouldn't be alone.*

Brian and I are so relieved.

She has more:

> *All this crazy lung stuff has made me very breathless, which is probably the scariest of all – I don't know whether I can walk, drive, get up the stairs... Basically, within three weeks, I've gone from feeling pretty much okay to really rough.*

Eating, moving, etc. has all become a challenge. The docs want to start me on oral chemo a.s.a.p., but the NHS has refused funding. So we're going down the private healthcare route with everything we have – should hear by Friday (28 February).

Otherwise, the docs will be looking to prescribe meds to keep the symptoms under control – for as long as they can. So – in black and white – that is the situation as things stand...

Shirley's whole circle of support from all round the world – friends, Secret Helpers, church, family – read on in dismay. Then they read on:

Thankfully, I can see a whole new dimension that is coloured by hope and God's amazing love for me. I'm on an adventure with God, and although things seem pretty bleak from the outside... I know we're heading somewhere amazing. Thank you, as ever, for journeying with me. Your love is amazing... I feel so blessed to see Christianity in action all around me. Much love!! Xxx :)

I was speechless, and no doubt the others reading this were too.

———————————

Katy texts:

Hi everyone. So – following some Doodle magic – the best date for the next prayer meeting is Tuesday, 4 March. Venue TBC. Everyone welcome to join us – particularly if you can lead us in some worship. Let us know if you can come! Otherwise do pray where you are ... And fast – if you can – to add extra fight to our battle! Let's keep praying, people...

Katy's text has no sooner been posted than Shirley adds:

Venue will be cat-free! Will you join me?!? I've been thinking about praying in faith for these specific things at the moment:

1. a definite treatment plan from the docs;

2. to be well enough to go to my birthday dinner this weekend;

3. to be able to go to the Randy Clark conference in London at the beginning of March;

4. to be able to go to South Africa in March/April; and

5. that I can go to Bethel worship school for two weeks in June.

A couple of these seem pretty outrageous... But we've seen answers to some outrageous prayers already! Also, feel free to add anything of your own to the list...

Amanda and Mark from next door pop in. Shirley gratefully warms her fingers round the mug of vegetable soup that Amanda's brought, and they chat for a bit. "Mark says the dogs nearly caught a rabbit in the woods; I'm so glad it was *nearly*!"

When they leave, they're shaking their heads at such obvious deterioration.

Quite tired after their visit, Shirley slowly types what's on her mind:

Yesterday (26 February), Nick Crowder challenged me to "come clean" about my symptoms – not that I've been hiding anything, but so we're all on the same 'hymn-sheet' – ha ha.

I was in a great place – until I woke up exactly three weeks ago with excruciating back pain. Over the past weeks, the pain has moved but remained severe. I'm taking 60mg morphine twice a day plus other pain top-ups.

Next day, John drives Shirley to Oxford for her scheduled scan. She's glad when it's over. On the way home, she can't resist texting.

John's comments in the traffic on the drive home really funny. You can imagine.

We both appreciate John deeply – but not in traffic.
Texts fly in all directions.

Am feeling pretty good. Do need treatment of some sort to start to feel better. And I'm frightened that I won't be able to hold it all together anymore. Shirley.

Praying that you will. "My hope is in you" (Psalm 39). What a wonderful thing. Lots of love, Mum.

Praying for a bunch of ministering angels to fuss round you, Thy. Nick.

You have been on your own and had to care for yourself – and now God has brought in so many carers to love and care. Oh, how your Father loves you! Lots of love, Mum.

Chloe-cat is a real nuisance as she likes to sit on me. Shirls.

Praying for Chloe-cat's salvation. Spending so much time on my knees. Mum.

Chloe-cat's habit of hefting herself on to Shirley's legs means she does have to go. Bee, who also goes to Greyfriars, offers to take her. The cat came as a kitten to Shirley when newly married and has been with her ever since. What a sad goodbye. Shirls tears up; and, infinitely gently, strokes and cuddles the black cat. Our hearts ache and grieve at another loss. But Bee's boys are delighted to have a new pet in the family.

CHAPTER THIRTY-NINE

The Other Shoe Drops

"Shirley and Nick sip some wine and begin to talk."

AT THE CHURCHILL HOSPITAL IN OXFORD, CLAIRE IS CON-cerned. She doesn't know why Shirley's symptoms have developed so quickly or why she's feeling so unwell – breathless and in pain. So, on 28 February, Claire promises to phone Shirley as soon as she has studied the PET scan.

We are all on tenterhooks, waiting to hear. Many of us have spent a lot of time there nowadays, stretched to capacity. This day, two days before Shirley's thirty-ninth birthday, does nothing but lengthen into a very long day. And still the phone doesn't ring.

When evening comes, Shirley and Nick sit scrunched up on the couch. They natter about everything and nothing. Even though they are expecting it, when it comes, the shrill ringing startles both of them. And it is Claire.

Once the hellos are done, she asks, "Shirley, is someone with you for this call?"

Nick and Shirley look at each other, eyes growing big. Their eyes lock, wordlessly.

"Shirley, I'm so sorry to have to tell you that even though the treatment brings some regression, the tumours are so aggressive that whenever we stop chemo to allow your body to recover, they are advancing faster than we are destroying..." Claire's soft voice trails off and she falls silent. Emotion colours each of her simple words. It seems that while oral chemo could win Shirley just a little time, that is all they can hope for. "I think you should call your parents in South Africa – to come immediately."

Later, Claire tells Nick:

> *I've never made such a call before – not in my entire career. Nor did I ever wish to. But my overriding concern was that, since the cancer was so far advanced, Shirley might not have lasted the weekend.*

Nick and Shirley just sit there. Apparently, the scan "couldn't be worse". Slowly, the world begins to spin, like a sick merry-go-round. It's business as usual out there, but in here? Here, Shirley's been told her life will be over – really soon.

Nick finds himself thinking about the promise he believed he'd received from God in Nuffield Hospital in September, standing beside Shirley's bandaged leg after her op. *This can't be right. God said he was going to heal her and restore her – I know that, don't I? I just know he is. I'm so sure of this that I will stake my life on it.*

Shirley's thoughts are tortured too: *I'm so, so disappointed. And I'm angry, God. You've given me all this really great stuff you're speaking to me about – not just the things I've cooked up, but really great volunteering opportunities that seem perfect for me – everything I've always wanted to do! Where is this all going, God? Am I really going to die? I can't believe that you would take... someone like me – tears bubble and then roll – who just wants to love you and serve you, and let me die?*

She sniffs, then cries, then sobs. The intensity of emotion rips at her body. In no time at all, Nick's tears mingle with hers. Then very slowly, after quite some time, the storm of emotion abates and all is quiet.

Shirley and Nick sip some wine and begin to talk. Nick is amazed by Shirley. *I've never seen anything like this. Such great bravery, strength, faith.*

Even now, she's thinking of others, not herself! And she's actually talking about getting her will in order – and planning her funeral!

From that day – 28 February – Shirley starts to sort out her affairs with Nick's help. She knows time could be running out.

Nick writes:

> After Claire's phone call, we started weeks of intimate dialogue regarding Shirley's will, healthcare, etc.
>
> How she undertook these conversations with such calm – such an objective view – leaves me in awe. How can you discuss how you want to die, in what location, with who present, under what kind of treatment, and then plan your own funeral? At times, I was more of a wreck than she was!
>
> But I know that this is what God asked me to do. I could have run from such a task...
>
> There was more to it than dialogue and the plans. It was about her heart. Her heart was the part of her God so dearly and passionately loved. He wanted her to know that she was dearly loved and cared for – and that she had his protective arm around her, while she walked this journey.
>
> He had asked me, alongside her mother, to be his hands and feet, to surrender my own heart, and love and care for her unconditionally. So I – we – did.

———————————

On that Friday night when the news broke, once Shirley and Nick are calm enough, Shirley phones. "Mum," she says, "I think it's time for you to see if you can get a ticket and come back."

One week after coming home to South Africa at the end of January, all I wanted to do was to do was to go back. But I knew the ball was in Shirley's court. Since she's taken charge of her life – my great joy – all the big decisions are hers, which to me is so wonderful.

Right now, she struggles with so much; it's hard to understand just *how* much. I have waited for her to ask me to come. And as I put down the phone, relief that my wait is over overwhelms me. My daughter has invited me to share her last days.

When Shirley puts the phone down, she turns to Nick. "If I am to die, I want to die at home – and I want to die well."

CHAPTER FORTY

Shirley's Birthday

*"Having a party like this and knowing it's for her
makes her radiant."*

THE DAY BEFORE THE DEVESTATING NEWS FROM CLAIRE, NICK
texted me:

Secretly, do you know Shirley's favourite flowers, Thy?

Actually, as I thought about it, I didn't know, except that she loves
sunflowers. So that's what I told Nick.

Nick fills me in. "Before the news, things were looking good. So, with
her birthday coming up, we were planning to do it with some style, with a
small group of close friends. When the news came, I was busy doing the

invites and arranging a dinner at the Crown in Playhatch, one of Shirley's favourite places – perhaps because it's run by South Africans? We decided the news didn't change anything – we were still going to do it, if Shirley could possibly manage it."

As her Saturday night party approaches, Shirley struggles. Even her new bionic right leg is giving her trouble and she can hardly walk. Her body keeps weakening and breathing becomes more difficult. Pain pushes hard to break through all the medication. Only three very close friends know how bad things are.

Nick glances at Shirley, marvelling as he drives. *My life, she looks beautiful. I love the short, sassy wig and sexy smile. And she's so elegant – as usual. How can you not totally adore this remarkably brave, wonderful girl?*

Once inside, her fears over that she won't be able to walk from the car, Shirley very soon establishes herself as the belle of the ball. Having a party like this and knowing it's for her makes her radiant. She bubbles, giggles, jokes and laughs. Beautiful in her favourite wig, she jokes about the pleasant change the short bob makes from the flowing, shoulder-length locks lost to the treatment months earlier.

I know how much this party means to her. It's something she's always longed for. She's had so many sad birthdays. I'm so glad – so deeply glad – that this is happening.

Shirley smiles almost non-stop. She takes every opportunity she can to hug and be hugged. But she does, increasingly, rely on others to help her move. All she manages is a gentle step or two of a dance before someone helps her to a chair.

"Hey, Nick," Jo calls. When he comes over, she whispers, her voice filled with awe. "We are seeing a miracle."

"Amen, sister. I'll drink to that."

On Shirley's birthday a day later, Sunday, 2 March, Nick stomps up the stairs carrying a tray. Shirley's spent the night after the party at his cottage. Her eyes grow big as he plonks a tray full of flowers, champagne, and strawberries and cream in front of her. They feast – not without giggles and laughs – and remember the previous night.

Shirley takes it easy, staying in bed and thanking this one and that. She journals:

HAPPY BIRTHDAY DUDE!!!

She's absolutely exhausted, but terribly happy. She tries not to let her thoughts wander but concentrates on the deluge of blessing. Texts line up, waiting their turn. Cards collect, destined for the top of her already overcrowded piano at home. Phone calls sparkle with chuckles and sometimes peals of laughter.

A few days ago, Shirley listed going to her birthday party as one of her outrageous requests for prayer. Now she texts:

> *Hi, outrageous answer to one of my prayer requests: I got to go to my birthday party last night! :-)*

> *Believe me, a few days ago this felt impossible. Not only was I there, but I was the last to leave. Thank you, God!!! :)*

That Sunday afternoon, there's another celebration planned. Nick and Shirley make their way to Tonia's. Chris has baked a chocolate cake – these have made her quite famous – and Tonia's decorated it with candles and sparklers. Pippa tries to light the sparklers. And Dave jokes about setting the carpet alight. When it's all burning brightly, they sing *Happy Birthday*, with a lot more feeling than usual.

"Come on, Shirley," Tonia chides, "blow your candles out."

She does just manage, amid more laughter and teasing.

I've asked Chris to give her a huge bunch of flowers from Brian and me. I'm a little sad that we won't be there for Shirley's birthday, but it's the familiar old sadness of many birthdays that we haven't been together. It's wonderful to know that her precious friends have produced the perfect birthday in their love for her. Many times that day, I think happily of all that's taking place. I couldn't wish for better. I have managed to get a flight and know that I will be back with her on 6 March.

To Nick I write:

> *You have all been so amazing. Thank you so much. I hope to love on her, along with you all, very soon.*

Chris, along with us and others, has been so anxious for me to come back that she writes:

> *Just heard you arrive Thursday. So relieved, I burst into tears!*

─────────────

It comforts me to write a round robin:

> *What is most alarming is that Shirley's right lung is now filled with tumours and totally out of action.*
>
> *Because she is very weak, Shirley's wonderful friends have not allowed her to drive to Oxford. In particular, she asks Chris with her medical background along to help her understand what the doctors are saying. Tonia has had her move in, providing meals and welcoming visitors. So Shirley is not alone, especially at night. Katy and four-year-old Amelia visit. Nick and Chris listen, counsel, and pray…*

On 4 March, Shirley writes:

> *Just received a phone call from Oxford Hospital to say the NHS has agreed to release the oral chemo drug (Pazopanib) to me as early as tomorrow – provided I can cover the funding. Am talking to my private medical aid Bupa about this now, but – given the amount of money involved – this shouldn't be a problem. Thank you, God, for answering our prayers!!! X*

When she texts me, I respond:

> *Wow! I love him, don't you? Xxx*

As soon as she has the energy to write, Shirley confesses to her Secret Helpers:

> *I have to say, as trite as it may sound, I had a lovely birthday. I had a lovely weekend – because I still believed and do believe that God has this somehow – you know, that this is under his control. It is in his hands in some way that I can't see and can't understand.*

That same day, Katy – pregnant, to her and her Dave's great delight – opens the door to welcome all who have come to pray. Katy describes this meeting as "a new battle in the ongoing war to claim Shirley's healing". Her whole heart is in it.

Laura, sad that she can't come, fasts the day before. Then she prays with a friend at home at the time of the meeting. God gives her Isaiah 43:1-4 which she paraphrases:

Don't be afraid. You're mine. When you're in over your head, I'll be there with you. You will not go down. I love you – I'd trade creation just for you.[20]

From South Africa, I text:

We all love you, love you, love you, and are finding our own ways to say it. So be blessed. Praying up a storm with you all tonight.

Laura's in Oxenhope and Rami's in Cardiff, but Shirley brings them into the loop the next day on Secret Helpers:

So, as you've gathered, last night was pretty phenomenal. We were all overwhelmed by God's presence from start to finish. The time seemed to pass in an instant. We – okay, I – laughed again, most of the way through.

I'm left with the sense that God is doing something pretty incomprehensible... I don't know what, but it is good.

While we were praying, Nick Crowder saw ring upon ring of wagons drawn up protectively around a little girl – me – to keep me safe. The entire formation of wagons was surrounded by countless angels, keeping us all safe.

I can't remember the words that were used... The point was that we are all safe and the victory is secured.

Please correct me if I'm wrong, Nick... I am but a bear of little brain! Love you all, guys. Xxx

---

The next day, Shirley comes back exhausted after her scan in Oxford. Claire examines the results very carefully and sits down to write a report:

The PET CT scan unfortunately shows massive progression of disease within the right hemi-thorax with mediastinal shift and pressure on her liver. Shirley also has a significant increase in the size of her left-sided metastases.

She now has good palliative care input. I am pleased to say her pain is much better controlled today than it was last week when I saw her. She also seems more comfortable from her shortness of breath ...

---

[20] paraphrase loosely based on The Message translation

We have been through the risks and toxicity of Pazopanib. She knows there is a significant risk of pneumothorax and, given her lung disease, this is a possibility, especially given the rapidity of her progression. She also knows there is an increased risk of blood clots and stroke and also diarrhoea.

Relentless, the prayer offensive marches on. And on 5 March, Tonia and Shirley drive to Hammersmith to hear Randy Clark, who has an international healing ministry. He and his team talk to Shirley for twenty minutes. Then they pray. Many pray – specifically, for the oral chemo. Shirley shakes uncontrollably, overwhelmed by the Spirit. She's blessed with laughter once again. She reports:

This seems to be my new thing. Could be worse... :-)))

Both she and Tonia have such a touch from the Lord that, in Shirley's words, they "were so glad to have been to heaven and back".

To her beloved Secret Helpers, Shirley texts:

Here's another outrageous prayer request: Please join me praying that not only will I have one, but many more fantastic birthdays to come. X

CHAPTER FORTY-ONE

Rollercoaster

"Nick moved her bed downstairs."

I TAKE ONE QUICK LAST LOOK AROUND, THEN, ON LEADEN feet, make my way to the car. Yesterday, I stood before my open suitcase, struggling to know what to pack. It always takes me a couple of days to decide. But these few days have been some of the most difficult – perhaps *the* most difficult – of my life.

How do you pack something to wear for your only child's funeral? I look, half-heartedly, but find I don't really have anything. And there are even more excruciating questions. How do you care for your only child as she dies? How do you get through her funeral? How do you factor in packing up her house afterwards? And dealing with your grief? Saying goodbyes? And how do you go home after all that?

Yesterday's text to Shirley read:

So good to be back with you! I fly Wednesday p.m. and get to Heathrow 8 a.m. your time Thursday. John lined up to collect me. Praying. Love you tons.

It sounds hollow, but I cannot say what the real issues for me are. I'm so glad I'm on my way because I long to take care of her again.

Today I write:

May only those thoughts that have God in them – making them beautiful – enter into your head. No more sleeps! Hooray!

I board the plane after a difficult goodbye to Brian, and strap myself in. It is extremely hard for him to remain behind when our anguish is so real, and we comfort each other. What lies ahead for us is huge.

There's a text from a friend – just in time:

His love never fails, it never gives up, it never runs out…

And a text from Nick:

Since last Friday night, when Shirls got the PET scan results, her life has been very full on. It's been multiple, long sessions with me, working through the finest details of her will. And advanced healthcare planning. And a weekend of birthday celebrations. And moving between her home, mine and Tonia's. She could not settle until we had found somewhere for the cats to go – and even her goldfish!

So, let alone the well-wishing visitors, health visitors, doctor's appointment and today's update in Oxford, she is very tired. She's doing incredibly well. God is amazing (as your daughter is!). Please do not be surprised if she needs to sleep tomorrow and Friday. Having you there now will give her such peace of mind. Always available on the phone if you need to natter. Welcome back. Nick X

Nick is trying to warn me, and I am expecting it, but when I see Shirley I am devastated by her deterioration. She's so very pale. And above all, so weak – she hates climbing stairs. I notice she's eating very small meals. I text friends:

This is very sad – but S close to the Lord.

We watch TV together – and she finds and holds my hand. "Mum," she says, "I am happier than I have ever been."

Texts fly back and forth across the pond. Brian writes to Shirley:

Hello love. Glad you are home with Mum. Hope you have a good day. Lots of love, Dad Xx

I text Nats:

S says she loves Jesus so much.

Brian messages me:

Wakey, wakey! Praying very especially for you today. I know it isn't easy. Have a blessed day. Love you. Xxx

---

The day after I arrive, I stand in Shirley's kitchen. Supper is over. Now for the medication. I stand, staring at four little white pills in my hand – her first dose of Pazopanib. Once the NHS released the drug, Shirley wasted no time in getting it – and thanking God.

All day long, Shirley and Nick have worked on getting her affairs in order – I'm glad they're doing this, but also so sad that it has come to this. And now, tonight, pills with such poisonous content...

I remember Brian's text this morning:

Morning, sweetheart. Hope you slept well. God grant you the strength you need today.

Right now, I'm saying a huge amen to that. And thinking of Nick's words too: "Maybe, just maybe, the new oral chemo drug can stop the progression of the cancer in her lungs. But the side-effects alone could kill her."

I take the pills and a glass of water to Shirls on deeply reluctant feet. I remember Chris saying she would never take something as dangerous as this. So I ask her, "Why are you doing this, my darling?"

"Because I want to prolong my life as much as possible for God. He seems to be taking his time about healing me, and I want to make sure I give him all the time I possibly can."

Shirley asks me to have coffee in bed with her. We hold hands again and she reads from Sarah Young's devotional, *Jesus Today*[21]. She asks for a long life to love and serve Jesus – a sweet, gentle, humble, respectful prayer.

---

[21] Thomas Nelson (Nashville, Tennessee: 2012).

That's why she Skypes with Bethel, Bill Johnson's church in Redding, California. It's a good connection and the prayer team pray for her for a long, long time.

Every day now, I take Shirley's blood pressure, using a machine lent to us by Chris. Actually, I take it *twice*, and jot down the results. I want to make sure this is as accurate as possible and not distorted by moments of increasing anxiety – hers or mine.

Nick brings everyone up to speed later:

> *Within forty-eight hours – the effects of the oral drug are remarkable – a whole new lease of life, including dinner at the local Leathern Bottel. Only small portions! What a rollercoaster this is!*

Saturday, 8 March, dawns crisp and frosty. I drive us in to London. We are an hour early. So we sit in the parking lot, watching a mum and dad playing on the grass with two very frisky children. Shirley's very pensive.

"Mu-um," she says, "maybe we should go home."

I stare at her. We have come for prayer at the 24-7 healing rooms.

"I have suffered so much during the last eight months. So… right now… I've had enough. And I'm half-wanting to go to heaven. And… if God wants me to die… I don't want to stand in the way."

"Sweetheart …" I pause to think. Then I say, "Sweetheart, you won't be forcing the hand of God if they pray for your healing and he doesn't want it. God is good through and through. He will respond to the prayers as he chooses. And *always* as an act of love towards you. What happens will be a mighty expression *always* of the love God has for you."

We meet a young student, vibrant with love for God. She's rejoicing because when she was facing a double lung transplant, her lungs were completely and miraculously healed.

Oh, if only this happens to Shirley. My anguish is deep and long.

This young girl – lovely, long blonde locks falling over her shoulders – prays. Others pray.

Encouraged now, we drive home.

Shirley brings the Secret Helpers up to speed:

> *I've just been to the 24-7 healing rooms at HTB this morning. I was really encouraged. I do get the feeling, though, that my healing is a process that may take some time. I've been finding my latest symptom – feeling breathless – very scary, so can you pray for courage for me – however long it all takes. Love you all. X*

'Harry' arrives. At first, he hasn't got a name, but Chris soon sees to that. She stands in front of the oxygenator and tells us why, because of somebody she knew, he has to be called Harry. Shirls and I look at each other. Whatever... Harry it is!

Even the presence of the oxygenator from the NHS distresses Shirley at first. She doesn't even want to look at it.

Harry puzzles me, because I have to get him working. Later in the day, I text Brian:

Chris very helpful. Shirls nervous about side-effects of chemo. New pain in her side. We got oxygen working. Please pray. Lots of love.

Suddenly, Shirley takes a turn for worse. Nick alerts the troops:

Good morning, good people. Big push needed in prayer for Miss Glameron, please. She's having increased trouble with her breathing. Now it's a big effort to get around the home. Thankfully, she now has a fab oxygen machine on wheels (currently called Harry). He (she?) helps relieve the pain from the struggle to breathe. Please pray that the breathing gets much easier again – and that there will be peace of mind in abundance.

Later Nick is very glad to send another text:

Update from my post this morning: A humongous thank you for your thoughts, prayers, incense-burning and general lovefest of goodness toward our Shirley Cameron, from all four corners.

The day closes with smiles, eased breathing, six visitors, one doctor and more wonderful flowers. And faithful Harry – pumping quality oxygen from the corner of the room.

Tomorrow quite an expedition to Oxford for check-ups. Continued cover for Shirls and Mum – and as little walking required as possible – though a little is good each day, to keep her toned up and ready to hit the dance floor in due course! Onward and upward. X

Gaynor is one of the six visitors:

Just back from a Shirley visit, and as I always say, I leave in a better place than when I went in. You looked radiant, oxygen suits you! Continued prayers and praise going up. Xx

Sometimes the changes from one day to the next are really big. On Tuesday, 11 March, I phone the local Macmillan nurse at nine and ask her to come because I'm alarmed. Later on, we drive to Oxford and pray more earnestly than usual – to find parking easily. And for a wheelchair.

Much later and back home, exhausted, Shirley curls up in bed. While friends visit, I duck off to Boots to get her new prescription.

A copy of Claire's report on the last consultation arrives for Shirley's GP. Claire writes that after five days on Pazopanib, the side-effects have been mild. And Shirley's Oramorph and other pain meds help with relief from both pain and breathlessness – now her major problem. She cautions that it may be four to six weeks before there's any evidence of a definite response to the chemo treatment.

Claire also notes that on average Shirley's blood pressure is 130/100. Consequently, she suggests one medication and, if this fails, something else. Shirley's blood pressure repeatedly gets alarmingly high. So her GP takes up the battle, frequently changing her medication.

At the end of this awful day, 12 March, Shirley looks up pathetically at me. "I just want to feel well again – even for one day," she pleads.

I'm quite overwhelmed.

Shirley tries hard but finds it an absolute nightmare to get upstairs. Even though she's using oxygen, we rest every two steps. And I keep the oxygen flowing freely along the plastic tubing – fortunately, there's miles of it. She's very frightened. And so am I.

She decides to sleep downstairs on her old leather couch.

I text Brian and Nick, alarmed and sad. For such a long time now, every text has ended, "Please pray."

Next day, I have the comfort of my early morning text from Brian. I'm able to reply:

Shirls slept well on couch. God enfold you in love today. lol Xx

Next day, Chris and I breathe deeply as we stroll round the lake at Dinton Pastures. The fluffy heaps of cumulus clouds reflect in the still waters below. Leaves flutter around us. It feels like a wonderful few moments of escape to me. Before we head home, we indulge in scones and cream. Chris offers me a weekend in their flat in Bournemouth.

"Oh, how kind of you – thank you so much. But I think I would find it hard to be away from Shirley for so long, and perhaps she might feel the same. I suspect we could see a real decline soon – and that there may not be too much time left."

"Oh, Thy. But the offer is still there, if you change your mind."

"Perhaps, while someone sits with Shirley... It's about me being able to sit down to a meal in someone's home for an hour or two, or going out for an afternoon, as I did with Tonia, and as we are doing now. Or going for a walk, while someone is with her... I find these little things work wonders for me, and I'm not away for too long."

Nick has been taking care of Shirley, so we expect him still to be there when we get back. And he is, grinning from ear to ear. He has plonked Shirley in a chair and single-handedly brought her double bed downstairs – bit by painstaking bit.

He's put up a screen to half-cover the front window, giving Shirls privacy but ensuring that she can still look out at the sunset over it. He's rearranged the couches too – and done all the necessary electrics so that Harry can do his work. Shirls has lights and chargers on tap for all her devices, and can plug in the heating pad Rami's lent her for the persistent aching in her legs.

When we come in, Nick and Shirls are sitting on the bed. They're sipping wine, giggling like two naughty children. *Look what we've done* is written all over their faces. What a joy to come home to this – all done and dusted.

But for Shirley, this step is not at all easy. Nick tells the Secret Helpers:

Scaling the stairs has become too traumatic and exhausting. The tumours are squeezing the life out of her. So – for her – this move downstairs is one of submission to the unfolding scenario. But, again, she faces it with such strength and humour.

As evening falls, I climb up on to the bed beside Shirley. We've had supper – only the things she wants to eat. I don't fuss or try to make her eat. We pray together for a really long time.

"Mum, what about my broken dreams?" Shirley asks again.

"Darling, let's give them to God," I reply – as I did last time. "He knows how precious they are to you – and they are very precious to him too. He knows how to handle them. Let him take care of them for you."

I marvel that her greatest desires have changed so much. Her greatest desire – her dream now – is to serve and love God. She no longer resists the magnetic pull of his love.

CHAPTER FORTY-TWO

Deterioration

*"Shirls lights up and manages to bubble,
like old times."*

AFTER NINE DAYS IN THE UK, I SEND OUT A ROUND ROBIN. I TRY to capture something of the devastation:

> *In the time I've been here Shirley's deteriorated markedly. She's battling to breathe and we have Harry, the oxygenator, on more and more.*

> *We realise that, as we try to bless her, time might be very short. The love for her is beautiful to see. Flowers keep coming. I'm so pleased there's beauty all around her.*

She so badly wants a bath. So – on Sunday afternoon – we struggle upstairs. And it's such a joy for me to see her luxuriating in the warm water. All of it takes a long time. But it leaves her happy though beyond exhausted.

Nick finds a company that makes a little chair to put in the bath. He plans to help her – once I've dressed her in a bathing costume. I'm so touched that he goes to all this trouble for her. And so sad he has to take the little chair back.

The biggest concern now is side-effects such as high blood pressure, a stroke or a hole in her lung. And she can't concentrate.

She keeps saying that her walk with Jesus keeps her "so happy". Praise God for the way he came powerfully into Shirley's life a year ago – after all the years he pursued her – and has absolutely transformed her.

I pause and pray in my heart that her delight in him will grow to eclipse the circumstances.

What I find so moving is that she's so concerned over our pain!

When I arrived in the UK, the tree outside Shirley's front door was pregnant with blossom. Since then, the white blossoms continue to suggest a beautiful Shirley to me – in a wonderful white wedding gown. And make me glad, as I come and go – shopping and fetching medicines.

Every morning now, at about eight, I try to come down the stairs quietly. Not easy. I don't know – I *fear* – what I might find. Sometimes Shirley's kept Harry on all night. And sometimes she's sleeping quite peacefully. For ever so long, sleeping well has been a considerable challenge: long nights with horrible, empty, frightening hours. And monster-filled dreams.

I make a cup of coffee and go back to have my quiet time with God. Words fail to express the pull I feel in every direction. It's really lonely, as others can't understand the path I'm walking as a mum.

As God calls me aside, I thank him for peace and strength. I have none of my own. I am so willing to come to him because he always refreshes and strengthens me. It's real intimacy with God, morning after morning. This is what enables me to understand, to some extent, what the one I love is going through. And what others who love her are going through too. I watch them and they bring me such joy. Nick, Chris, Katy, Laura, Jo, Gaynor, Tonia, Rami and others minister constantly. I marvel that they share the very spiritual truths she needs, just when she needs them. I know God wants me to be blessed by this and content – and I am.

As God takes care of me, time after time he enlightens me with amazing truths. I realise anew that in essence Jesus has successfully deleted all the destruction from his Father's world through his life, death, resurrection and ascension. Therefore, suffering – like the devastation of my child – was dealt with once and for all. As I realise this, I feel a sudden, inexplicable surge of joy. But more than that – in the process of my probably losing Shirley, I am getting to know Jesus better.

I was struck, the moment I got back to the UK, by the birdsong. It was as if the birds had to outdo themselves at the beginning of spring because they'd been silent for so long. Now every morning they lift my spirits for the day. But it's my time with God that becomes manna for the day – one day at a time.

I go down to wake Shirley and help her begin her day. Usually, she asks sleepily, "Just ten minutes more?" I find this so precious as it reminds me of the little girl who couldn't get up. "Just ten minutes more," she would say.

I get my muesli and sometimes a cheese omelette. By then, she's ready for her small bowl of cereal and Twinings cranberry and blood orange tea. I sit on the couch beside her bed while she tells me what clothes she wants – and where I can find them.

Caroline kindly brought a basin for Shirley to wash in. She's in and out nearly every day, keeping us supplied with fruitcake and very efficiently producing whatever we need. How many times we just have to say how grateful we are for her!

I spread towels everywhere and Shirley stands to wash and change. She hates the taste of toothpaste so I'm allowed to put only very little on her toothbrush.

As the days go by, this little routine exhausts her more and more. Getting her to the toilet becomes increasingly difficult. Her legs become more and more painful – rubbery, perhaps because of the chemo. So I stand in front of her, scared that she might topple forward, and hold her crutches ready. Then, while I feed out tubing from the oxygenator, she shuffles slowly down the passage.

Soon it's necessary to put a chair halfway along the route so that she can take a rest between bed and toilet.

As Shirley's use of morphine increases, so does what she calls "morph brain". As a result, her friends receive fascinating texts from her. She assures Gaynor she will pay her what she owes real soon. She types out the alphabet to send to Tonia. She keeps texting Katy about her new boyfriend – handsome, attentive and gorgeous in every way.

Shirley tells her friends:

> *I'm very sleepy and dozy. I apologise for texts, etc. that some of you may receive that don't make much sense. Morphine-tastic!!! :-).*

But the morphine also gives her nightmares. One morning she is very scared, so I hold her hands and listen.

"Mum," she says, "I dreamt about these enormous, horrible monsters coming at me. They... they..." She shudders and tears trickle. I sooth with gentle words and then prayer.

When Shirley can't get out of bed anymore, I help her, sliding her unresponsive legs and feet over the edge. I see her struggle to get into her slippers. So one day I suggest, "Why bother, Shirls? The floor's carpeted."

Quite outraged, and morphine-inspired, she replies, "Mum, because men pee on the floor."

As the pain increases, our morning routine changes. For now, after I wake her, I rub and rub her legs, so thin and white, until they feel a little better. There's talk of thrombosis, or new cancer, but it seems more likely that this is a side-effect of the Pazopanib.

When I get a chance, I phone Bindy, Shirley's local Macmillan nurse, to ask for a commode. "Don't tell Shirley," I say, "but let me hide it in the back room. I think we're going to need it very soon." Bindy also supplies a packet full of emergency medicines – injections and things – which I keep at hand on the sideboard. This is in case we have a crisis; then when a doctor arrives, all he might need is already here.

On 13 March, Brian sends me this text:

> *Hello love. I was so distressed after talking to you last night. You looked so tired. I hope today is an easier one for you. God bless. Lots of love, Xxxx*

I'm so sorry I am not there with them; Nats is getting engaged and her ring should arrive any day! A few days later I text her:

Excited to hear you have a date and venue for the wedding!

Shirley's friends don't miss a beat. After popping in for a while, and bringing Shirley's special smile out of hiding, Gaynor brings the others up to speed:

Shirley was sleepy today, after a couple of tiring days. She's been sleeping well at night. And she's as peaceful and positive as ever. Nice knitted woolly sheep – whoever sent that? Prayers for the oral chemo to kick in a.s.a.p. would be cool...

The little sheep comes from California. He represents the sheep Jesus cares for. He's unique in that he can take off his coat. So Nick and Shirls have great fun.

Laura, in Oxenhope, feels the distance. She writes:

I love it that every time I mention you, the people I am with are compelled to pray for you. I feel that is such an indication of how much God loves you. X

Shirls responds:

Hi all. I'm so encouraged by everyone's prayers, thank you. Still feeling really rough and waiting for the oral chemo to kick in... Should be another week or so. X

Every morning, I watch a little robin hop from the top of one post to another, always in the same order, around the neighbour's garden, red chest fluffed out. Shirley tells me he never changes his routine. Not so with her situation. This morning, because of the flow of oxygen from Harry, her nose suddenly begins to bleed profusely. She's most distressed; partly because she's never had a nosebleed in her life, so for her, this is a new horror. Fortunately, I know what to do: cold cloths and ice cubes. But my heart is so very sore for her.

Man of sorrows, did you also feel the tears well up when pain intruded with a heavy hand? Of course you did.

Shirley talks me through creating a fish pie; Nick's coming for supper. "Not spag bol, Mum. That's what he lives on!" It takes many trips getting instructions from her in bed, but it turns out really tasty. I can see she's enjoyed actually doing something.

Laura, Jo and Shirley (a.k.a. "Charlie's angels") consider going out to a pub with Nick ("Charlie") next day for Sunday lunch; but sadly, Shirley's just too ill. Nick arrives with cooked chicken and salads. Jo brings a yummy pudding of fruit, yoghurt and crushed meringue.

Shirley's hair has been growing for quite some time now. It's very soft and downy and, as they arrive, none of them can resist stroking it. They all pile on to the bed and connect – now serious, now chuckling. Shirls lights up and manages to bubble, like old times. Once again, I'm happy – and sad – for her.

CHAPTER FORTY-THREE

The Inevitable

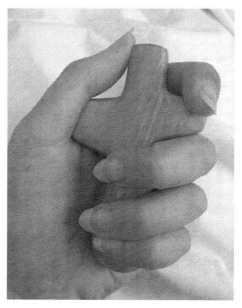

"It's as if she's on the cross,
but also bearing the cross with her beloved Saviour..."

SHIRLEY PLEADS WITH GOD FOR ANOTHER SHOT AT LIVING. TO me, the question becomes: will it be here, where we manage it imperfectly, or in heaven, where we do it absolutely perfectly? Only time will tell. Deep in thought – and pain – I journal:

> *As Shirley suffers, Christ operates in her as her Lover and Saviour. It's as if she's on the cross, but also bearing the cross with her beloved Saviour – victory over destruction.*

I text Tonia:

In this very sad journey, as it has now become, I keep wanting to see God's hand at work and be comforted by it. One such comfort is the way you have been ministering to Shirley. You – and the others. I am so thankful. I know all of you, who are giving your love to Shirley, are carrying quite a load. I so badly want to help. It won't be for long, by the look of things. Shirley comes alive and thrives on your visits.

Next, I send another round robin – one that is nearly impossible to write:

Please pray for Brian as he too makes this most difficult journey to the UK. Pray for us all as we face the horror of such suffering. It seems that God is calling Shirley into his presence. I may be wrong – and I'd love to be wrong – but, perhaps, it's time that we pray for wonderful anticipation in her of her homecoming. Pray that she is blessed more and more with the realisation of the wonders and blessings ahead. And that she can stop worrying about us, because God will comfort us.

Propped up on her bed in the sitting room, Shirley tells Nick, "I'm really anxious about Dad coming and him being here every day. I don't want to stop him coming but, as weak as I am now, I don't know if I can handle it."

They talk for a long time about the past, her childhood, the feelings, anxieties and fears she has. She has carried it all for so long. And festering, it has closed down her relationship with her father. In essence, the blockage is unforgiveness and resentment.

"What is it that you want?" Nick asks.

"To be at peace," she replies like a shot, "and to wipe it all away. Yeah, to be at peace with where we all are now – Mum and Dad are all I have."

"Then why don't we pray, Shirls? Why don't we ask God to bring that peace to you and to enable you to forgive? To reconcile and let the bad feelings and memories go?"

With tears on her pale, soft cheeks, Shirley nods slowly. As they pray, Nick is sure he sees Shirley's shoulders drop as though a great weight has been lifted from them.

She wipes her tears away. Her enchanting and mischievous smile breaks across her face and she says, "Nick, I feel so light, I feel so happy! Why have I been so s***wed up in my head about all this stuff? Why didn't I just give God my heart years ago rather than keeping him in my head? I do hope it's going to be okay with Dad; I'm sure it will be, I feel a lot better now!"

Before Brian's arrival, Shirley calls me over. I perch on the edge of her bed, full of trepidation. I know that she and Nick have been so busy – almost daily. Now she says, "Mum, I want you to know that I have been able to make provision for you and Dad in my will."

I want to run away. It's outrageously abnormal. But she holds my focus.

"You and Dad will inherit sixty per cent. And, as the only beneficiary of my dread diseases policy, you personally will receive a great deal."

I want to interrupt – this is too awful – but she stops me.

"It makes me so happy to be able to do this for you."

My face creases in distress. I manage to thank her, I think – just briefly, so clumsily – and stumble away into the kitchen to do I-don't-know-what.

Brian arrives on 27 March. And now, more than ever, rides the roller-coaster with us. Nick picks him up from the airport. The sadness and pain written across Brian's face touches Nick deeply as a father who has also travelled a traumatic journey with his own daughter.

The devastation and deterioration Brian sees since he last saw her is hard for him to digest. Or bear. Shock paralyses heart, mind and soul. Slowly – very, very slowly – he begins to take some of it in.

I'm grateful for precious times together. Every morning, we enjoy a sweet time of prayer and sharing Scriptures. I store these memories, putting more and more into a special place of safekeeping – an area in my heart dedicated to these unique days.

It's terribly traumatic for Brian to see Shirley's intense suffering. And his ten-day visit goes far too quickly. He has to go back to sort out visa issues and line up an emergency visa so that he can return at a moment's notice.

Once back home, he messages Shirley. She responds:

> *Thanks for your lovely message. Thanks also for a good time together, for fitting in so well, and for all your help so sweetly given.*

After three weeks on Pazopanib, Shirley texts about the expedition to Oxford planned for 28 March:

> *I'm having an X-ray before my appointment. It would be awesome to get a good report, specifically that the tumours are shrinking. I'm also desperate to regain my breath and strength... and to be able to get out of bed and move around more. Please would you pray... and*

stand with me... asking and believing for these things in Jesus' name.
X

Brian watches in horror as the expedition begins. Nick eases Shirley out of bed and into a borrowed wheelchair – that's how bad her legs have become. I've carefully dressed her and struggled her limp feet into her trainers. Doing that takes me back to struggling to get her feet – then still so little – into her shoes as a tiny girl.

The expedition is bruising. Getting the X-rays done challenges us. It's a difficult thing, in the tiny cubicle, to get Shirley out of her clothes and into her X-ray gown. Nick wheels her in. While I wait, I wonder how on earth she's going to stand up but, somehow, she does.

At the end of a crushing day, texts fly. Shirley writes:

> *Well! It was an expedition to Oxford all right – with my legs just refusing to work. Nick and I got very good at the waltz! Strictly Come Dancing, here we come!*
>
> *Overall, the news is good. The docs want to get me off morphine (so no more comedy texts and messages, sorry). And... given my scan... I should not be breathing as easily as I am.*
>
> *I fully believe this is an answer to prayer... Thank you, God.*
>
> *Love you all, hope you're out enjoying the sun. I'm hoping to get into the back garden and soak up some rays...*

Nick fills in the details:

> *Today was a very hard day for our most incredible Shirley – not with the lungs, but the legs.*
>
> *For some reason, the transition from bed to wheelchair, to car, to wheelchair, to X-ray, to wheelchair, to doc's treatment couch, to wheelchair, to car, to wheelchair and finally back to bed... Well, if ever you saw a most incredible, remarkable woman undertake the seemingly impossible, then we saw it today. Shirley, you're a legend!*
>
> *So – with that totally unacceptable leg situation – we ask that prayer focus be laser-aimed at the legs.*
>
> *A few days ago we asked for laser-prayer on the lungs, as Shirley's breathlessness was scary. She couldn't move from her sitting position in bed to being sat on the edge of the bed without seriously laboured breathing. She was on oxygen for a lot of the day, every day.*

Today – with all the extraordinary physical effort she's had to make – not once did she need any oxygen, not once, not at all, her lungs worked just great!!!

Thank you for your prayers for – clearly – they are heard. As God choreographs this most remarkable journey, he wants us to be part of it – because he knows we love Shirley.

So he asks us to pray – together let's pray – with expectation.

Laura sips coffee as she joins in:

Hey, beautiful friend. My word for you is 'boldness' – "the trait of being willing to undertake things that involve risk and danger; requiring or exhibiting courage and bravery".

Shirley, I want to honour and applaud you for the way you have journeyed this cancer path – such a rollercoaster – with dignity, grace, joy, courage and boldness...

But Shirley has the last word:

I can breathe a bit better! David said, "I praise you because I'm fearfully and wonderfully made" (Psalm 139:14).

Let's pray that, through the oral chemo, God's healing power continues to restrict the flow of blood to the tumours, and that they shrivel up and die – as my body is restored to its healthy, original design. Thank you, Jesus.

On 29 March, Shirley says:

Guys, my legs are so much better, it's unbelievable! Been for two (slow, wobbly) walks today. Much easier getting in and out of bed. Am so grateful. Hoping for an even easier day tomorrow!

Chris pops in and Shirley lights up. I make tea. As they chat, Shirley says, "What an amazing God we have – to have changed the horrors of this cancer into quite a lot of blessing."

"Yes," Chris replies, "and what an amazing person you are – to have allowed God to transform you into such a blessing."

CHAPTER FORTY-FOUR

The Shadow of Death

"Tonia has taken me out too –
to the charming village of Goring..."

SHIRLEY IS SO MUCH BETTER THAT SHE'S GONE TO A PUB FOR lunch with Katy, Gaynor and Jo. And my heart is so, so glad. She gets to be normal one more time and to gorge herself on their lovely chatter and laughter.

Tonia has taken me out too – to the charming village of Goring, where she has her hair done. She's kindly arranged a blow wave for me, which means I finish long before she does. So I take a little walk, exploring the streets in rare but precious sunshine. Next, I follow the deep green, lazy Thames – taking pics – to the weir and back.

265

As I walk, I revisit the last five weeks. Once Shirley started the Pazopanib, over a month ago, her breathing began to improve. We stopped taking Harriette with us – two very portable oxygen cylinders, in a nifty blue backpack, supplied by the NHS. Now that the oral chemo has kicked in, Shirley uses oxygen only sporadically – and sometimes not for hours. She can take short trips – to sit beside the Thames in Henley, or to visit a friend for a cuppa. We seize the moment to indulge in all the foods Shirley likes, as her appetite's much better. The pain in her chest is gone. And she's cut the morphine right down. The two or three months of better health seem to be happening. Sadly, the X-rays – very soon after starting the oral chemo – do show increasing lung disease. And we live under another shadow of a possible stroke, since even the several changes in medication don't completely control Shirley's increasing blood pressure. There's also a further, more immediate shadow. The chemo begins to make her legs ache more and more.

As Tonia and I drive back, she shares about the years she spent in the Goring area. We're both looking good, but Tonia's looking particularly 'glam'. I feast on the country roads, occasional green tracery of overhanging branches, and grass waving gently in the breeze.

The next day, I text Lynn:

Busy day. Big grocery shop. S a good day with less leg pain. God is very close.

And later:

In these long, sad days, there are special moments – like your texts – that I treasure. Called the doc and he was reassuring. Please pray about my struggle with exhaustion. Lots of love.

Brian texts Shirls:

Hope today is not too tiring for you. Lovely talking to you last night. God bless, Dad.

Claudia writes:

When you cannot trace his hand, trust his heart.

I respond:

How absolutely beautiful. What a dear faithful friend you are! Really standing in the need of prayer.

And, later:

We are feeling very small. Lol.

Every day, so many texts come and go – to and from Shirley's phone in its sky-blue cover. I notice, though, as I vacuum, dust and clean, that she's frowning.

"What's it, bunny rabbit?" I ask.

"Mum…" She's very pensive. "I'm very touched. I've just found out that some of my friends have vowed to stand beside me and fight with me before God. No matter where my journey leads. They so want me to keep fighting too…"

She has to stop. It's a while before she can continue.

"I don't want to let them down… But… I just can't… anymore."

Tears follow well-worn paths down her alabaster cheeks. She's put up such an amazing fight – picked herself up after every blow, and us, so many times.

I feel so sad. But though I don't want to, I do understand. "Oh, Shirley," I murmur, "you care so much about disappointing them…" I take her hands for a moment. "But remember, it's the Lord's fight. He will fight for you."

We've learnt that fear takes many forms – some new to us. Tentatively, Shirley asks, "What happens when the drug no longer works? What then?"

I climb up on the bed beside her.

"Of course, I don't want to die… I still don't… but… where I'm at now… I fear the *process* more than *dying*."

How hard it is not to be fearful of that! What is so real at this stage is the wonderful grace which alone has carried her – us – this far.

Hesitantly, tenderly, I say, "I think – *hope* – I understand."

Quiet tiptoes around us for quite some time. Then Shirley shares another deep concern.

"Mum," she almost whispers, "Nick's going away this Saturday (29 March) for ten days. Will I ever see him again?" Floodgates open. Nick's going to Rio to assist with a Street Child Football world cup for street children staged just before the real world cup.

"I don't know what to do," he told Shirley. "I don't want to leave you…"

At the last visit to the oncologist Nick had managed a private chat with her.

"I'm supposed to be going to Brazil next week for ten days. I'm so torn as to whether to go or not..."

Claire had smiled, placing a caring hand on Nick's arm. "Go, Nick. Shirley will be here when you get back, I'm sure of it. Yes, she's deteriorating quite fast, but a break will help you help her when you get back."

"I want you to go," Shirley responded. "You've worked so hard organising this... You must go. Really!"

I know she's being totally and typically unselfish. And it's costing her a great deal. How beautiful such unselfishness is. And how wonderfully happy she is when he gets back.

Nick comes in every day now. I watch her light up the moment he arrives. His business partners have told him to take whatever time he needs.

I think of our conversation of a day or two ago: "Nick, you are giving Shirley everything you possibly can, totally, no holds barred. No human being can give more."

———

On Saturday afternoon, 12 April, Helen Dibley moves in behind Shirley's piano. Quietly at first, but later in full voice, she and Shirley sing the worship songs they particularly love. What a blessing to be there. Later, I journal:

While Shirley still has breath to sing, all her songs are songs of such heartfelt, fervent praise.

Shirley tells the others about Helen's visit. Next time Helen comes, Jo, Gaynor and Katy make sure they're there too. They sing with passion until they're tired out.

I find myself watching Shirley – and so does Gaynor:

I saw Shirley touching heaven many times. I will never forget a prayer she said, while lying in her bed, with tears streaming down her face. She thanked God for revealing himself to her – and loving her so much. Despite her suffering, she was so joyful to have gone deeper in his presence. And this was more than fulfilling enough for her.

For me, it's another very beautiful experience; another one to remember, balm for my aching soul.

On another Saturday afternoon, not long afterwards, Helen Sparks comes to help Shirley plan and practise the worship for her funeral. This time, quietly, I jot down random words, phrases and snippets of all sorts. I want to keep as much of this afternoon as I can in my heart forever.

At this point Helen and Shirley beautifully celebrate in their song the absence of evil and of fear because God is with them.

As the Spirit falls, Helen's heart explodes, "Pour your perfect love over Shirley. We declare there is no fear in Shirley. There is no fear in this room. Pour out your light and love on Shirley, on Thy. Thank you that our God is with us." This is her song and it is so sweet.

Shirley's tears flow. They know to be gentle as they course down her pale cheeks. Now the words they sing focus on God's permanence, faithfulness and steadfastness. He is always there when they call and it is his love that is their anchor. They sing about their longing to be with God, to be in his love, rather than anywhere else. They sing to the Holy Spirit, telling him how welcome he is.

As we fall silent, God graciously accepts the invitation.

Helen arrived overwhelmed at being asked to practise the worship for the funeral. She leaves even more overwhelmed.

On the lighter side, Jo – or Joey, as Shirley calls her – kidnaps us. We cross the bridge at Henley and park. Shirls and Jo giggle as they people-watch. The many swans and ducks – perennially hungry – people-watch too.

"That kid's on Ritalin – I just know it! Look at the faces of his family as he hops from bollard to bollard. And it's weekend so he hasn't had any today," jokes Jo.

A little later, a pregnant-looking man wobbles past.

"I wonder what he's having for dinner. Roast lamb with heaps of potatoes," speculates Shirley.

"Nah, I think he feeds on bacon pizza, with lashings of cheese, mushrooms and salami," suggests Jo.

Quiet in the back of the car, I enjoy it all hugely. As always, I'm so glad for the pleasure all this gives Shirley. *Thank you, Lord – she's holding her own.*

Sadly, when we stop at the George on the way back, Shirley can barely manage to get to a bench beside the river and back. Outings like this soon become a thing of the past.

Every night, Shirley watches TV. I crawl up beside her on the bed. Often, she finds my hand to hold. Together we watch *MasterChef, Shaun the Sheep* and *Indiana Jones and the Lost Ark*. When we watch that for the third time,

I get a little restless. But what I really find hard, for different reasons, is watching all that the TV screens about cancer.

Often, when Nick arrives, and after the banter fizzles out, he crawls up beside Shirley on the bed to read *Harry Potter* to her. These days, concentrating – and reading – becomes very difficult, perhaps because of the increasing doses of morphine. Many times, they both make me smile – because they've fallen asleep.

Shirley begins to falter over the exercises the physio wants done; largely, because she feels so awful much of the time. She manages to rinse her mouth with salt water though. We guess at how many times a day and how much salt, but she wins – no mouth sores. She also manages Wilf and Shelley-cat. But she's so gentle with them that when she really needs to move them off her, she often relents. "Just five more minutes – okay?" she says.

To me, as gently, she says, "Mum, when my friends come, you don't need to leave. You can join us." The soft, gentle quality of her voice, when she calls "Mum" nowadays stirs my soul and settles into my heart, among my other treasures.

With a very full, loving heart, Laura writes:

Shirls is really tired now. Every day – as things present themselves as mountains – Shirls continues to face them, because she wants to admire the view from the summit!

And we continue to step in with fresh strength. Faith as small as a mustard seed is enough, and – together with Shirls – we are mountain movers.

Cancer is a beast of a bully! The disgusting squatter is trying to call Shirley's lungs "home". I don't think so! Let's banish the cancer back to where it came from.

Shirley, we love you, we are with you – heart and soul. And we celebrate your tenacity to hold on to your anchor, the King of kings and Prince of Peace.

My special quiet joy is to see how friends, as God's chosen spokesmen and women, come, perch on her bed and encourage her.

Nick tells others:

The house is constantly soaked in the Holy Spirit. People come here to know his presence. There's a remarkable sense of peace.

Shirley just keeps giving out. So the peeps come to be with her. They just find it so good to be here.

A district nurse called Katy tells me she keeps making excuses to come back. And God shows me Shirley is like a fountain – giving and giving and giving. It reminds me of what Larry Crabb says in his book:

Spirit-given confidence that God is there and worthy of absolute trust breeds freedom to release what's most alive in you ... At some point you realise these are springs of living water! You find yourself released to be the person you've longed to be – loving, joyful, peaceful, patient, kind, and gentle.[22]

---

[22] *The Pressure's Off,* p. 181

CHAPTER FORTY-FIVE

As the Shadow Lengthens

"Shirley can see the sunsets."

ONE MORNING, I WAKE TO AN INISTENT, URGENT BEEPING sound. It must be Harry. And he's in distress. Deep panic grips my guts. Looking at him doesn't tell me anything. I page through the little booklet about him. Somewhere in there, I know, is a number to phone. *Ah, here it is... But wait – is that noise really coming from him? It sounds familiar...* I explore. *Oh, thank God! It's the phone – and it's telling me it needs charging.*

As the days go by, I become increasingly aware of my responsibility. I have no medical knowledge at all. So far, Shirley has put her healthcare in my hands. I don't want her feeling nervous or frightened because of my limitations. So I say to Nick, "Please ask Shirls if she's okay with me looking after her. I won't take it amiss if she wants something different and professional."

Not too long afterwards, he comes back into the kitchen. "Thy," he says, "she trusts you absolutely. Actually, I've just checked this out with Katy and Jo. And she's told them the same. They think it goes back to the role you've always played in her life. Though separated by so many miles, you have always been close. You love her so much. And she loves you hugely; you have always been her safe place and retreat when things get really awful. You are her one unfailing support. Sometimes she did wonder if you fully understood her boyfriend issues, for one, but that did not shake her trust in you. You were always her sanctuary, the one with whom she could be completely vulnerable."

"This is... What can..."

"Thy, she so values and cherishes you. You are her rock, Thy, her constant. Please never forget that."

As I hear this, I have no idea what my emotions are – or how to describe or handle them. What I do know is that I now feel reassured and empowered to deal with this situation.

Lying in bed, Shirley can see the sunsets. And her four goldfish too. While so beautiful, the sunsets bring on sadness – at least, for me. Then circumstances threaten to overwhelm. Tears drip-drop from the corners of the soul.

We can't go to church because of Shirley's weakness and low white cell count. But we can pray – we have the sweetest prayer times. And we detail our thoughts. Shirley pulls out her beloved diary – rapidly filling up – as the right place for the résumé of her cancer. She records her pain meds and her journey with pain. She journals her heart and mind and soul.

Major challenge: God's promises only mean anything to you if you trust the person doing the promising. So, I began this journey asking: Is God good? Have lots of Bible verses and promises, but until I really, really believe God is good, these promises mean nothing.

Good, hard look at what I think about God – good, or just another deceiver? Once I made my decision, I found a degree of peace. I made myself stick to it. At times, felt tangible / physical presence of God comforting, bringing peace. This was my decision to trust God.

> *Realised people are God's hands and feet. As such, they apply his love to me.*
>
> *Felt overwhelmed by love and grace of others.*
>
> *And by God's real involvement in keeping me safe.*
>
> *Core idea: If God loves me, I have no need to fear. He only wants the best for me – and his love is huge. Therefore, his care for me is / will be huge. Therefore, I'm not afraid because God loves me!*

I turn to my dairy too. At times, pain fills my heart, clogging it up. I document the comfort that soaking in worship songs brings, now that we stand face-to-face with death. I remind myself to say nothing but yes to my potter as he gently works with me every day.

I record my change in status: for the first time, I feel as if I have come into partnership with Jesus as a sufferer. I am weak; but all he requires of me is to take the next step, as he does. This is the path of life, a reality check, what life is really like. We cling to his hand, also acquainted with grief. It is also a journey into rejoicing – how impossibly hard to believe, but it is. That Jesus, in his finished work, atoned for all of Shirley's great suffering is wonderful beyond words.

I write another round robin:

> *Meaningful times with the Lord are difficult. I can't concentrate. I know if I don't do it before nine in the mornings, I can forget it. Many times, God speaks.*
>
> *And thank you, Lord, for lovely times of worship with friends.*
>
> *Thank you, Lord, for the very precious times Shirley and I have together – more treasures to store in the attic of my heart.*
>
> *Pray with me about the very real fear Shirley – and I – have about what happens when the drug is no longer effective. What is so real to us, at this stage, is the wonderful grace we have received so far.*

Shirley keeps us all up to speed:

> *Feeling so ill. Gut-wrenching fear. Restless.*
>
> *Please help me, guys. The mystery of my painful legs continues... except that now I have only one weak, painful leg... and it's not the one that was operated on either?!? It's still enough to make moving and walking a nightmare. Last time we prayed for my legs, they improved massively... Can we do it again?*

Next day, 7 April:

Hello, can I hijack our group to ask for emergency prayer for Katy Lyne, whom most of you know. Katy's been unwell for ages with chest pain and coughing. She's cutting her holiday short today to see the docs, as she's suffering terribly from asthma. She'll hate me posting this... But she's been such an incredible support to me... it's the least I can do. Xx

In turn, I text:

S has severe pain in localised spots on left leg. Waiting for oncologist to phone.

Shirley reports:

Today, 8 April, the leg saga continues. The oncologist explains that, apparently one of the side-effects of the oral chemo is cramp. (Aha! That's what this feels like.) Solution is either to lower the chemo dosage... hmm... or keep me dosed on enough morphine to take the edge off. Neither option is great... Please, can we pray for a God-intervention? Love you all. Xx

Two days later:

Guys, just an update... docs have advised that I up my morphine intake so that I can move more easily. Obviously, I have to watch that I don't take too much and get zonked... and send any texts!!!

Not successful today... was in a lot of pain this morning and morphine made me sleep half the afternoon.

Later that day:

I've been so focused on my leg pain... But... about my breathing... it's so good! Over the last couple of days, I've become really sure that my breathing is improving. I'm so grateful and relieved that the nasty, breathless feeling is gone.

Thoughts and prayers go to Katy Lyne, who is still struggling with a bad chest. Much love, everyone!

"Skattebol, how about some tea?"
"Really, Thy! What kind of a word is that?"

"Nick, every South African loves it. It's a special term of endearment and it means, roughly, 'ball of treasure'. Appropriate, don't you think?"

"I'll say! Now let's get your beautiful daughter into her chariot and get on the road to Oxford."

It's a gruelling journey and this time it's longer. Of course, it can't be, really, but I feel sure it is.

At the Churchill Hospital they do more scans, and Shirley copes well. Nick drives us back via a scenic route, and we enjoy McDonald's.

The next day, 16 April, Shirley can hardly move, and struggles – on crutches again – to get to the toilet. So we continue to be tossed to and fro.

We sit for hours in dull reception rooms. We feel time moving ponderously, grinding minute by grinding minute. Sinister treatment outcomes, etched on many faces around us, discourage us.

Claire believes that the increasing, excruciating pain in Shirley's legs is caused by the Pazopanib. I appreciate her dilemma: *Do I reduce the pills? Less pain – but the tumours will grow faster. Continue as now? But Shirley's suffering from her legs will steadily increase.* What a situation. Very, very reluctantly, Claire decides to reduce the chemo by a quarter. I feel she's right but find this incredibly hard. This means the cancer will plunder and pillage almost unchecked.

Once home, I fetch meds from Boots immediately (never mind the traffic) because Shirley's pain is so bad.

In his heartache, Nick turns to Jo and Laura. "As usual, I went round to Shirley's. I knew she'd love it if we talked about everything and nothing – which we do really well. I come up the path to the front door, aware of the white blossom on her tree. The next thing, as I turn the corner into her 'bedroom', I see her looking up at me with a weak smile. And I see death all over her. She's been transfigured from a vibrant, fighting warrior of faith. What I now see is that she could pass within hours – days, if God is gracious. She's in a place somewhere between life and death."

"Oh, Nick…" Laura is tearful. "Standing with you in prayer…"

"It's all so sad – the cocktail of drugs, the oxygen pipes up her nose, 'Harry' faithfully chugging away behind her… But then, on the other hand, there are the fervent warriors praying for her night and day, all over the world." He stops and chokes up.

"Hang in there, Nick," encourages Jo.

Last night, we tied a pot and soup ladle to Shirley's headboard. She was scared I wouldn't hear her from upstairs in the night. Now she can make a really big noise. But tonight, I move downstairs, duvet and all, to sleep on the couch behind her, which is where I will stay from now on.

Often, Shirley wakes in the night. I wake too. It's that thing mothers do – we're fine-tuned to wake every time our baby wakes. Many times, she needs me.

The leg gets increasingly worse and I rub it more and more. I notice that Shirley needs oxygen more often too, and sometimes her mouth is blue. Nearly every second day, I call the doctors for her pain and her problems with blood pressure.

As breathing is becoming so difficult, the district nurse teaches Shirley how to breathe deeply from her upper thorax. She tries valiantly, but it's too tiring.

Because of Shirley's difficulties to breathe I'm so struck by the song that claims every breath we breathe is given by God. Every breath given her becomes doubly precious.

Every breath becomes very, very precious.

One morning, we talk about Psalm 23 and "the valley of the shadow of death". I realise we now linger there. I'm quick to point out, though, that we can't stay there permanently; we go through it.

"Mum," Shirley says, her voice full of emotion, "you do know that I'm dying?"

"I know," I somehow manage, trying not to choke.

"Mum, please, will you help me die?"

I'm stunned. Then, "Of course." What a world of emotion – pain, horror, shock and distress – packs into my reply. "I'll do absolutely everything I can for you, my darling."

"Thank you." Silence. A long silence. Then, "Thank you, Mum. I love you."

CHAPTER FORTY-SIX

A Love Story

*"God was so present, the Holy Spirit so tangible.
Anything – her healing – could have happened."*

SHIRLEY STARTS THE DAY WITH A CHIRPY LITTLE TEXT:

Today is the day we start filming!

Through his contacts with HTB, Nick has arranged for two media production students to come and film Shirley's testimony.

I text Brian, knowing how anxious he must be:

Broken night until 2 a.m. After more meds, S – and I – slept well for seven plus hours. She's really anxious as to whether she can do this – because she's so breathless.

Brian texts Shirley:

Hello sweetie. I'll be thinking of you especially today. I hope the filming goes well and doesn't tire you too much. Lots of love, Dad.

For two whole days, at huge cost to herself, Shirley has been cutting down on drugs, especially morphine. It's her greatest desire now to tell her story as well as she possibly can to glorify God. It is a final, powerful attempt to give God her best. To do it well, she needs to be drug-free – for a clear head and an open heart.

On Wednesday night, four nights before the filming, Nick and I load Shirley into her wheelchair and then into the car to take her to Chris's for worship and prayer. Although weaker than a kitten, she's not willing to give in or cancel.

Many help us into the house, while I guard her oxygen supply from Harriette. It just cannot be interrupted.

For a good few moments, I stare, entranced, at a piece of pottery placed on the hearth. Grey hands cup a burning tea light. They form a shallow steeple round it, pointing heavenward – caring, protective, poignant. And comforting.

I sit beside Shirley, struck by how pale and sick she looks. She's hardly aware of her surroundings, her eyes falling closed again and again. I'm sad to see that as the ten of us worship, Shirley's lips don't move in song. It's the first time ever that I can remember her not taking an opportunity to sing. While the rest stay on to pray, we stay only twenty minutes – an amazing twenty minutes.

"Oh, Thy," Nick says later, once we have Shirley settled in her bed at home again, "God was so present, the Holy Spirit so tangible. Anything – her healing – could have happened. But it didn't – just a depth of peace present that was beyond understanding. At one point, Jo thought… that she was going."

Chris texts:

Wednesday night, the experience of God's presence with the tangible sense of God's love in the room for all of us was unforgettable.

Shirls, may you continue to feel peaceful as you rest in him. May you know he is holding you in his everlasting arms.

Next day, Shirley manages to text too:

Fabulous prayer time yesterday evening, thank you so much. I know we all felt God's presence powerfully. I had a much easier night. I'm continuing to believe and pray that my breathlessness will improve but, at the same time, I'm very peaceful. There's not a lot I can do! I'm trying just to rest and trust. Thank you for pouring out your love on me last night – it was very, very precious. Xx

This prayer and worship meeting, besides blessing Shirley in very many ways, turns out to be the very best preparation for the filming ahead, with all its challenges.

The day before the filming, 26 April, I ask, "Would you like me to wash your hair?" I know it's going to be difficult, but I also know she'd really like that. And that I'd like to do it for her.

"Oh, would you? Thank you, Mum," she says.

So I rig up a back support for her with the sponge wedge she's had for her legs, and with cushions and heaps of towels. I help her turn – slowly, gently, but still on her back – until her head is propped up over the edge. I shampoo and wash, every movement an expression of love. I get lots of things very wet but, at last, she's back on her pillows, tired but so pleased with the results. For one thing, her head feels so good.

That same day, Nick rounds up the troops:

Just as a reminder, filming starts tomorrow, Sunday through Monday. Big faithful prayers for something truly remarkable from our Miss Glameron – that she may feel and know her faithful God's presence. That the words flow from her heart. That her lungs fill and work like fireside bellows! This in tonight – from the film crew: "Working on visual ideas and tailoring the video to the purpose. It's going to be incredibly powerful."

Tom responds:

We will pray. Spent some time with her today and was so encouraged by the peace and overcoming power of Jesus. Shirley has been teaching us so much without realising it. She mentioned how loved she felt – what a journey this is for so many.

Then Nick and Shirley draw up the questions he needs to ask. She depends on them – she is simply too weak just to talk.

Early on Sunday morning, I help Shirley get settled on the couch. I juggle cushions and help her cover all the tubing with a pretty floral grey and cerise scarf.

Nick meets Zack and Freddie at a local supermarket coffee shop. He wants to prepare them. He finds it hard to hold back the tears.

"She's dying, guys. We don't know how long we have left with her. She's so weak, so we need to be so careful how we do this. She has to set the pace."

Soon there's some strident knocking at the door. The introductions over, Zack and Freddie set up their equipment. Zack bends his tall frame over the camera to get the lighting right. Freddie fiddles with the curtain behind Shirley and finds the right spot to sit – a suitable cushion on the floor. He runs his fingers through his curly brown hair. And they are ready to start.

Nick leans forward. "There's such peace in your home. And people comment on how peaceful you are. How come, Shirls? Where did that come from?"

"There were times, you know... in the hospital especially... when I was so afraid and I just needed to cling to a promise or two from God. Then God's peace would... almost, like, *tangibly*... descend on me. It was, like... okay; I can feel God's peace; and I can do this next bit. I remember having a week when I was really peaceful." She nods. "And I didn't know why. It was in the Nuffield, after the op. I really can't explain... other than that God just drew near to me at that point... and gave me what I needed, and answered my prayers."

Shirley smiles and lights up the room.

"Actually, every morning... I wake up and I'm not sure what kind of day it's going to be... hmm... so once I've tested that the legs and arms sort of work" – she chuckles – "and I can breathe, I kind of go, 'Okay, it's going to be a reasonable day.' I'm breathless... Every morning I wake up and I just... hope that the breathlessness will be gone. Hmm... yeah... otherwise, I'm peaceful."

Nick gives her time to catch her short-rationed breath. When she's ready, Zack and Freddie switch on again. "What about prayer?"

"Many times... many, many times... I'd be so tired and exhausted, not able to concentrate... too down and out, really. I used to beat myself up quite a lot about that. I know when I really dig in and have a good prayer time, it does me huge good. So it was hard not to be able... physically... to do that. But my friends and my supporters keep saying to me, 'We'll pray for you. You just stand and we'll hold your arms up. You know we've got the words when you don't.' Without those touches of prayer and that support behind me… hmm… it would have been a lot harder." She nods her head for emphasis. "Support like this has been so beautiful to me about the community of God."

A cat meows loudly somewhere down the passage. Wilf is hungry and his feeder is empty. Shirley giggles. And I smile. Everybody but Wilf is trying to be so quiet.

Shirley takes a few rather shallow breaths. Next, Nick asks about prayer and healing.

"All of this has taught me… There's an old hymn with the words, 'It is well with my soul.' When I have touched my Father's hand… my Daddy's hand in prayer… you know, and I've opened my heart, he's reached out to me. He's comforted me. At those times, I know it is well with my soul. Hmm… that's what I long for, that's why I keep going back!"

A slow, weak little smile. Then she says, "You asked about prayer for healing? I fully believe God can heal me, at any second…" She laughs softly. "I don't understand why he hasn't… yet. But I'm not going to rule that out. The fact that I'm not healed… so many months down the line… doesn't mean my prayer hasn't worked."

She stops breathless.

"It just means that it's not God's time… It's not right yet. I believe that… with God… anything is possible, anything is possible, at any time."

"What do you base that on?"

"He says that about himself. Also, I believe his promises. Secondly, the Bible records amazing things that have happened. And, thirdly, I've seen a few of these, and so have my friends. I've met people healed from cancer. It does happen today, I believe that."

Shirley nods again. She runs her fingers through Shelley-cat's long, soft fur.

Nick changes direction. "Seven months into this, the leg op done and dusted, and the cancer redoubles its efforts. What now? How did you feel?"

"So frightened. The prof said I'd responded well to the chemo, my body was fit and strong, with few nasty side-effects. So they were going to be aggressive… until I told them to stop. It made me realise that we might have a lot longer to go than I hoped… But I still felt that we were going to get there, still felt we were going to get through this."

"How were you going to do that?"

Her special chuckle. Then she says, "Not in my goodness! If I had to, I was going to drag myself through somehow! I just believed, with God's support, we could get there. You know, anything would be possible… and, you know, that this healing was going to come."

"The real shocker was the PET scan in January?"

"It was hard; it was very hard. I felt disappointed, angry with God. I didn't understand why he was leaving it to the last minute. I think more than angry, I just don't understand." Shirley shakes her head. Tears flow – hers and ours. "Where is this all going, God? Am I really going to die? I can't believe that you would take... someone like me..." – she sniffs; more tears escape; we haemorrhage tears – "...who just wants to love you and serve you... and let me die! You know, what's that about?"

The sniffs morph into quiet, aching sobs.

"I have a tissue here somewhere..." Nick finds it and passes it to her.

"What didn't help was" – more tears – "I had this terrible sense of lost time... that I haven't lived my life the way I ideally want to. And I was just so, so longing for the opportunity to do it again and do it right... and do it for God."

The floodgates open – tears everywhere, some of them sliding through the cracks in our broken hearts. Shirley struggles to breathe, holds Nick's hand, and calms down slowly.

It's a good time to give her a break.

I get up from her maroon borrowed wheelchair. It's out in the passage, from where I've been able to watch and try to pray out of sight.

Now I make tea and coffee. Zack replaces the toilet-paper rolls he's used to quench his nose – streaming because of the cats. Under other circumstances, we would have laughed. But here, now? We can't.

Not too long and Shirley's ready to go on. She asks me to rearrange her scarf. Nick takes up his perch on the end of her couch again – not too comfortable, but out of sight of the camera.

"So, you get this really bad news – where'd you go from such a place, Shirley?"

"Well, the other side to all this is heaven. This has comforted and helped me so much. I'm actually going to a better place, you know! I have really started to think more and more about it. Of course, I'm scared: I don't... I don't... I don't know what it's like... and I don't want to say goodbye to all my friends. But I believe that heaven is awesome... no more suffering, no more hardship, no more dying, no more pain. I just can't say enough how grateful I am to God that we get to go there. What an amazing end to a life... even a life like mine, which... you might say... had lots of flaws and didn't really come up to standard in various areas. Hmm... I still get to go there…" She nods endearingly – emphatically. "I still get to go and be with Jesus. That is just one of the most precious things.

"We've just had Easter. Easter's been" – she chokes up – "so special… because… without what Jesus did on the cross… none of us would have any hope at all. So, yeah… in many ways I'm not afraid of dying, I'm afraid of the process… just so many things about my body not working the way they should… just being in pain… not being able to breathe. All these things have been really hard…"

Shirley chokes up again but, characteristically, she nods to emphasise every word. Then she waves at the camera, asking them to stop.

"Is it okay that I sound so teary?"

Freddie and Zack, pretty choked up themselves, reassure her. There's a lot of emotion all round.

"You mention heaven and how that comforts you – but is it reality?"

"I see heaven as… sort of… the ultimate gift. I don't understand much about it. I don't think anybody does. But there is a mansion and God has prepared a place for me. I think there will be things for me to do. There'll be a whole bunch of my beloved people and… hmm… we'll be with the Father and the Son. I don't think we know how big that is. It will just be… it will just be… awesome. So… yeah… I look forward to it; I look forward a lot to going there… Some people may look at my situation and say, *what a disaster, how awful…* but it's not. It's not, you know."

She stops to rest, catch her breath, sip some water.

"Okay, there's disappointment… sadness… 'cause I've not got to do all the things I've wanted to do… not made right some of the things I wanted to make right. But at the same time, there is heaven, and that makes it all okay, it really does… well…" – she chuckles ever so gently to herself – "not *all* okay, but it makes it largely okay… if I'm to be perfectly honest."

Shirley's getting very tired, more and more breathless, and needs to rest more frequently. Nick takes Zack and Freddie off to get some lunch. I do what I can to help her. Her eyes close softly. Very tenderly, I stroke her hair and hold her hand until she drops off.

When the men come back, chatting easily about this and that, Shirley works hard to focus.

The camera rolls, and Nick asks, "This is all unfolding in less than twelve months. What's happened to Shirley – the Shirley that was (before last year in June) and the Shirley that is (now)?"

"I think it's fair to say I wasn't a very happy person... No, I think it's safe to say... I wasn't a happy person."

She's thoughtful for a moment.

"I was a Christian and going to church. But wherever I looked for love... I couldn't quite find it. And I wasn't quite sure that God loved me. I felt like I'd asked and asked and asked... and God hadn't really heard me. It felt like I was doing something wrong. The hurt and frustration with all of that just kind of built up and built up... to the point where I had a big fight with God..."

Shirley chortles – like a dove softly cooing.

"About... gosh... a year and a half ago, I just said to God, 'I believe you're there... but I don't believe you care about me, cause how come you've just ignored me? How come you've not answered any of my prayers? Dealt with my pain? And I don't see you present in any way.' As a result, I was making some pretty bad decisions... hmm... mainly out of hurt and anger..."

She nods slowly and deliberately.

"I'd say the biggest transformation is that I learnt that God loves me..." – more nodding, really emphatic – "really, truly loves me... I just find it astounding that God would use something like cancer to show me that. You know... what kind of a God can do something cool out of cancer? That's mind-blowing to me. I don't believe God sent the cancer. But I believe he used it to show me how loved I am... through other people, and then by reaching out himself to me... when I was able to hear him and see him and feel his touch. It's been the most incredible journey of discovery, of discovery that... you know... all those years when I thought I was alone, I wasn't... I wasn't..." A smile, somewhat watery, breaks across her face, much like a gentle dawn. "This is why I want to go back and redo... I think most of us, most of us do... in some area."

Nick sits for a moment. Then he asks, "And now?"

"I think that... hmm... I regarded God as basically there to make my life comfortable. I loved him, but it was all very lukewarm... and it wasn't meeting the desires of my heart..." Slowly, she shakes her head – really sorry. She pauses. She has to. Then, "I'll never understand God's ways!"

Amazingly, laughter bubbles up from deep inside.

"God is so much bigger... Do I wish he'd healed me? Of course I do! Do I wish he'd answer that particular prayer? Well, it goes without saying... But at the same time, I trust him, I trust that he knows best..."

She looks up and melts Nick with her smile – and then turns to the camera.

"Before, I was convinced *I knew best, thank you very much...* and now I know God does. And that trust just makes things bearable, makes things doable..."

She's pensive for a while. And we are all very still.

"This journey you have walked with God – where did that start?"

"I've known about God all my life, but it's not been an easy relationship. I've never... I've never quite got it... I've never quite got the fact that God loves me... until now. I think this is the thing about God... I think that he never stops giving opportunities to help you grow and learn and realise... to bring you closer to him."

"You've just turned thirty-nine."

"Yup."

"What has been the purpose of your life?"

"What my specific purpose has been..." – a charming little chuckle escapes – "has been a bit of hit and miss, I think!"

She shivers a little, close to exhaustion. I'm really anxious.

Nick signals a break.

A while later, tomato and cheese sandwich in hand, Nick climbs back on to the end of the couch. "You've come to believe God loves you. In what ways does he show it?"

"So, so many ways. I'm single, live on my own, left South Africa fourteen years ago... Without help from my friends, and from my church community, and without financial help... I would have been in a really, really bad way. Also, one of the things... at my work... was a new sort of healthcare package, about six weeks before I was diagnosed. I now get critical illness payout, income protection cover... hmm... I get a payout, should I die... It's just a fantastic package of benefits. Without that, I would have had to sell the house... I honestly don't know how I would have coped." Shirley shakes her tired head. "It's just phenomenal how God took care of me financially... let alone the rest.

"Before all of this happened, I was fit and whole on the outside... Twelve months ago, you could have looked at my life and thought, *she has so much going for her.* However, inside I was very, very broken and hurt. But... since I got cancer... God has turned all of that around."

Shirley pauses in thought and wipes her damp face.

"Oh, Shirley," Nick asks, deeply moved, "how have you coped with it all?"

"I think the thing which has really, really underpinned me... if you like... is just my belief that God is trustworthy. His Word has a lot of really cool things to say about my situation... You know: *I will never leave you nor forsake you... I will send my angels to take care of you... I will not let your foot slip... I have a plan for you...* All of those things I can trust because God is trustworthy.

"I believe He's fighting for me. I've become increasingly helpless... bedridden... and not really able to do a lot for myself. I've had to let go... accept I can't do the fighting; it's just not in my power anymore. In Exodus, it says God will fight for me. And I found that really, really encouraging... the fact that I can be still, and God will take care of things.

"One of the really hard things is the sense of helplessness. I'm in a position where I can't sort things out; I can't make myself better..." She laughs, almost to herself. "I can't do even simple things for myself. This has left me feeling quite panicky at times... Then the reassurance that God will fight for me... God will sort it out for me... has just been like this incredible weight off. In my weakened state, I can just lie back... I can just be a child, really... and just allow him to do all the hard work. God is asking me to be still. I think its 2 Corinthians 4:16 that reads, 'Therefore we do not lose heart. Though outwardly we are wasting away, yet inwardly we are being renewed day by day.'"

The sun begins to dip low. It's been a grey, sometimes drizzly day, but now weak sunlight filters in. Freddie and Zack pack up. Nick makes the arrangements for tomorrow. He struggles Shirley into her wheelchair and across the room to her bed.

I drum up some supper. Shirley doesn't want any, and I leave them. I need to gather my thoughts and to lean into the peace I know I have somewhere in my heart.

Later, Nick and I share a glass of wine. I cry, and I share about Shirley's very difficult past (which is not new to him) and my great joy about where she is now. It's not long before Nick leaves too.

I text Lynn:

Thank you, dear family in South Africa, for especially beautiful flowers – brought by such a super guy [Lynn's nephew lives in Wimbledon, and arrived during the filming]. Shirls and I are both so touched. How loved we feel!

Pray S settles and sleeps deeply and long. Her BP is high and she's very tired.

I make Shirley as comfortable as I can, rearrange her pillows, and we settle down to sleep – or at least try to.

Drained, Nick parks and makes his way into his cottage in Shiplake. A glass or two later, he gets round to bringing everyone up to speed:

Hey, all. You hear about accomplished actors and actresses having multiple takes to capture the perfect delivery. Well, our Shirley just [rolls] them out and – oh my – on Day One, we have some quite remarkable content in the can.

What is astounding though – why do we ever doubt? – is that your prayer cover enabled Shirley to get through a very gruelling day. She spoke more fluently and effortlessly than she has since her breathing first deteriorated.

She drew tears – and smiles – from the guys. Her faith and peace ran to her very core and became tangible. Tonight she's exhausted, though very happy. Please pray for a deeply refreshing sleep, peace of mind and ease of breathing. What a love story where, through all the difficulties, she embraced Jesus more and more as altogether lovely.

We finish tomorrow.

CHAPTER FORTY-SEVEN

Finishing the Story Well

"...a photo of Shirley with her medal
after the London Marathon."

NEXT MORNING, I TEXT BRIAN:

> *S only woke once. Phoning doc to come see her. Filming from 11 till*
> *2. Lots of love.*

Zack and Freddie begin by taking stills – the cards on the piano, Shelley-cat drinking from the kitchen tap, Harry pumping out oxygen, the goldfish, a photo of Shirley with her medal after the London Marathon.

Once again, Nick wrestles Shirley from her bed to the couch in the window. She manages a small bowl of cereal before I help her settle back on comfy cushions. I brush her short hair ever so gently, position her cannula and tuck the tubes out of sight – just as she prefers them.

She takes up from where she left off. "So here I am... twelve months on... and my body is pretty broken and busted on the outside. It's not behaving the way it should. I'm sad about that but... on the inside... I feel whole... I feel loved... and I know peace."

She smiles at Zack behind the camera, and at Freddie, once again on his cushion.

"Once I came to really believe God loves me, some very nasty things became bearable. It just helped me to look away from... *Okay... I'm having this treatment and it makes me feel gross... I don't feel good.* God's love helped me to lift my eyes to a future where God loves me and... therefore... things are okay. To know that this is not forever... I think that is the most important thing... just to know that my God loves me... and that he is going to make all of this right."

There's a knock at the front door. I usher in Shirley's doctor. Everyone takes a break while, very concerned, he attends to her. He leads Nick and me out into the garden.

"It's not looking good, I'm afraid," he says, the collar of his jacket pulled up against the rain that's started to fall. "Her breathing is so much worse and vital signs are really quite weak. She may not have much longer."

The doctor, sad too, leaves us. With his news ringing in our ears, Nick and I return to Shirls, hold hands and pray. Then it's back to work.

"But you have been angry with God, haven't you?"

"You know, it's a funny thing... I've not been angry with God much. We've come a long way. I just have a really calm certainty that God loves me and it's going to be okay. It carries me like nothing else. And God dealt with the fear. You know, whenever that fear came around... It hung around for months and months... It was like this constant thing I couldn't get rid of. Hmm... When it did come, I came to say... *you will not have your way because God loves me.* You can let your mind go absolutely mad in a situation like that... You can imagine all the worst things! But I was able not to... because God loves me."

"How do you know that, Shirley?"

"A number of ways: I've felt it... hmm... I've seen it in action, in the love of other people around me. I mean... the amount of love and generosity and kindness that has been poured on me has been..." She chuckles softly, just a little of the Shirley-chuckle we all love so much. "I still get teary when I think about it. It's just... the most humbling thing... to see God's love for me in action. He's sent people to carry me... and to hold me... and to help me. Basically, he's not let me come to harm... in the sense that he's not let anything drastic happen to me... and he's not let me be broken.

"One night in hospital, after getting comfortable at last, I was in a deep sleep. For ages, I felt I needed to wake up to do something important. I didn't want to... I was so warm and snug. At last, I had to get up. And I was horrified to see that someone had switched my IV off. I called the nurse immediately... and she was most upset. Much longer... and there could have been serious kidney damage... organ failure... even death... God woke me with a dream to save me.

"He's kept me safe, you know, and let's not joke... I was pretty sick. For a start... I was a pretty ill puppy, with all those nasty drugs in me.

"The biggest message at every stage has been that God loves me... God loves me... God loves me. All my praying friends were pouring into my life, 'God loves you, Shirley.' I couldn't... oh... I couldn't turn a deaf ear to that. So I don't need to spend time questioning... or doubting... or going round in circles. I don't understand why... hmm... but I believe he loves me. It's just been the foundation... or the central truth that has changed my life."

Finished at last, Shirls warmly thanks Freddie and Zack. Subdued, all set off for home.

Friends wait expectantly to hear from Nick. True to form, he's no sooner home than he posts:

> *Dear all, Day Two of filming went so well. But the increased demand on Shirls has taken its toll. She's elated, but she's really finished. We pray for her peace, her breathing to be with greater ease, for her to know that she is safe... and for pain meds to kick in big time.*

Laura writes:

> *I know you will have given your all – and then some. What an inspiration you are!*

Gaynor responds:

> *Truly amazing and inspiring!! Well done, Shirley Cameron!!! X*

Rami in Cardiff also comments:

Not by might, nor by power, but by my Spirit, says the Lord. Hugely impactful – you will be used to bless others in ways we haven't yet understood. We love you – and stand with you. X

"Mum," Shirley calls feebly from her bed, "please, will you now give me all the meds… loads of morphine, never mind morph-brain… and whatever you can. Please. I've done what I wanted to do… And I don't want to… just can't… suffer any more."

As quickly as I can, I bring it all to her. I'm thinking, *Oh, Shirls! No pain meds for four days! Why?* I pretty much know the answer but ask anyway, "Shirls, wonderful girl, just why did you do that?"

"To make sure I could tell my story with a clear head… I love God so much and it was one last thing I could do for him… So I wanted to do it well."

I kiss her hand.

"Lekker slaap." (Sleep well.)

"Thanks, Mum."

CHAPTER FORTY-EIGHT

Journey's End

*"What a wonderful thing the relationship
between you and Shirley has become."*

THE PHONE RINGS ON TUESDAY MORNING, 29 APRIL. I STARE AT
it for a moment, quite startled.

"Hello!" It's Shirley's consultant in Oxford. "Can I please speak to
Shirley's mum?"

"This is her speaking," I say, worried now.

"I'm really concerned that Shirley's lungs are deteriorating so fast. From
my years of experience, this shouldn't be happening. So we need her to come
in for a PET scan a.s.a.p." I hear distress in her voice.

"She's too sick, Claire," I tell her, "even if she came by ambulance. Can scans not be done at a local hospital here?"

Also playing through my head is something Vicky said to me: "If they bring her to the Churchill Hospital, they won't let her go home again." All she needs to keep her comfortable is being done here by the local district and Macmillan nurses. And above all, this is what she wants.

There's a lengthy pause. Reluctantly, Claire agrees.

Nick sets the ball in motion for a visit to a local hospital on Wednesday, 30 April.

Every day now, I see Shirley take a huge step down. She's been on even keel for a while, but not anymore.

For weeks now, it's not been unusual to wake up sick to my stomach and feel nauseous all day. Now I wake up to live in horror all day long. Horror is a place and I'm always in it. I have to get up and get on with it. But I keep crying out, "Lord, help me in this horror."

I journal:

> *Just as you think you have handled one challenge and can take a breather, another looms large. Much of the time, I have my feelings firmly out of the way. I cannot begin to let them loose. That does not mean that I don't feel fresh pain when I see Shirley suffering more. But I can't allow myself to express my sorrow.*
>
> *Every day is totally unpredictable. I keep control through a sort of diary, see to Shirley's medication, call the doctor to give another injection, wash and make her comfortable, dash off to shop when she's not alone, and on and on and on. Totally exhausted, I cry out that this is impossible. Every day – and night – God carries me through.*
>
> *As things get worse every day, I can't despair – because I don't know how much worse they are going to be tomorrow. I can't afford to fall apart yet.*
>
> *That this life will all go on and on and on fills me with horror; that it should end – and what that will mean – fills me with dread too.*
>
> *Because of grace, I have learnt to wait. God has made the impossible possible a number of times. I have learnt how weak I am. He has pointed out that his grace is sufficient. I have learnt the tangible and*

trustworthy quality of peace and at no stage has it left me – not even now.

But, day by day, I wonder when to call Brian – and how quickly he will be able to come. Tuesday night, I suggest to him that he get ready to come next week.

By Tuesday, I just know we need a hospital bed. I know I can't lift Shirley, wash her and reach her from the sides of her double bed anymore. I ask the district nurse in the morning and the bed arrives in the afternoon.

At first, Shirley's not very happy. I wonder if she feels trapped when the sides are up?

I marvel how whatever we need is just there, the moment we need it: commode, bedpan, catheter with its bag hidden in her scarves, injections within half an hour, morphine pump attached and refilled daily, Caroline helping me with bed-baths. Name it and it's there, on time.

Today, as Caroline finishes up, Shirley says, "Thank you. You're a star."

"No, you're the star," Caroline replies.

As I let her out, she says to me, "What a beautiful, wonderful thing the relationship between you and Shirley has become."

Thank you, oh thank you, God.

On Wednesday, 30 April, we set out to have X-rays done in Ascot, at a local hospital. The skies are fittingly grey and disgorge their woe in fits and starts. How truly grey it all is – very, *very* grey.

I wrap Shirley in her comfy old navy-blue dressing gown. Nick struggles her into the wheelchair. I tug on her socks and sneakers and tuck a warm rug over her pathetically thin legs.

We transfer her oxygen supply from Harry the oxygenator to Harriette, the two portable tanks in their canvas backpack. As I do the transfer, I can sense Shirley feels anxious the moment she's off oxygen but relaxes at the sound of a returned comforting hiss.

Nick builds a ramp with the strong plank he now keeps at the door. He wobbles the chair down it to Shirley's car – driven as close as possible, across the roughly cut grass. Rain-drenched, he wrestles Shirley into the car. Cold and wet, I hold a futile umbrella and clutch Harriette, making sure Shirley has oxygen. I am thoroughly miserable.

Too weak to do anything else, Shirley sags into the seat. Nick swings her limp legs in for her. We are aware that Amanda looks deeply sad as she watches from next door. We bump slowly over the uneven ground and drive off.

At the hospital, we don't want Shirley to have to wait. She stays in the car with me while Nick goes in to organise all the details. The minutes tick slowly by. Shirley begins to get a little restless. She's so uncomfortable. But, as always, she doesn't complain. As I wait with her, I'm so aware of how sick she is, how gruelling this trip is. I find myself wondering why she's doing it.

"Because Claire can't decide what to do next," she struggles for breath, "if she doesn't have the data she needs."

How typical of her, I think, how gutsy, and how determined she is to cooperate to the full – no matter the cost for her.

At long last Nick appears. He's explained the situation and managed to get all the paperwork done. Because it's so serious, they have agreed to take her straight away and spare her a very long wait in a queue. He gingerly transfers Shirley to a wheelchair again. We walk the long corridor straight into X-rays, where they're waiting. He and I wait and watch behind a transparent screen. They help Shirley into position and she barely hangs on until it's done. The spectacle of her clinging, skeleton-thin frame fills me with horror. What a relief when she can collapse into her chair. Her chest is heaving and, oh, how she gropes and gropes frantically for life-giving air.

We expect to be dismissed, as in the past, to go home to wait for results. So we gape at the radiologist who reappears. She's extremely agitated. Stunned, we stare at her. I've never seen a radiologist behave like that. They stay deadpan. So we are highly alarmed. She can't be more emphatic: "These X-rays must be seen by a doctor today." She emphasises every word – and then vehemently repeats what she's just said.

The hospital contacts Claire in Oxford who, very sadly, concludes that nothing more can be done.

Shell-shocked, then somewhat numb, we drive home. Shirley is as pale as alabaster and limp as a rag doll. Nick and I each weep silently.

Once indoors, and everything is done to make Shirley relatively comfortable, Nick brings scores of anxious friends up to date:

Dear wonderful, faithful friends, the doctors say they cannot drain the lungs as this will undoubtedly create further complications. The procedure, even if conducted at home, would also be too distressing at this point.

Shirley is now no longer taking the oral chemo as it's hardly effective any more. From yesterday, her pain medication has been increased significantly. She wants us to pray that "the fluid in my lungs be miraculously removed, my breathing improve, and for increasing peace and restful sleep".

Sitting here with Thy, all I can honestly say is that God's peace in this place is tangible. May our joint prayers decrease discomfort and increase this wonderful presence for her. Thank you all.

I text Brian:

Come now – as soon as possible.

That night, at about midnight, Shirley asks me for the takeaway menu as she wants to order slap chips. I steer her round to being satisfied with orange juice.

"I love you, darling," she says. She says that many times nowadays, and also asks how I am. In fact, she's very concerned about us all.

Next, she texts her beloved Helpers:

Hello to all of you. Latest X-rays show fluid in my lungs; please may the doctors have wisdom as they decide what to do. Much love!!

Replies soon follow:

Reaching out now – praying for you to feel the depths of God's love and safekeeping in all this. He is with you – there is a friend that sticks closer than a brother. Rami

Praying for you, lovely. Gaynor Xx

On it! Sending lots of love and prayers for rapid improvement, peace and complete healing. Carolyn Xxxx"

The days of lying beside Shirley reading Harry Potter are past. Nick cares for her, holds her hand, loves her non-stop. At one point he says, "My darling, you are dying. If you want to say anything – see anything in place – while you're still able, we need to do this now."

Softly, Shirley responds with this and that – sheds tears from a dwindling supply – and, haltingly, manages to highlight again, "Before this cancer... I was so seemingly fit on the outside but broken on the inside... But... somehow... God has used this to totally restore me... I may be broken on the outside now... but I am so healed and at peace on the inside... and draw much comfort from the fact that I'm going to a better place."

Her chest heaves. Even a few words make her out of breath. Nick lays his hand on her chest and prays, pleading with God. Slowly it settles, and he watches her fall asleep.

Nick has promised to stand by her – in every way he can – and he's doing just that. He's here for hours every day. No one has ever had a better best friend.

For a very long time now, any exertion, even just lifting her, has caused Shirley's chest to heave. Alarmed, she pants and struggles for air. She beckons, and night or day, I lay my hand on her chest and pray. Nick does too. I hold her hand until the breathing calms down. At first it takes two minutes, then three, and later much longer. Usually, once she can speak again, she squeezes my hand, lets go and whispers, "It's okay," and then, "I love you, Mum." And I respond, "I love you too, sweetheart."

First Bindy, the local Macmillan nurse, and later Claire, the district nurse, aware of my increasing tiredness, suggest a night carer. But Shirley objects. "Please, no! Who will pray with me then?"

Brian arrives on Saturday, and a very sombre Nick drives him from the airport. *How can I prepare him for this?* Nick asks himself, as they turn in to Sandy Lane.

Nick texts:

> *Dear all, Shirley had a second very disturbed night. Medication to enable rest and sleep administered twice in the last 12 hours. She now recognises little of her surroundings and is being nursed by Mum constantly.*
>
> *Please – can we all come together with increased prayer? For her peace, and her rest in mind, body and spirit. Today her father arrived from South Africa. Please pray for Thy and Brian as they now walk this path with their loved and cherished daughter.*

Brian is utterly appalled to see Shirley. Together, we wince over what her body has become. She can hardly manage even a sentence at a time. Fortunately, she does recognise him.

That afternoon, she signs to us to move her bed sideways to see the TV better. She mimics hitting backwards and forwards. We all look at each other, totally puzzled. Then it dawns on us; she wants to watch Wimbledon.

I am upstairs when I hear Brain come up into what was Shirley's bedroom. He cries out – howls – his anguish. I stay still, waiting quietly. I know this is a very private moment, but my heart breaks for him.

Later, Brian stands beside her bed, bereft. He squeezes her hand. "I love you," he says.

"I love you too."

Perhaps her words are audible. Perhaps all she can manage at this stage is to mouth them.

CHAPTER FORTY-NINE

Homecoming

"…every time I passed the tree, the white blossoms suggested a beautiful Shirley in a wonderful white wedding gown."

SUNDAY IS A VERY IMPORTANT DAY TO SHIRLEY. WITH NICK'S unhesitating help, she's planned not only the details of her funeral, down to the worship, text and tributes, but also for communion before she dies. She has drawn up a list, and Nick has invited the people special to her for Sunday afternoon.

That morning, the first thing that strikes me is how dreadfully ill Shirley looks. She looks like death now, with parchment for skin and staring eyes. I half wonder whether it is an inappropriate invasion to have others see her in this state. *Surely some things are too private?* What calms me is the fact that communion, for her, will cement once more her love for God, her need for him now and her complete surrender to him. This is about her and God. And her closest friends can say goodbye, because she can't cope with visitors anymore.

Brian and I swallow down some breakfast. We tidy up, stuffing my duvet out of sight next to my black leather couch bed behind Shirley's. We top up the cat feeder, much to Shelley-cat's and Wilf's satisfaction. I then water and tidy the many lovely vases of flowers, positioned carefully so that Shirley can see them. Brian wipes the tabletops in the kitchen and unpacks the dishwasher; then he feeds the goldfish.

We hover round Shirley's bed, trying to keep her comfortable, moistening her dry lips, giving little sips of water by means of a syringe, holding her pale hands, singing to her and praying over her. As it has for days, peace continues to pervade the house – like an especially sweet diffusion from heaven. The early afternoon May sunlight brightens the room.

Subdued, friends slip in and gather round her bed. She can no longer speak but seems to know they are there. Her eyes are round, big, bewildered. The skin over her high cheekbones is like delicate white porcelain. Love for her flows through in the gentle words spoken softly, tenderly. Again, no one can resist, so they stroke her short, soft, fluffy newly regrown hair.

Dan finds a natural gap in the quiet conversation round her and begins the communion service. Mindful that I am anxious that she might choke, he places a tiny particle of bread on her tongue and moistens her mouth with wine. "Take and eat this in remembrance that Christ died for you – and feed on him, in your heart, by faith, with thanksgiving."

Jesus has made her "so happy", as she has said many times of late, and we rejoice with her.

"Drink this – in remembrance that Christ's blood was shed for you – and be thankful."

Each of us eagerly endorses every word with our whole being – for her sake.

One by one, the friends drift away, finding tea and coffee in the kitchen and gathering in a close circle on the lawn. Tears flow. There have been so many tears these days, months.

I stay alone beside Shirley for a while, torn between joining the others outside, even very briefly, and not wanting to leave her even for a moment. Not sure if I'm doing the right thing, I eventually go out to where they are standing, arms about each other, heads bowed. The circle eagerly breaks to draw me in. I join the 'group hug' and am enveloped by their love. But I can't stay away for long. So I am back beside Shirley when Gaynor comes to say goodbye.

She holds Shirley's hand, telling her how much she loves her. I remember the times Gaynor sat on Shirley's bed and was counselled and blessed by Shirley. Now she says, "I will never forget you. You have taught me so much about God."

Jo follows. "I love you so much, Shirley Pearly," she murmurs, stroking Shirley's hand. I am quite overawed when she too says, "You have taught me so much about God."

The filming was only a week ago. Since then, not unexpectedly, her physical deterioration has been horrific. But she continues to be surrounded by people full of tenderness and gentleness. We are all trying so hard to do all we can to drench her in love. It is beautiful to see.

Her words "I'm so happy" ring in our souls. We are single-minded and united in loving her.

"My darling, may only those thoughts that have God in them (making them beautiful) enter into your head," I whisper again beside her.

Shirley has asked that her last days be filled with the worship songs she loves. So I ask Nick to set up her music player gently beside her. Her head lolls to one side and, every time, I'm anxious to adjust her pillows. Her mouth gets very dry, so I dip her toothbrush in water – as her nurse Claire showed me – and gently moisten her mouth. I talk soothingly to her all the time, stroke her hair, hold her hand. Claire says that's the best thing now.

Sunday night, after the communion, Shirley can't settle. Every half hour, she pulls herself up. Brian and I each hold a hand, talk to her and pray, until she lets us lower her back on to the pillows. Eventually, I crawl into bed and Brian falls asleep upstairs. But every half hour, Shirley sits up, pulling on the railings of the bed, writhing and restless, eyes so bewildered. I get up for her but decide not to wake Brian. I want him to rest. Who knows what tomorrow will hold? Each time, I stand beside her, talking quietly, singing and praying. She can hardly speak but her distress is obvious: "Help me."

Oh, my darling, all your life I've tried to do that. That's all I've ever tried to do.

When dawn peeps over the trees, ushering Monday in, I'm relieved. I text:

> *Pray for us all as we face the horror of such suffering. It seems that God is calling Shirley into his presence to receive her prize. I may be wrong – and I'd love to be wrong – but perhaps it is time that we pray for a wonderful homecoming for her.*

The peace and grace in her home – is this the Kingdom breaking through into the present to 'fetch' her?

At half past five, I phone for a doctor. It takes him less than half an hour to come. After the injection, Shirley falls asleep at last. The household stirs and tiptoes round her. Brian and I breakfast on muesli and omelettes. It's going to be a hard day, but we are never far from Shirley.

These last months, I've admired her beauty a million times. She's always been beautiful. But now, somehow, she seems to be more so, only different. While she's been so roughed up by cancer, she's also been set alight by grace. I've traced the delicate curve of her eyebrows, admired the high cheekbones and slender nose, stroked the slim hands, and smiled at the left ear folded back in the womb and never come straight – all without moving a finger. Now I caress from my heart – still without moving a finger.

Her skin is as white as bone china and her features as delicate. Eyelashes, newly regrown, rest on her cheeks again. Most of the time her eyes are half-closed. When they open, they are bewildered, puzzled, sometimes a little frightened. They haunt us.

Almost unnoticed, Shirley slips off somewhere and becomes deeply restful. Last Saturday, she would become aware of us talking in twos or threes out of earshot and ask, "What's up? What's going on?" – but no longer. Back then, Nick said, "Oh, Thy, she never takes her eyes off you. Every time you leave the room, she asks, 'Where's Mum?'" But now? *No longer.*

All Monday afternoon, Nick, Chris, Brian and I hover round her bed. We take turns to caress and minister. When it's my turn – nobody's organising this, it's just happening – I bend so that she can hear. "Softly and tenderly, Jesus is calling," I sing. "See on the portals, he's waiting and watching, calling, 'Oh, Shirley – come home.'"

I share Psalm 23. "Though I walk through the valley of the shadow – through the valley, Shirley." I also tell her of my love for her. This I do more or less every time I draw near to her.

Brian, Nick, Chris and I won't allow her to be without one of us. We draw alongside her with Scripture, stroke her, pray over her, sing to her, love her.

Scripture says, "Love is invincible facing danger and death. Passion laughs at the terrors of hell. The fire of love stops at nothing – it sweeps everything before it."[23] Shirley is awash in our love, directed by heaven and choreographed into a dance which we lovingly weave around her.

That night, as Nick stands holding her gentle, white hand, he's very aware of the worship music playing softly. As he gazes at her he thinks, *the beauty of heaven adorns her.* But he's very confused. *'My God, my God, why have you forsaken me?' Why did you give me such a strong conviction all those months ago that she would be healed and restored?* He remembers when, after the leg op, he put his hands ever so gently on the deeply bound leg. *At that moment, I just knew that I knew God was going to heal her – a wave of certainty washed over me like warm water, tears just flowed down my face. On the way home, I couldn't stop crying with such a sense of awesome wonder and thanks...*

His thoughts run on to Claire's call, two days before her birthday. *Shirley was being told her life is to finish, imminently. And now this? So I'm thinking, this can't be right? God is going to do an amazing healing. I know that; I know he is; I would forfeit my life on that belief.*

A knock at the door breaks in on his thoughts. It's the night carer arranged by the district nurse. Today she's prevailed on me to make use of this service. I'm so tired that I actually agree to this. We fill in his paperwork, settle him in a chair, and Brian and I kiss Shirley goodnight – one last time – and go up to bed.

I text Lynn:

S going home. Pray with us.

We climb into bed fully clothed, thinking we won't sleep – but we do.

Nick sits next to Shirley, stroking her hair softly, from her forehead back down the side of her face, her skin slowly becoming nearly luminous. Her breathing rattles gently in her chest. He soothes the dryness of her lips using a wet tissue. Tiredness and emotion overwhelm him. Only the present seems real. Time passes. The carer sits patiently next door in the kitchen.

Nick's back begins to ache from sitting on the edge of the bed. He can no longer keep his eyes open, Quietly, he calls to the carer, "Could you just

---

[23] Song of Songs 8:6 (MSG)

for a few minutes stroke her hair while I go outside for a few moments of fresh air?"

The candle Nick's placed on the garden bench flickers in the night breeze. He gazes up at the dark sky, wrapped in the silence all around him.

"Come now!" The carer is standing in the door. "Come, come quickly!"

With a few bounds Nick's back at Shirley's bedside. He takes her hand and puts his face close to hers. Then he races up the stairs two at a time. When he shakes me, I'm immediately fully awake. We fly down to her, again taking the steps two at a time.

Shirley's chest rises, hesitates and falls under Nick's hand.

"She's gone... No... wait."

He takes my hand and puts it over her heart. There's the softest puff – an amazing thing, whisper soft – a gentle, last breath.

Then she's gone.

And heaven rejoices.

Nick quietly moves away.

I stay, kiss her forehead, thank Jesus. I come back many, many times – we all do – just to look at her, sometimes to touch and to love. I pull her little blanket straight, pray, hover and pray some more. I don't know what I feel – numb, I guess.

We hear Nick on the phone to the doctor and Christian undertakers he has selected. Then he comes back to stand beside her. *As I rest my hand on your chest, I felt the last breaths – the last flutter of your heart against the palm of my hand. So many times, you held my hand so strongly in yours. Oh, God, why do you take her from us?*

For some days now, I've been eyeing a little wooden cross Shirley kept beside her bed. Its sides are rounded and smooth, so that it's comforting to hold. Now I can't find it. So eventually, I settle on her little white ceramic cross. I fold her hands – how quickly they begin to get cold – around it now.

I hear a text come through to my phone. It reads:

My dearest Thykie, it is two o'clock on Tuesday morning. I just can't get to sleep because I am constantly aware of you three. And all I can say is that right now my heart is overwhelmed with love for you all. I don't know – but my Father knows exactly what's happening. Love you with the love of the Lord. Spaantjie Xxxx

Chris and John leave into the dark night. Brian and I go back upstairs and collapse on our bed. Nick falls on the sofa behind what is an empty bed with its oxygenator and bottles now completely redundant.

Nick wakes at 4.15 am, as dawn begins to break. He turns and sees the empty bed. *It is real; she's gone. Shirley's gone.* Tears run down his stubbly cheeks, his mind flashing back with such clarity to the moment in the hospital when he heard God say, "I will heal her, I will restore her." Extreme sadness, the most extreme sadness, overwhelms him.

"Then why is she dead, God? Was that just me making that up in my sheer desperation for her healing? Would you lie to me? Why would you do that? You *wouldn't* do that. Why is she dead, why have you taken her when you said that you would…"

A voice resounds, deep, irrefutable and out of nowhere: "I have healed her. I have restored her. I have taken her home to be with me."

The vision God now gives Nick is as clear as if it's taking place in the same room. Shirley stands before him, her hair really long, the smile on her face radiant. She's wearing a denim jacket and flowery dress. Nick can't get over how radiant she is. And peaceful and happy – the Shirley she was created to be.

Peace envelopes Nick. Great happiness floods his heart. God has worked tirelessly to bring her to this place. And he has completed his full restoration of her.

Two weeks ago, while driving, Laura asked God how she could encourage Shirley. She explained to me, "I felt God share with me a picture of a bride before her wedding day – preparing to meet her bridegroom."

In April, I saw the tree outside Shirley's door pregnant with blossom. From then on, every time I passed the tree, the white blossoms suggested a beautiful Shirley in a wonderful white wedding gown. And I would thank God that Shirley is a bride of Christ – in whom he delights.

Today, Chris and John come quietly up the path beside Shirley's tree, which is now dropping white blossoms like confetti. We all cry and hug and talk with hushed voices. Chris gently whispers to Shirley, "I'll never ever forget how beautiful you are right now."

Beside Shirley once again, Nick sees "a most remarkable picture of her in heaven. No mind could conjure up such – it just makes me smile".

He writes:

And God answered my question. The spring dawn chorus was ringing in a new day – and she was in heaven. I saw her there, as clear as I see one standing before me on this earth. God had healed and restored her, he had spent these months bringing her back to him, preparing her and her heart for an eternity with him; his bride was complete.

As we wait, we begin to text:

Shirley was taken into his loving arms at 1.35 a.m. this morning. Her last days were full of expressions of our love for her. What a love story, where – through all the difficulties – S embraced Jesus more and more as altogether lovely. Lots of love, Thy.

Dear friends, today is Shirley's day, the day that our loved one and dear friend has been taken home and rests in peace in her heavenly Father's arms. Early this morning, Shirley's mother, father and I were at her bedside at home as she drew her last breath. There has not been one person, who has come into her presence or heard of her journey over the last eleven months, who has not been moved, inspired or touched to the very core by this remarkable woman. Her natural beauty even in adversity, increasing depth of faith and sense of humour to the last made her the unique and wonderful person we knew. Please know that your support, love and prayer carried Shirley through the valley of the shadow of death for eleven months; her depth of gratitude had no bounds, and – consequently – ours too. Nick

Replies soon come back:

That is such a vision of how she is now – happy, free, and in the presence of her Jesus. No more tears, no more suffering, no more pain. We grieve for ourselves, but we rejoice for you, dear friend. Katy

Oh, Nick – now smiling her smile and singing in heaven: Shirley has been an inspiration in facing her journey with so much courage. She has a new body – alleluia. Chris

Even as her body grew weaker and its light dimmed visibly, she shone ever brighter each day of this journey. The last time I saw her, she was lit from within despite the pain – and she looked utterly beautiful, glowing with the light of heaven. Rami

What grace you have been given, my darling – dying grace. Mum [Thy]

My beautiful friend, you have fought the good fight, you have finished the race... Believe me, now you leave a devastating hole, as you are irreplaceable. I celebrate the crown of righteousness you now receive from the one you love, your Bridegroom, your Saviour, your King. You are forever an inspiration. Laura X

After attending to Shirley, the undertakers prepare to take her away. One of them, a kind man to whom I warm immediately, squeezes my hand. "I want you to know I'll make sure the cross she is holding stays in place in her hands."

"Thank you," I murmur, so glad of that because that's where it belongs.

Chapter Fifty

Celebration

"The St Joseph's lilies sweeten the air with their gentle scent."

NICK WRITES TO ONE AND ALL, "SERVICE OF CELEBRATION, 11.00 a.m., Wednesday, 14 May, at Greyfriars Church. After the committal at Reading Crematorium, there will be light refreshments – selected by Shirley for you – at the Crown in Playhatch. She also asked that, instead of flowers, you support her favourite charities."

As near as he can, Nick carries out Shirley's every wish. She used to say Nick loves a project – and will be "on it" in no time. The difference about this one is his heart. He recruits the band she wanted. He liaises with the church; organises flowers and tea, ushers, the composition and printing of a leaflet, amplification – you name it. He arranges with Dan to preach on the text Shirley chose: Hebrews 12:1-2. She ran her race and finished the course. Now she wants to encourage us to do the same.

Tonia is to lead the service; Jo, Laura and Nick to pay tribute; Chris, Katy, and Brian and I to lead in prayer.

Nick draws me aside. "Thy, the girls are asking about dress."

"This is a celebration – or Shirley would want it to be. So let's dress accordingly."

"Shirley said so too! I'll text the girls."

Dear Friends, with respect to dress code, Shirley would say "more life than death, more wedding than funeral". Though we miss her terribly, this is a celebration of her life. Let's make it so.

So the girls arrive dressed for a wedding – Gaynor in fresh apple-green, Laura in red and Jo in sky-blue.

As Chris and John drive Brian and me to the church, I know all is ready, thanks to Nick, and exactly what Shirley wanted. I'm glad 14 May is a sunny day. One thing Shirley didn't like about England was its grey skies. And we need sunshine to celebrate, don't we?

When we arrive, the coffin – so like Shirley to choose a light-coloured wood and simple trappings – stands in a pool of light at the foot of the steps. The St Joseph's lilies sweeten the air with their gentle scent. As I wait, I imagine the little white cross, embellished with blue, in her hands. And I'm glad – another special little gladness in an ocean of sadness.

"The cut we want playing beforehand is on here." Nick hands in the CD at the sound desk in Greyfriars. "Like incense rising before you, lifting up my hands in sacrifice, oh Lord Jesus, turn your eyes upon me."[24]

"Hillsong?"

"That's it."

The service begins – one last act of love from Shirley for all of those she loved. The worship is intensely sincere and personal, the songs those that spoke to her on her journey. The lyrics begin with a reminder of God's unchanging grace. They describe Christ as the cornerstone. They emphasise God's firm grip on us, no matter the circumstances. They uplift us by reminding us that the Father eternally sings a love song over us.

As Shirley's pastor and friend, Dan encourages us from Hebrews 12:1-2. "Shirley has fought the good fight, she has finished the race, and now she takes her place in the great crowd of witnesses to cheer us on in our race of life – a life that continues through death; a life centred on Jesus."

---

[24] *A Beautiful Exchange;* Joel Houston; © 2009 Joel Houston / Hillsong Publishing

Nick, along with Laura, Jo and Shirley ("Charlie's angels") share their hearts and bring tribute.

Nick speaks first. "Shirley touched and inspired to the very core with her natural beauty, increasing depth of faith, sense of humour and gratitude for all others did for her. She was truly genuine, honest and understanding. In this, you discovered a depth of strength and bravery that I believe few knew."

Jo's tribute comes next. "Shirley touched so many lives, especially mine. This whole year, she just shone as God took her on an amazing adventure of faith and trust. She came so much more alive than I had ever known her – more Shirley-like than I had ever known she could be. She lived to the fullest, loved more deeply, involved herself more fully, and became more fulfilled in all she did."

Then Laura. "Shirley was a ray of sunshine in all our lives. She could light up a room and make you feel better, regardless of what was going on in her life. She was always generous with encouragement – which increased as her suffering increased – the friend who made sure you were never far from a kind word. Her imperfections, weaknesses, fears, insecurities and unanswered questions came to be satisfied by Perfect Love. So many times this last year, she said, 'I'm so happy.' She did not leave with feelings of abandonment, disappointment or despair. She was full to overflowing of the great hope for what was to come."

Gaynor collects messages from those attending:

Thank you for once again thinking of blessing and loving us – this time, in the service you put together. Margie

Thanks, Shirls, for being so kind to put together your funeral service – with your thoughts fixed on those who'd be there grieving. That's typical of your kindness. Andy

Gorgeous Shirley, how fitting that you should leave us in such style! The service today was gorgeous... so you to make it all about us, and all about God's love for us. We were all touched by how loved we are and excited by our future in heaven with our Saviour. Louisa

I have never witnessed anything quite like it. Thank you, Shirley, for all you showed us along your journey. We saw you being transformed through all this by Jesus' love – in a fashion that gives hope for the future, whatever it holds. Tom

Standing at the back of the church, Nick and the undertaker exchange a few words.

"In all my years," he confesses, "I have never been to a funeral like this. I have never seen anything like it. It was more like a wedding than a funeral — she must have been a very special person?" He looks deep into Nick's eyes.

"Oh, yes," Nick responds, "a very special person, with a very special faith and relationship with an extraordinary and faithful God."

As we drink tea in the hall, Chris wanders over to Katy. "That was amazing – like we were all meeting at some celebratory wedding."

"I know. What an atmosphere – just indescribable." Katy sips her coffee thoughtfully. "Unless you were here, you could not really understand." She sniffs a little.

"Our love for her was so tangibly present. I haven't actually got the words to describe it."

Jo wanders over. "As we were worshipping, I saw a host of angels rejoicing with us here in the church. I've got to paint what I saw."

Later, Jo gives the painting to me.

Brian and I walk behind the coffin of our only child – for me, a moment of horror. We battle again with unreality – a battle we are to fight again and again in the time to come. *How can our darling Shirley be lying there? How can we be attending her funeral? It cannot possibly be true – can it?*

The journey to the crematorium is a blur. I keep looking at the message carved into the wood above the curtains: *Resurgam* – "I shall rise again."

"I know, I know you will, my darling," I whisper. And I am so glad.

As we get ready to leave, the organist plays Psalm 23. Spontaneously we take hands and from full hearts begin to sing:

> *The Lord's my shepherd ...*
> *And I will trust in You alone,*
> *And I will trust in You alone,*
> *For your endless mercy follows me,*
> *Your goodness will lead me home.*

Faith, rejoicing, peace and hope, so fervently expressed, encircle us.

Once we are back at Sandy Lane, tired and battered, I write my last round robin:

Her choice of songs, the testimonies and prayers, text and message by Dan, everything was profound. A sense of victory and quiet joy prevailed. Her previous pastor and the undertaker each said the same thing, though in different words:

"I have never experienced such a service before. It was beyond wonderful."

So I find myself saying: "Well done, Shirley-girl. Once again – with your usual style – you pulled it off with excellence. And what is so wonderful is that you did it all for love – your love for God and your love for us all."

CHAPTER FIFTY-ONE

Resting Place

"Her ashes scattered here, her haven on earth,
on a beautiful summer's day…"

NICK, BRIAN AND I PACK UP SHIRLEY'S HOUSE. "IT'S AS IF WE'RE invading someone else's privacy," Brian murmurs. "Like we're dismantling someone's life," Nick adds. This is more of the 'very hard'. We've got to know 'very hard' so well by now. I invite Shirley's friends in to select what they would like as a memento. I know she would want that.

Brian and I are given a week in the Lake District. I'm so pleased, because that's where she wants her ashes to be scattered. And I want a fresh memory of where she will be.

Just before Brian and I fly home, we all meet for dinner at the George – in the sunset over the lazy Thames. I am so touched to see that the girls are wearing some of Shirley's things – Gaynor a belt, Jo a ring and Katy a scarf.

A friend drives us to the airport. We've packed two extra cases of Shirley's things to take home to keep near us. As we take off, I have a picture of Shirley, face up in a vortex, swirling steadily away from me and growing smaller and smaller – and I'm utterly undone.

———————

At the end of May, we arrive home to a huge bowl of flowers – sent by the Secret Helpers. We arrange a second memorial service in Cape Town – using as much as we can from what Shirley put together. Friends and family come. Again, we are blessed.

Two months somehow slip by. The days are full of pain, grief and agony. Almost immediately, Brian goes back to catch up on a month's backlog at work. He continues to feel numb – struggling with reality.

I sit. I can't function. When I can, I write a bit in my diary, trying to describe my feelings. I share about my numbness and intensely debilitating pain. I also miss Shirley's friends terribly. And, in a strange way, I miss my life as it was with her during the final couple of weeks. Word fail me when I need to describe how much I miss her.

On 2 July, Nick texts:

> *I've just picked up Shirley's ashes. I thought she would love a last drive-by along her favourite stretch of the Thames in Henley – bonus that it is Regatta week – on the way home.*

Sleeves rolled up, he changes gear. He drives along the sparkling Thames, drinking in sights and sounds. The busy boats full of happy people are a huge contrast to his present mission.

He remembers many other such drives; they'd chat and laugh in the easy way that was so typical of them when they were together. Nick chokes up as he remembers the warm banter between them, and his blue eyes tear. He remembers her long, wind-blown hair and her pushing her sunglasses up her slender nose.

In another passionate attempt to pay tribute to her – as he did at the funeral – he now plays Hillsong's *A Beautiful Exchange*. The song emphasizes that the surrender of self by Christ first and then of us to him in response are the supreme expression of love.

Now the words capture something else; they capture the essence of Shirley's own transformation from near tragedy to perfect triumph.

At last, Nick turns into his narrow driveway. He turns off the humming motor. Then, like the gentleman he is, he walks round to Shirley's side of the car, loose stones crunching under his feet, and opens the door. He unbuckles the seatbelt. With infinite care, he lifts out the navy-blue canister with its sky-blue bow on top and carries it carefully, tenderly, into his old farm cottage. He puts the canister down very gently on the couch in front of the fireplace. Shirley used to pack the grate and nurture the flames until the leaping yellow tongues made them both cozy. Then they'd watch DVDs together. Tears roll down Nick's roughly shaven face.

I watch Nick's video footage of this love-filled journey from the undertakers on Facebook. The bow is blue, which makes me glad. It's her favourite colour. I tear up as I watch the video over and over again. I'm sure others do too.

Under the video clip, Nick comments:

Happy memories of an awesome girl.

Chris responds:

Wonderfully comfortable and luxurious for our Shirl – no doubt, she's smiling down on you, Nick, as you give her such a ride – and shouting, "Whoopee!"

Jacqui says she's drying her eyes but smiling a big smile.
Suzy writes:

Putting the gorgeous Shirls in the front seat of a soft top is the best thing. When I go, I would love someone to do the same for me.

Nick responds:

Well, I couldn't put her in the boot! What else would one do?

I write:

Oh, Nick. Can't you just hear her comments about the boot idea? How funny she would have been!

Katy warmly agrees:

I can hear her giggling about this too. She'd have loved it! Xxx

---

The next day, Nick drives Jo, Laura and Gaynor to Wastwater; Jo in the front seat, the precious canister between them. At this point, their minds are full of the same things. And they find it so easy to chat, rag each other, giggle and laugh often, in Shirley-fashion.

"You know how much I've been dreading this, Nick." Jo adjusts her sunglasses.

"Because of saying goodbye?"

"Partly that. But largely, I guess, climbing Middlefell. I am so unfit, and I've dreaded being left behind, or not making it, and letting Shirley Pearly down. There are very few people who could get me to climb a mountain, but Shirls was one of them."

Gaynor, anxious for another reason, chips in, "To be honest, I was a little hesitant too. I mean, how do you look forward to – or even think about – what it will be like to scatter your friend's ashes?"

They are all very emotional.

Gaynor adds, "Although I know that God is sovereign and intends only good to come of this trip, I was slightly scared of my own emotions, I guess."

Nick comforts and encourages. His caring for them all extends to me too; as he stops for petrol, he sees a number plate which reads "THY" and sends me a pic. I'm so touched.

When they arrive at the Bridge Inn, it's pouring with rain.

"Please, Lord," Nick prays as he unpacks the car, "let it be a fine day tomorrow, the sun shining and a breeze blowing north-east so Shirley can fly above Scafell Pike, the largest of them all."

The next morning, Nick enjoys a few moments alone in the fresh, crisp morning air. Then he texts:

Today, I am joined by Jo Harbidge, Laura Ryder and Gaynor Burton to climb Middlefell. It overlooks Wastwater in the Lake District. We are going to scatter Shirley Cameron's ashes there. She loved this place – her heaven on earth.

After an impressive English breakfast, they drive to the foot of Middlefell. They park next to a working farm, pull on backpacks and head up beside a clean, bubbling stream. The blue sky with huge, fluffy cumulus clouds promises a good day. They lovingly take turns carrying the canister in one of Shirley's rucksacks.

Together, they have prayed that God will give them love tokens, one for each of them. And he does. Jo comes upon a shimmering black-and-yellow dragonfly, beautiful and still in the morning light. It obliges and doesn't fly away until they are done with their photo shoot. Along the way, green bracken uncoils furry new leaf tips, a few yellow buttercups stud the grass, scarce thistles display purple buds and cerise foxgloves wave when there is a little breeze. Yellow lichen brightens up the rocks. Sheep – now white, now black – pull at long, green grass. Carefully packed stone walls hem them in.

And the silence is broken by the bubbling of the crystal-clear stream they follow.

It's a stiff climb, once they turn up right from the river. So, when they find a flat patch of lush green grass, they flop down. For a while, they lie on their backs, pensive, drinking in the beauty all around them. Then they tuck into the sandwiches provided by the inn. When they add some chocolate bars, bananas and cold, fresh water, it turns into an impromptu feast.

Gaynor later journals:

> *Fun and chat over lunch. Already plenty of Shirley-style whoops as we climbed.*

Refreshed, they head for the beacon at the top. The views are stunning – a very blue tarn to the left, the Wastwater lake to the right.

"Thank you, Shirley, for choosing such a great place."

While the sun was hot on their backs before, now at the top they're cold, the wind blowing north-east. *Just what I prayed for,* Nick thinks to himself. So they pull on their turquoise and blue jackets.

The girls stretch out on the grass again while Nick unpacks. He pulls the stones of the beacon away to get to its heart. Very carefully, tenderly, he puts inside the gifts he has brought – a drawstring bag with precious contents from Katy, a rough stone and a smooth stone egg from Chris signifying Shirley's transformation, a small piece of slate with a loving message from Carolyn and a carefully sealed little wooden box from him. He also puts inside a little rounded wooden cross, like the one I wanted her to have.

Before setting out, Nick asked me for a verse I'd like to leave with Shirley, typed it out and slid it into the hole he'd drilled into the cross from the top. Finally, now, he puts in the tribute he has written:

> *The remarkable, effervescent, beautiful*
> *and wonderfully talented*
> *Shirley Jeanne Cameron.*
> *2 March 1975 – 6 May 2014*
> *Her ashes scattered here, her haven on earth,*
> *on a beautiful summer's day – 5 July 2014*
> *Now healed, free, and at peace with her Father God.*

Next, Nick sets up his video camera on his tripod. When he is ready, Jo phones us in South Africa.

All afternoon, I've been praying on and off. Now it's amazing to talk to Nick on top of the mountain, at this most precious moment for all of us. There's only one thing I want to know: "Is the Holy Spirit there? Do you feel his presence? Is he with you?"

The answer is a resounding "Yes, oh yes!"

And I am so glad.

They spontaneously form a circle to pray. Then they move to the edge, carrying the canister. Jo takes it and hugs it a number of times while they sing and worship. She kisses it and hugs it again before she hands it over to Nick. I'm so, so glad – so *very* glad – she does that. Even at the very last, there's someone to demonstrate love for her

Nick opens it – it's just a little stubborn – and steps forward. Then, in a wide arc, he scatters the ashes into the north east wind towards Scafell Pike. They are deeply silent as they watch the earthly remains of their dear friend drift off over the water and mountains she so dearly loved. Laura finds herself thinking, *this was just what Shirley would have wanted – to fly!*

For a long moment, they stand, heads bowed, deeply moved, crying a little but rejoicing for her. A whole mix of emotions pulses through them. What a tough time it's been for everybody. Now there's release, freedom, sorrow and sadness. Slowly, very slowly, it dawns on them that they won't see Shirley again – not for a while. But, as they text:

> *We sang and prayed, and underlying everything was joy and peace. The journey back down was actually only slightly more thoughtful – but joyous and beautiful too.*

Sometime later, when they take a rest on the soft, long green grass, Gaynor starts the journal they want to put together about this journey:

> *We're at the top!!!*

> *From the moment we all got together and started travelling, it just felt right. This was a journey we were making together – as friends of Shirley's – to honour and respect her and her last wishes.*

Gaynor changes Kokis[25] – one that works, instead of the dry one.

---

[25] felt-tipped pens

> *But was it really for Shirley? We have been blessed with so much beauty – a dragonfly for Jo and flowers for me.*
>
> *Shirley is more than fine!!! But, maybe, through her, God has led us to this place – a pilgrimage for us, a journey of discovery. Maybe it's about what Shirley discovered, for us to discover the God that loves us massively – and cares so much and will never let us go.*

Jo takes over:

> *I'm so pleased to be up here, and not too much of an ordeal! In fact, it was beautiful – such an amazing day – the weather, the views. Every corner, God was inspiring me more and more – mountain stream water, his love and sacrifice washing us so clean. The joy of looking back! And forwards: steep and hard-going – but to be taken one step at a time.*
>
> *Shirley knew what she was doing, asking us to come here. It's so still, so beautiful, so perfect. God's love is perfect. It is complete in Shirley now – and I long for the day when it will be so utterly complete in me too.*
>
> *Sat here, looking out over the lake, with the mountain and cloud shadows dancing along them. It feels like a taste of his glory fulfilled.*

Jo draws what she sees and adds Scriptures. Then she passes the book to Laura:

> *Shirley definitely had her head screwed on straight when she brought us here – natural beauty as far as the eye can see – a giant lake holding the reflections of heaven. Maybe she even chose this spot so that heaven and earth would meet. It was he who saw this lake landscaped before any eye caught its wonder.*
>
> *Our God chose to share a precious treasure – Shirley – with each of us, to be impacted, shaped, loved, encouraged and befriended. Shirley is inviting us: "Please worship him with me now, sing of him – and the love he displays. Please do not mourn my loss, but celebrate my finish. Please join with me to declare his glory and the riches of his grace." How can I not do as she asks?*

Nick scrawls:

> *My heart is full of praise for God's creative genius in his conception of Shirley, for giving her such an eye for beauty, for gently moulding*

her character and heart. It always had to be gentle treatment, given the delicate nature that he gave her. How wonderful, that she reached her full potential!

This is a majestic place... she was a majestic lover of God.

Gaynor pens a last word:

I felt Shirley – in heaven – wanting to encourage us: "Guys, this is just a taste! You have to know it's amazing here! Wastwater is like the hem of heaven – spectacular."

It's as if God – through Shirley – planned a perfect experience for us all. The sun really did shine!

Nick remembers sitting on the couch in Sandy Lane with Shirley when, among all her other planning from the time of her birthday onwards, she planned her last days in detail too.

"Why Wastwater, Shirls?" he asked, holding her hand as they looked at a Google Earth image of it.

"Because it's where I have always felt closest to God. It's so beautiful but desolate. So it speaks to my heart, not of what I thought I wanted to be, but what I have been. It gives me such hope for what God has for me at the end of all this, whatever that may be."

Now he pictures her sitting on a rock looking pensively out over the lake. And he hears her saying, "God loves me – he loves me, loves me, loves me..."

Epilogue

CHRIST ALONE, CORNERSTONE
WEAK MADE STRONG IN
THE SAVIOUR'S LOVE

IN HONOUR OF SHIRLEY CAMERON, 1975 - 2014
FOUNDING MEMBER OF
MERCY UK CORNERSTONE COMMUNITY

*"...you've seen the plaque in the passage
and asked what that might mean."*

ON 1 JUNE 2016, AT THE OPENING OF THEIR NEW WING, Arianna Walker, Chief Executive of Mercy Ministries, Oxenhope, paid tribute to Shirley.

"I want to make a special mention of Shirley – you've seen the plaque in the passage and asked what that might mean. Shirley was a good friend of Laura who works here. She fought a really great battle against cancer – she did everything very well.

"She left us a significant amount of money and we knew that it was going to be for something specific – not just helping with the running of Mercy in general. It needed to be for something that we could name, that we could point to and say, 'That is what she has built.'

"It was a time when we hadn't even talked to many people yet about the plans to expand. And then, suddenly, when this money came, we realised we already had some things in mind. It was the seed that gave us that impetus to be able to go, 'Okay, we're going to do this, and we're going to build something.'

"So Shirley, even in her death, has brought life, not just to this building, to this site, but to the many, many people who are going to come through here and be trained and be brought back to life.

"We were wondering what the name of this building should be, and Kathleen suggested Cornerstone – the foundation to provide for the two arms to our ministry; and, of course, Jesus our Cornerstone. What I didn't know was that Shirley's favourite song was *Christ Alone, Cornerstone*."

The plaque reads:

> *Christ alone, Cornerstone*
> *Weak made strong in the Saviour's love.*
> *In honour of Shirley Cameron, 1975 – 2014*
> *Founding member of Mercy UK Cornerstone Community.*

To see Shirley's video testimony or access other free resources related to this book, please scan the QR barcode below with your phone:

Or visit

www.onwardsandupwards.org/mum-please-help-me-die

What Shall I Read Next?
Recommendations from the Publisher

A Prayer Companion Through Cancer
Kate Strickland
ISBN 978-1-78815-671-4

This prayer book has been written for all those suffering with cancer. Over 70 prayers cover the many stages of the unwelcome journey: from diagnosis to facing treatment, from recovery to remission. Kate recognises that the battle against cancer is both physical and emotional. Her prayers acknowledge and tackle the complex feelings and experiences often encountered by cancer patients; her words giving an authentic voice to the inner struggles, whilst holding on to hope in God.

My Mighty Son
Virág Wheeler-Mezei
ISBN 978-1-911086-54-3

This is the story of a journey that few of us have to take; it is only for the bravest. When Virág became pregnant, no one could have been more delighted and thrilled than she and her husband James. Luki – or Luke – was born and seemed a very healthy baby. And then their lives changed suddenly and drastically; Luke was admitted to a local hospital and then transferred to Bristol for radical emergency brain surgery for an aggressive brain tumour...

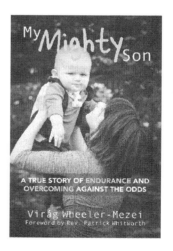

Books available from your local bookshop or from the publisher:

www.onwardsandupwards.org